AMERICAN
METROPOLITICS

AMERICAN METROPOLITICS

The New Suburban Reality

Myron Orfield

Brookings Institution Press
Washington, D.C.

ABOUT BROOKINGS

The Brookings Institution is a private nonprofit organization devoted to research, education, and publication on important issues of domestic and foreign
policy. Its principal purpose is to bring knowledge to bear on current and emerging policy problems. The Institution maintains a position of neutrality on issues
of public policy. Interpretations or conclusions in Brookings publications should
be understood to be solely those of the authors.

Library of Congress Cataloging-in-Publication data
Orfield, Myron.
    American metropolitics : the new suburban reality / Myron
Orfield.
       p.   cm.
    Includes bibliographical references and index.
    ISBN 0-8157-0248-5 (cloth : alk. paper) —
    ISBN 0-8157-0249-3 (paper : alk. paper)
    1. Metropolitan areas—United States. 2. Metropolitan
government—United States. 3. Urban policy—United States.
4. Sociology, Urban—United States. I. Title.
HT334.U5 O72   2002
307.76'4'0973—dc21   2001007582

9 8 7 6 5 4 3 2 1

The paper used in this publication meets minimum requirements of the
American National Standard for Information Sciences—Permanence of Paper
for Printed Library Materials: ANSI Z39.48-1992.

Typeset in ITC Stone

Design and composition by Circle Graphics
Columbia, Maryland

Printed by R. R. Donnelley and Sons
Crawfordsville, Indiana

CONTENTS

FIGURE

TABLES

BOX

MAPS
Following page 16

Following page 48

Following page 160

For my Mother and Father
Jeanne, Sam, and Will

FOREWORD

After years of academic neglect, corporate indifference, and political hostility, metropolitan thinking has reemerged as a potent force in the United States. In the past decade, a growing chorus of scholars has published influential studies on the costs of sprawl, the interdependence of cities and suburbs, and the virtues of metropolitan governance. Regional employer alliances like Metropolis 2020 in Chicago and Silicon Valley Joint Venture have fought for metropolitan approaches to transportation, housing, and work force challenges, issues of central importance to the business community. Governors such as Maryland's Parris Glendening and Pennsylvania's Tom Ridge have pursued "smart growth" policies to curb sprawl, preserve farmland and suburban open space, and promote urban reinvestment. And Congress has made metropolitan governance and planning a significant element of transportation and environmental policy.

The new metropolitan thinking contends that the shape and quality of metropolitan growth in America are no longer desirable or sustainable. Current growth patterns undermine our efforts to achieve fundamental environmental objectives, threaten our ability to build competitive regional economies, and exacerbate deep racial, ethnic, and class divisions in our society. These growth patterns are not inevitable but rather the result of major government policies that distort the market and facilitate the excessive decentralization of people and jobs. It puts forward an integrated agenda to change the "rules of the development game" at the federal, state, metropolitan, and local levels of government. This is a powerful paradigm shift, a sweeping rethinking of the costs and consequences of metropolitan growth in the country and a compelling vision of how to achieve environmental quality, economic competitiveness, and racial and social justice in metropolitan America.

Now comes the hard part. Assuming that current policies are the problem, then politics—or a reimagining of politics—can be the solution. But how can that happen in a world where the conventional wisdom states that "all suburbs are the same" and "strong city/suburban/rural coalitions are not possible"?

Perhaps no individual has done more to advance the possibilities of new metropolitan coalitions than Myron Orfield. In 1997 the Brookings Institution Press published Orfield's seminal work, *Metropolitics: A Regional Agenda for Community and Stability*. The book chronicled, in part, his efforts as a Minnesota state legislator to pioneer innovative metropolitan solutions to land use, taxation, and governance. Using the latest spatial mapping technology, the book painted a stark, visual picture of socioeconomic disparities in metropolitan Minneapolis/St. Paul and a handful of other metropolitan areas. It gave visual expression to such scholarly terms as "inner ring suburbs," "metropolitan decentralization," "spatial mismatch," and "fiscal disparities."

American Metropolitics: The New Suburban Reality applies Orfield's innovative analysis to the top 25 metropolitan areas in the nation. Based on his mapping of socioeconomic trends in each of these areas, he has developed a useful typology of the three different kinds of suburbs found in metropolitan America—at-risk communities, bedroom-developing places, and affluent job centers. By Orfield's calculus, a progressive metropolitan agenda of land use and fiscal and governance reforms would benefit a supermajority of citizens and jurisdictions in each of the metropolitan areas he has studied.

This book will go a long way toward altering the conventional views of the role, function, and composition of central cities and their suburbs. It explodes the lingering myth that suburbs are monolithic and points the way to new city/suburban alliances aligned around true self-interest rather than outmoded ideologies and divisions.

These are big, exciting, and provocative ideas. They deserve serious study and debate in the academy. More significantly, they present a challenge to political, corporate, and civic leaders to remove the geographic blinders that limit the potential of American politics and build a powerful constituency for change that is worthy of this nation.

BRUCE KATZ
Director, Center on Urban and Metropolitan Policy
Brookings Institution

ACKNOWLEDGMENTS

This book is based on careful statistical work and analysis, but it is also based on experience gained traveling the United States over the past six years. After the publication of my first book, *Metropolitics: A Regional Agenda for Community and Stability* (1997), a study of demographics and reform in my native Twin Cities, many groups in other U.S. regions requested that I undertake local research studies and help them with advocacy efforts on regional issues. In the past five years I have traveled to almost every part of metropolitan America. I have met with government officials and planners from all types of cities and suburbs; civil rights, environmental and antipoverty advocates; business leaders; all types of religious officials; economists, sociologists, geographers, and political scientists; bond houses; chambers of commerce; and of course, thousands of citizens. I have toured America's ghettos, barrios, and slums, its gentrifying neighborhoods, gated communities, and all variety of bedroom suburbs. I have listened to thousands of human stories about decline and development, of local and regional politics. I have made many remarkable friends and acquaintances. During this period, I have worked on 30 studies of places in the United States, each in its own way a small book, like the original *Metropolitics*. Most of these reports and the underlying research are located on the web at www.metroresearch.org and they are also listed in appendix C. My travels and the work on these reports have given me an education in this country and its regions, its politics and its people, that I could not have got in any classroom or in any other way. For this I would like to thank my clients, my funders, and the hundreds of individuals and groups who made it possible.

This book and the studies noted above were written not by any individual but by the talented team of people at the Metropolitan Area

Research Corporation (MARC, www.metroresearch.org) and its partner organization, Ameregis (www.ameregis.com). MARC is a nonprofit region research and advocacy center. Ameregis is a geographic information systems (GIS) research and demographic consulting firm. In particular, Tom Luce, director of research at Ameregis, worked with me to create a more rigorous methodology and approach to support many of my evolving concepts. He was instrumental in the very difficult task of building a national database for the 25 largest regions. Tom is one of the leading experts in the United States on the fiscal condition of cities and suburbs, and those who know his work will see his impact clearly in these pages. With these and additional data, Tom has plans to publish an even more detailed study of the fiscal conditions of regional communities with Brookings in the near future. I am also grateful to Tom for his assistance and patience during the seemingly endless process of turning a rough draft into a final manuscript. Ben Oleson, Anne Discher, Lisa Bigaouette, Kevin Shively, Paige Kahle, Steve Smela, and Craig Hagensick provided valuable research assistance. At various times, Jenny Jones, Jennifer Bradley, Kathleen Lynch, and David Mahoney helped edit various parts of the manuscript. I am also grateful to the people who are the infrastructure of MARC and Ameregis. Lisa Bigaouette's substantive and organizational skills were helpful in securing funding for many of our projects. For her efforts on behalf of the work of metropolitan reform, I can never adequately express my thanks. Cheryl Hennen skillfully kept our books in order, our bills paid, and our financial course steady and safe throughout the project.

A very talented group of GIS professionals at MARC and Ameregis made the maps in this book and the more than 420 additional maps that accompany the book on MARC's website. Very special thanks goes to Andrea Swansby, GIS director at Ameregis, who supervised the massive collection of data and created an orderly process to study and map the large regions of the United States. Aaron Timbo used his mapping and programming skills to improve the accuracy and speed of our mapping. Liesa Stromberg redesigned our map layout, making it more intuitive, more beautiful, and easier to reproduce. A wonderful and talented staff, including Bill Lanoux, Mike Niemeyer, Micah Brachman, Laura Wendt, Jeff Matson, and Scott Laursen ably assisted these three.

I would also like to thank those who read the manuscript and provided helpful, insightful comments: Anthony Downs, Bruce Katz, Robert Burchell, Hal Wolman, David Rusk, Helen Ladd, Susan Wachter, and john powell. My brother, Gary Orfield, not only read the manuscript, but has continued to advise and help me in all sorts of ways. His scholarship on race in America has had a profound influence on my thinkings about metropolitan areas.

The board of directors of MARC, Bruce Katz, James Brown, David Rusk, Tony Downs, john powell, Bill Morrish, Paul Moe, and Pat Diamond also deserve thanks for their support of this project. Particularly important in this regard is Bruce Katz at the Brookings Urban Center, who has strongly supported my work on this book and many other projects. I hope to continue working with him in the future. David Rusk also provided strong support and guidance, and Jim Brown, john powell, Bill Morrish, and Tony Downs shared their invaluable time and experience. Pat Diamond and Paul Moe provided sound advice and support to keep MARC running at the highest level.

Also at Brookings, Amy Liu, Jennifer Bradley, Kimberly Gibson, Kurt Sommer, and Rob Puentes have been helpful in refining the messages of the book and developing interest and attention for it. At the Brookings Institution Press, Vicky Macintyre ably copyedited the manuscript, Carlotta Ribar proofread the pages, and Enid Zafran provided the index.

I would like to thank the Ford Foundation, the U.S. Department of Housing and Urban Development, the Rockefeller Foundation, the Charles Stewart Mott Foundation, the John D. and Catherine T. MacArthur Foundation, the McKnight Foundation, the Local Initiatives Support Corporation (LISC), Deutsche Bank, and Mid-America Regional Council of Kansas City for their support of this project. It would never have occurred without them.

In addition, the Brookings Urban Center acknowledges the support of the Ford Foundation, the George Gund Foundation, the Joyce Foundation, the John D. and Catherine T. MacArthur Foundation, the Charles Stewart Mott Foundation, and the Fannie Mae Foundation for the center's work on metropolitan growth and urban reinvestment issues.

From 1990 to 2000 I served in the Minnesota House of Representatives and in 2000 I was elected to the Minnesota Senate. Representing the people of the 60th District, I have had the privilege to learn about policy and politics of metropolitan reform from the inside. During my time in office, my constituency has supported me unwaveringly on reform—no matter how controversial or difficult the issue. For this I give them never-ending thanks. Serving as an elected official, pursuing with some success the reforms one most believes in, is one of life's greatest privileges.

I have had to spend time away from my family in researching and writing this book. But Samuel and William, with their shining eyes, infectious chuckles, great questions and new words, tiger-like wrestling skills, and beautiful true hearts are more important than all of this or than anything to me. I miss every moment that I am away from them. My wife, Jeanne, has held us all together by staying home with the boys. In addition to being my best friend and, with the boys, the center of my life, she is a lawyer, a writer, and the daughter of a former governor. She has more savvy, grace, and political skill, both developed and inherited, than I will ever possess and is my closest adviser and confidante. For her constant support, counsel, and love, I owe more than I have. I would also like to thank my parents, Myron (Sr.) and Lindy Orfield, for their constant love and support throughout the 40 years of my life.

I hope that this book helps people see their country in a new way and make it better.

INTRODUCTION

Once a country of farms, small towns, and big cities, the United States today is a nation of regions. More than 8 out of 10 Americans live in one of 300 metropolitan areas. Nearly half the population lives in the 25 largest regions. Within these 25 regions, thousands of cities compete fiercely with each other, with little common social, political, or economic strategy.

An evolving pattern of intense, unequal competition and inefficient, environmentally damaging local land use threatens every community and region, undermining the nation's promise of equal opportunity for all. Geographic stratification has already had devastating consequences for the minority poor. Now it has begun to diminish the quality of life of working- and middle-class Americans and to circumscribe their opportunities. Sprawling development is gobbling up land with no corresponding growth in supporting infrastructure—schools, roads, transportation, sewerage. This unplanned growth endangers public health, the environment, and the quality of life for people in every region. Protests against the current pattern of development show that no group—not even the wealthiest suburb—is fully satisfied with the status quo.

American Metropolitics details the evolution of social and geographic stratification and wasteful development in the United States and offers an alternative. The plan laid out in this book, based on cooperation among metropolitan communities, would strengthen all communities and regions, opening opportunities for economic advancement and social mobility for all citizens.

Metropolitics, the new metropolitan politics explored in this book, borrows ideas from both major political parties. From the Republicans,

1

it borrows the foundation of regional governance, coordinated regional land planning, and fiscal equity that they pioneered in the post–World War II period. Many government solutions proposed in this book were first enunciated, a generation ago, by good-government Republicans. Metropolitics shares their distaste for waste of money, land, and human potential and their goal of less complex and more efficient government. From the Democrats, it borrows a strong commitment to ending overt discrimination based on race and class, and an environmental agenda for preserving natural areas and cleaning up the air and water.

American Metropolitics is divided into three sections: "Metropatterns," "Metropolicy," and "Metropolitics." "Metropatterns" illustrates the increasing social separation and wasteful, sprawling development common to all U.S. metropolitan regions. Social separation and sprawl limit opportunity for poor and minority residents, diminish the quality of life for all residents, and degrade the local environment. Compelling evidence in this section also challenges the notion of a homogeneous monolith known as "the suburbs." It reveals at least four types of communities, each harmed in some way by the common pattern of development:

—*Central cities* (28 percent of population in the 25 largest U.S. regions). These communities have inadequate local resources and high concentrations of residents needing social services. The most heterogeneous group, central cities include both strong and gentrifying cities such as Portland, Oregon, and Seattle and weak or declining cities such as Detroit and Milwaukee.

—*At-risk suburbs* (40 percent). This group has present and growing social needs and draws two-thirds of the central cities' per-household government resources. Often more fragile than the communities they surround, the at-risk suburbs lack amenities such as large central business districts, gentrifying neighborhoods, large parks, and cultural resources. These are the places that decline most rapidly when socioeconomic stress begins to appear. They also are the least likely to rebound from decline.

—*Bedroom-developing suburbs* (26 percent). These are high-growth communities that lack sufficient resources to build schools and infrastructure. Dubbed bedroom communities, they are built for young middle-class families with school-age children. Many residents must commute long distances to work. The high ratio of children in these communities contributes to overcrowded classrooms and low per-pupil spending. Without a strong commercial tax base to help support pub-

Compelling evidence challenges the notion of a homogeneous monolith known as "the suburbs."

lic spending, these places find it difficult to provide adequate services such as schools, roads, and sewer systems.

—*Affluent job centers* (7 percent). These communities have few social needs and extensive public resources. They are considered the most attractive communities in a region, creating a steady flow of jobs, expensive housing developments, and upscale retail outlets. They contain proportionately about five times more regional office space than any other group of suburbs. But that attractiveness comes at a price: their roads are congested and valuable open spaces are being lost to relentless development. Ironically, many residents of these communities have been the leaders in the movement against existing patterns of development, imposing development moratoriums and devising other strategies to restrict development.

"Metropolicy" begins with a critique of the most significant efforts to address the problems of concentrated poverty, sprawl, and inequitable distribution of resources: most notably, urban renewal, public housing programs, and federal empowerment zones. Such past and current efforts have been and will continue to be ineffective because they do not address the complex, regional nature of those problems. "Metropolicy" lays out a comprehensive regional agenda to deal with increasing social separation and wasteful development patterns throughout the country. It also presents a strategy for advancing that agenda in a politically possible and palatable way. Three types of strategies guide this agenda, and each is discussed in detail: *increased fiscal equity among local governments,* with an emphasis on reinvestment in central cities and older suburbs; *coordinated regional land-use planning,* with a strong emphasis on affordable housing; and *improved governance and leadership at the regional level,* to help facilitate the development of policies that benefit all types of communities.

Finally, "Metropolitics" outlines a political strategy to pursue this agenda. That strategy recognizes the fundamental importance and volatility of U.S. suburbs—especially those in decline and those growing without sufficient schools and infrastructure. Its basic premise is that regionalism not only is possible but also represents a way to renew reform-oriented legislation on planning and fiscal equity in the United States. An analysis of metropolitan *swing districts*—legislative districts that regularly switch from one political party to the other—provides important evidence of a political environment ripe for reform based on a regional approach. About 80 percent of the swing districts in the 25 largest U.S. metropolitan regions are in fiscally or socially stressed suburban communities, which makes them the true pivot points of American politics.

To that decisive group of voters, regionalism means lower taxes and better services. For older suburbs, it means stability, community renewal, and less social stress. For rapidly growing communities, it means sufficient spending on schools, clean water, and infrastructure. Even the wealthiest and most isolated areas of metropolitan United States find regionalism appealing. Those communities may appear to "have it all," but they are leading the popular revolt against sprawl in many parts of the country. Regionalism offers them the most realistic way to preserve their community's original character and proximity to open spaces.

PART

1

METRO
PATTERNS

**METRO
PATTERNS**

METRO PATTERNS

Metropolitan areas are very diverse places. City/suburban disparities have been well documented, but differences among suburban areas have not. In region after region, problems associated exclusively with central cities in the national psyche have moved into inner-ring suburbs. As metropolitan areas have continued to grow more quickly in geographical area than in population, growth pains in those outer reaches have taken on prominence in the public consciousness. Many suburbs have come to recognize that they now have as much, if not more, in common with large cities than with their suburban counterparts. Coalition building in state legislatures is beginning to change to reflect this flash of recognition.

How sharp are the divisions in metropolitan areas? Can suburban areas be categorized in ways that are of more than academic interest? What portion of metropolitan populations live in suburban places that fit the long-held image of the suburbs—largely white, low-poverty, low-density, and growing bedroom communities? Are suburban areas a mosaic of affluence with small pockets of fiscal and social stress, the converse, or something more complicated? How effectively have states responded to fiscal and social disparities across cities and towns?

These issues are explored in chapters 1, 2, and 3. Chapter 1 begins by documenting the extent of social separation (by income and race) as reflected in schools in America's 25 largest metropolitan areas. It goes on to analyze the fiscal resources at the disposal of the more than 5,000 cities, towns, townships, and unincorporated areas in those metropolitan areas.

Chapter 2 examines the fiscal health of the central cities in those metropolitan areas and compares the cities' and the suburbs' ability to raise revenues and their public service needs and costs. Finally, a typology of municipalities is developed, grouping suburban cities, towns, townships, and unincorporated areas according to their tax capacities, needs, and costs. The characteristics of the groups that emerge are then used to examine suburban diversity.

Chapter 3 compares the regions to each other on the dimensions of (1) social and racial segregation, (2) fiscal equality, and (3) sprawl. It finds that regions doing comparatively well on any one of these dimensions tend to be doing well on the others.

CHAPTER 1

SCHOOLS AND TAX WEALTH: LEADING INDICATORS OF COMMUNITY HEALTH

Metropatterns presents a typology, or classification, of America's suburbs. This classification scheme relies on a technique called cluster analysis, which groups places according to common characteristics of social and physical need and locally available tax resources. The characteristics used in *Metropatterns* are a community's tax capacity, poverty, density, age of infrastructure, certain characteristics of the school population, and growth in population and tax capacity. The two features especially important in the cluster analysis here are schools and local tax resources.

ELEMENTARY SCHOOLS

Schools are a powerful indicator of a community's current health and of its future well-being. First, when a community's schools reach certain thresholds of poverty, middle-class families of all races choose not to live in that community. Second, a community's school children are likely to become its next generation of adults.

For several reasons, such change in the overall community is likely to lag behind changes in local schools. As communities become poorer, flight is not immediate. Rather, as the number of poor school children grows, demand for local housing gradually declines. Think of it this way: Americans move a great deal. Housing in stable communities is in continuous demand. As schools gradually gain more and more poor students, middle-class families' demand for housing in the community softens. Housing prices reflect this. As poverty continues to increase, demand slackens further. As the school population becomes noticeably poorer, nonpoor families with school-age children are likely to leave first because changes in the schools affect them most. Some nonpoor families may choose to abandon a school system but not the community itself, by putting their children in private schools. In the end, despite frequent local claims about a large percentage of children attending private schools, few households can afford the additional expense.

Poverty rates among school-age children therefore tend to rise more quickly than the overall poverty rate. A community with schools in transition may also continue to draw nonpoor households without school-age children (empty-nesters, for instance), easing the increase in overall poverty rates. Eventually, however, when schools reach certain thresholds of poverty—and its attendant racial segregation—middle-class families of all races with children that have residential choices will leave the community, and they will eventually be followed by other middle-class segments of the housing market.

Poverty and its consequences underlie social separation, but it is difficult to separate poverty from race and ethnicity—particularly for African Americans and Latinos, who are strongly discriminated against in the housing market.[1] (Because Asian Americans face relatively low levels of housing market segregation, they are not included in this discussion.)[2] In 1996 about half of all U.S. schools had black and Latino enrollments of 10 percent or less.[3] Of those schools, only 7.7 percent reported more than half of the children living in poverty. Meanwhile, 8 percent of U.S. schools had black and Latino enrollments of 90 to 100 percent. Of this group, 87 percent had poverty rates above 50 percent. "In other words," as housing researchers Gary Orfield and John Yun have noted, "the students in segregated minority schools were eleven times more likely to be in schools of concentrated poverty, and 92 percent of white schools did not face this problem."[4]

Sadly, analysis of racial data for elementary school students in the 25 largest U.S. regions shows that once the minority share in a community's schools increases to a threshold level (10 to 20 percent), racial transition accelerates until minority percentages reach very high levels (greater than 80 percent). Change occurs fastest at levels of 20 to 50 percent and proceeds inexorably until schools are highly segregated.

1. Massey and Denton (1993); Orfield and Logan (2001).
2. Orfield and Yun (1999); Massey (1993).
3. Orfield and Yun (1999).
4. Orfield and Yun (1999) and www.law.harvard.edu/civilrights/publications/resegregation99.html.

As racial and social change spreads through the older suburbs and satellite cities, an especially distressing pattern emerges. The gradually expanding black and Latino middle class, in pursuit of the American dream, begins moving away from poverty and into the suburbs. In their search for new homes, they are frequently steered to areas where their presence will be the least controversial.[5] When black and Latino residents reach a critical mass in a neighborhood and its schools, white homebuyers, *perceiving* the community to be in decline, choose not to buy there, and, before long, whites already living in the neighborhood move away. Businesses and jobs soon follow. The consequent decline in demand causes housing prices in the neighborhood to fall, and poorer individuals (whites, blacks, and others) move into the homes vacated by the middle-class whites. The earlier perceptions become reality. In a short time—often less than a decade—the black middle-class migrants find themselves in the same kind of neighborhood they sought to escape just a few years earlier.

Spurred by the growth of the country's nonwhite population, the already rapid suburban racial and social change is likely to accelerate. According to census statistics, nonwhite enrollment in the United States stood at only 11 to 12 percent between 1940 and 1960, but jumped to 36 percent by 1996 and is expected to reach 58 percent by 2050. The two most populous states, California and Texas, already have a majority of nonwhite students in their schools.

The close relationship between racially segregated communities and areas of concentrated poverty has been used to support flawed conclusions about blacks and Latinos. Some people, associating an influx of minorities into a community with social and economic decline, conclude that minority residents somehow contribute less than whites to a community's health and stability.

Nowhere was this tragic misconception better illustrated than in a segment from the television news magazine *NBC Dateline* about the white-collar Chicago suburb of Matteson, Illinois, 20 miles south of the Loop.[6] In the early to mid 1990s, black middle-class families began to move to Matteson, a community of large, attractive suburban homes, open space, and good schools. These blacks were, by most important demographic measures, at least the socioeconomic equals of Matteson's white residents. Some were, in fact, better off than Matteson's whites.

When black and Latino residents reach a critical mass, white homebuyers perceive the community as in decline, and soon white residents also move away.

5. See Yinger (1995).
6. Tom Brokaw Special Report, "Why Can't We Live Together?" Dateline NBC, June 27, 1997.

But as soon as black households became a significant percentage of the population, there was a sudden sell-off of homes by white residents. Asked why they were moving, the white sellers replied, "Because the schools are getting worse and crime is increasing." On the evidence, neither claim was true. School test scores and the crime rate remained unchanged. However, once the white residents left, demand for middle-class housing in Matteson cooled, because the black middle class was not large enough to sustain market demand. Not only did the schools become more segregated, they also became much poorer. This is why "white flight" invariably means poverty.

There is an unhelpful myth that the black or Latino middle class has achieved a separate, stable prosperity, apart from the white mainstream.

There is an unhelpful myth that the black or Latino middle class has achieved a separate, stable prosperity, apart from the white mainstream. A companion report that discusses this myth in reference to parts of Prince George's County in suburban Washington, D.C., finds that the county is actually a telling example of the process of racial and social change in America's at-risk suburbs.[7] In 1996, 47 of the county's elementary schools had a non-Asian minority student population of 90 percent or more. Students qualifying for the free-lunch program fell below 20 percent in only three of these schools. As a rule, middle-class families with residential choices do not select communities in which more than 20 percent of the school population is poor. A student is eligible for free lunch if family income is 130 percent of the poverty line or below. They are eligible for reduced-cost lunch with incomes up to 185 percent of poverty. Because the federal poverty line is so low (roughly $12,000 for a single mother and child in 2000), free or reduced-cost lunch is a slightly more realistic measure of family stress. It is also a statistic that is updated yearly.

In 31 of those 47 high-minority elementary schools, less than 50 percent of the children were eligible for free lunches. Since a majority of students in those schools were not poor, theoretically the schools could be called middle-class minority schools (although, again, most middle-class families with residential choices would not choose schools with these levels of poverty). However, nearly all of the schools were in the midst of rapid downward social transition: in 11 of the 31 schools (36 percent), the number of students eligible for free lunch increased by more than twenty percentage points in just seven years (1989–96); and in 24 of the 31 schools (78 percent), the number increased by more than ten percentage points over the same period. Those are big changes. None of those schools were socioeconomically stable.

7. See Orfield (1997).

In 57 of Prince George's County's elementary schools, minority students constituted between 50 and 90 percent of enrollment in 1996. Thirty-two of those schools (56 percent) experienced an increase in minority enrollment of more than 15 percentage points between 1989 and 1996. Only 7 of the 57 schools showed changes of less than 10 percentage points. In 41 of the 57 schools (72 percent), students qualifying for the free-lunch program increased by more than 15 percentage points. The schools in the older suburbs of Atlanta showed a similar pattern of change: discrimination, racial succession, and neighborhood deterioration.[8] This process has torn apart untold numbers of urban neighborhoods over the past century and is now entrenched in U.S. suburbs.

Maps 1-1 through 1-24 show the shifting geography of poverty and race among elementary school children in six representative metropolitan areas: Atlanta, Chicago, Denver, Minneapolis–St. Paul, New York, and San Francisco. The six were chosen because they are geographically diverse and because their school-poverty and tax-capacity patterns from 1992 to 1997 were representative of patterns in other metropolitan areas across the nation. Both the percentage of students eligible for free-lunch programs and the percentage change in free-lunch eligibility are shown for every elementary school in the five regions except Chicago, for which these data were not available. Racial data were available for all six.

In all of the metropolitan areas shown here, and in fact in all of the 25 largest regions in the United States, high-poverty, largely minority schools show marked concentrations in the central cities and older satellite cities and towns. Moving outward, poverty increases hand in hand with increasing diversity. In several regions, suburban racial diversity appears to precede socioeconomic change. White people choosing not to live in areas where middle-class blacks and Latinos have moved is a very important part of the downward social change in communities. To reiterate, this is not because middle-class blacks and Latinos inherently destabilize a community. Rather, it is because the ranks of middle-class blacks and Latinos in most metropolitan areas are

8. In the 1980s, Gary Orfield's attempt to study middle-class black schools in the Atlanta suburbs met with two problems. First, although the region had one of the nation's largest black middle-class populations, there were only a handful of middle-class, predominantly black schools. Second, because the residential areas in which those schools were located were in constant flux, the schools did not remain middle-class long enough for him to study them. See Orfield and Ashkinase (1991, pp. 103–48).

currently too small to maintain a robust middle-class housing market if middle-class whites are not also interested in that market.

The Atlanta maps show significant school poverty in the interior of Dekalb, Clayton, and Fulton Counties. The non-Asian minority maps show a very similar pattern with respect to race. However, the spread of racial diversity is somewhat larger in geographic scope than the spread of poverty, reaching deeper into Cobb and Gwinnett Counties. As the maps measuring changes in poverty and race show, the most rapid changes are occurring in the places beyond the inner suburban subdivisions, namely, the outer edges of Dekalb, Clayton, Cobb, and southern Forsyth Counties.

In Chicago, many south- and west-side suburban districts actually had a higher percentage of blacks and Latinos than did the city itself. To the north, trendy Evanston has schools that are very racially diverse and struggling with social and economic changes. Like Atlanta, all of suburban Cook County is experiencing rapid racial change at the elementary school level, reaching even to traditional suburban power centers of Schaumburg and Palatine, the electoral base of conservative U.S. senator Peter Fitzgerald. In inner suburban Cicero, where a visit by Martin Luther King once precipitated a violent protest against housing integration, nonwhite students are in the majority. Park Forest was the locus of William H. Whyte's *Organization Man*, a classic study of the white-collar worker of the 1950s and his suburban life. Today, the schools are increasingly poor and diverse and, per household, the city has a fraction of the local resources of Chicago. Local malls had been empty so long in the 1990s that the city government moved into one of them. The rapidly changing suburb of Matteson, subject of the NBC documentary, is geographically so far into the suburbs that it is literally off this map.

In the Denver region, the economic and racial composition of inner suburban elementary schools is indistinguishable from those at the outer edges of the city. High-poverty schools are particularly centered in western Adams County, inner Jefferson County, and Arapahoe, Westminister, and Englewood County school districts. Even the northern part of the white-collar Littleton school district (site of the infamous school shootings) has several poor elementary schools. The race maps follow a similar pattern, with racial change moving slightly deeper into the suburban ring. The maps show the movement of poverty deeper into Jefferson County to the west and to the north through the Westminister and North Glenn school districts. Racial change is again moving hand in hand with socioeconomic change.

14

In Minneapolis–St. Paul, poverty-related change is occurring in most of the older suburbs, while racial change is concentrated in the southern suburbs of Minneapolis and the northern inner suburbs adjacent to Minneapolis's historic north side black neighborhoods. The most dramatic suburban racial changes have occurred in the heart of the Brooklyn Center and Osseo school districts. These districts serve the city of Brooklyn Park, whose mayor through much of the 1990s was the Honorable Jesse Ventura. Ventura, a former wrestler, was elected during a tidal wave of public discontent because of the rapidly worsening social conditions in Brooklyn Park, exemplified in protests over crime, the state of local schools, a troubled mall, and general decline. During this period, a citizens' group calling itself "the Legion of Doom" made a highly public push to limit affordable housing in Brooklyn Park. Ventura eventually became a supporter of regional tax sharing and metropolitan fair housing as tools to stabilize his community.

The vast mosaic of the New York region shows poverty and racial change moving in many directions. There are deep pockets of poverty in inner Long Island; in many of the New Jersey communities on the eastern shore of the Hudson River, in areas surrounding older industrial towns in the region; and to the north in Yonkers, Mount Vernon, and beyond. New Rochelle, the home of the 1960s fictional sitcom couple Rob and Laura Petrie (of "The Dick Van Dyke Show"), is facing dramatic challenges in terms of school poverty and diversity. The maps of racial and social change show powerful transformations deep into Long Island, through inner Westchester, and far into the suburban counties of New Jersey.

In San Francisco, the largest core of segregated poverty is concentrated in the city of Oakland on the east side of San Francisco Bay. A second, less extensive core is in the city of San Francisco. A third is centered in the south bay city of San Jose. Poverty and racial change are spreading quickly out of Oakland and through the school districts of San Leandro, San Lorenzo, and Hayward to the south and Berkeley and Western Contra Costa to the north. Similar changes are also pushing south out of San Francisco into the Jefferson and South San Francisco districts, and outward in all directions from the city of San Jose.

TAXES

Trends in a community's school population indicate critical local needs, and local tax capacity—or tax resources—is a good measure of the ability to raise revenues to meet those needs. Communities with copious tax

15

resources have low tax rates and great services. Resource-poor communities have just the opposite. Why is this? Think of it this way: if community tax wealth per household is $100, a 10 percent tax rate raises $10 per household for services; if tax wealth is $1,000 per household, the same rate raises $100. No matter how smart administrators are, and no matter how much reorganization they do (and all governments should constantly seek economy and efficiency)—even if they hire Bill Gates to run their city—they cannot avoid this basic math.

Most of the suburban places experiencing rapid school change and decline also have relatively few local tax resources. Moreover, these local resources are either declining, stagnant, or growing at a much slower rate than the resources for the region as a whole. What does it mean when schools are socially poor and local resources are meager and declining? It means that the community is implying to prospective homebuyers and new businesses, "Please come here. We have high and growing school poverty. We can tax you at a comparatively high rate and spend comparatively little on you." This claim is not likely to persuade a person or a business to locate there.

As maps 1-25 through 1-38 show, communities at the metropolitan edge are not immune from fiscal stress either. Many growing communities are gaining people faster than they are expanding their tax base and trying to provide streets, sewers, and schools with less-than-average resources. This fiscal stress at the edge is even greater when regions are "growing against themselves," that is, adding urbanized land area at many times the rate of population growth. While these edge communities do not have social needs of the poor and old infrastructure to pay for, they have significant fiscal and physical pressures related to growth.

The tax maps also help illustrate the problems related to the fragmentation of local government and intrametropolitan competition for local tax resources. Remember, each of the little boxes on the map is a separate government. Only the citizens living in that box, and no one else, elect each government. These governments are elected to respond to a central imperative of politics in any democracy: to provide the best services and the lowest taxes to their constituents. These governments are not elected to take care of other cities or other people. How do American local governments respond? They try to be efficient, to be sure, but their main tool for keeping taxes low and the quality of services high is land management through zoning codes, development agreements, and development practices. The developable land within such a locality is its resource for both present and future needs. In short,

Many growing communities are gaining people faster than they are expanding their tax base and trying to provide services with less-than-average resources.

LIST OF MAPS IN CHAPTER 1

Listed below are representative maps for the Atlanta, Chicago, Denver, Minneapolis, New York and San Francisco regions. A full set of over 400 GIS maps that include all of the 25 largest U.S. regions are available online at www.metroresearch.org.

MAP 1-1. ATLANTA REGION (CENTRAL AREA)
Percentage of Elementary Students Eligible for Free Lunch, by School, 1997

MAP 1-2. ATLANTA REGION (CENTRAL AREA)
Change in Percentage of Elementary Students Eligible for Free Lunch, by School, 1992–97

MAP 1-3. DENVER REGION (CENTRAL AREA)
Percentage of Elementary Students Eligible for Free Lunch, by School, 1997

MAP 1-4. DENVER REGION (CENTRAL AREA)
Change in Percentage of Elementary Students Eligible for Free Lunch, by School, 1992–97

MAP 1-5. MINNEAPOLIS–ST. PAUL REGION (CENTRAL AREA)
Percentage of Elementary Students Eligible for Free Lunch, by School, 1997

MAP 1-6. MINNEAPOLIS–ST. PAUL REGION (CENTRAL AREA)
Change in Percentage of Elementary Students Eligible for Free Lunch, by School, 1992–97

MAP 1-7. NEW YORK REGION
Percentage of Elementary Students Eligible for Free Lunch, by School, 1997

MAP 1-8. NEW YORK REGION (CENTRAL AREA)
Percentage of Elementary Students Eligible for Free Lunch, by School, 1997

MAP 1-9. NEW YORK REGION
Change in Percentage of Elementary Students Eligible for Free Lunch, by School, 1993–97

MAP 1-10. NEW YORK REGION (CENTRAL AREA)
Change in Percentage of Elementary Students Eligible for Free Lunch, by School, 1993–97

MAP 1-11. SAN FRANCISCO REGION (CENTRAL AREA)
Percentage of Elementary Students Eligible for Free Lunch, by School, 1997

MAP 1-12. SAN FRANCISCO REGION (CENTRAL AREA)
Change in Percentage of Elementary Students Eligible for Free Lunch, by School, 1992–97

MAP 1-13. ATLANTA REGION (CENTRAL AREA)
Percentage of Non-Asian Minority Elementary Students, by School, 1997

MAP 1-14. ATLANTA REGION (CENTRAL AREA)
Change in Percentage of Non-Asian Minority Elementary Students, by School, 1992–97

MAP 1-15. CHICAGO REGION (CENTRAL AREA)
Percentage of Non-Asian Minority Elementary Students, by School, 1997

MAP 1-16. CHICAGO REGION (CENTRAL AREA)
Change in Percentage of Non-Asian Minority Elementary Students, by School, 1992–97

MAP 1-17. DENVER REGION (CENTRAL AREA)
Percentage of Non-Asian Minority Elementary Students, by School, 1997

MAP 1-18. DENVER REGION (CENTRAL AREA)
Change in Percentage of Non-Asian Minority Elementary Students, by School, 1992–97

MAP 1-19. MINNEAPOLIS–ST. PAUL REGION (CENTRAL AREA)
Percentage of Non-Asian Minority Elementary Students, by School, 1997

MAP 1-20. MINNEAPOLIS–ST. PAUL REGION (CENTRAL AREA)
Change in Percentage of Non-Asian Minority Elementary Students, by School, 1992–97

MAP 1-21. NEW YORK REGION (CENTRAL AREA)
Percentage of Non-Asian Minority Elementary Students, by School, 1997

MAP 1-22. NEW YORK REGION (CENTRAL AREA)
Change in Percentage of Non-Asian Minority Elementary Students, by School, 1992–97

MAP 1-23. SAN FRANCISCO REGION (CENTRAL AREA)
Percentage of Non-Asian Minority Elementary Students, by School, 1997

MAP 1-24. SAN FRANCISCO REGION (CENTRAL AREA)
Change in Percentage of Non-Asian Minority Elementary Students, by School, 1992–97

MAP 1-25. ATLANTA REGION
Tax Capacity per Household, by Municipality and County Unincorporated Area, 1998

MAP 1-26. ATLANTA REGION
Percentage Change in Tax Capacity per Household, by Municipality and County Unincorporated Area, 1993–98

MAP 1-27. CHICAGO REGION
Tax Capacity per Household, by Municipality and County Unincorporated Area, 1998

MAP 1-28. CHICAGO REGION
Percentage Change in Tax Capacity per Household, by Municipality and County Unincorporated Area, 1993–98

MAP 1-29. DENVER REGION
Tax Capacity per Household, by Municipality and County Unincorporated Area, 1998

MAP 1-30. DENVER REGION
Percentage Change in Tax Capacity per Household, by Municipality and County Unincorporated Area, 1993–98

MAP 1-31. MINNEAPOLIS–ST. PAUL REGION
Tax Capacity per Household, by Municipality, 1998

MAP 1-32. MINNEAPOLIS–ST. PAUL REGION (CENTRAL AREA)
Percentage Change in Tax Capacity per Household, by Municipality, 1993–98

MAP 1-33. NEW YORK REGION
Tax Capacity per Household, by Municipality, 1998

MAP 1-34. NEW YORK REGION (CENTRAL AREA)
Tax Capacity per Household, by Municipality, 1998

MAP 1-35. NEW YORK REGION
Percentage Change in Tax Capacity per Household, by Municipality, 1993–98

MAP 1-36. NEW YORK REGION (CENTRAL AREA)
Percentage Change in Tax Capacity per Household, by Municipality, 1993–98

MAP 1-37. SAN FRANCISCO REGION
Tax Capacity per Household, by Municipality and County Unincorporated Area, 1998

MAP 1-38. SAN FRANCISCO REGION
Percentage Change in Tax Capacity per Household, by Municipality and County Unincorporated Area, 1993–98

MAP 1-1. ATLANTA REGION (CENTRAL AREA)
Percentage of Elementary Students Eligible for Free Lunch, by School, 1997

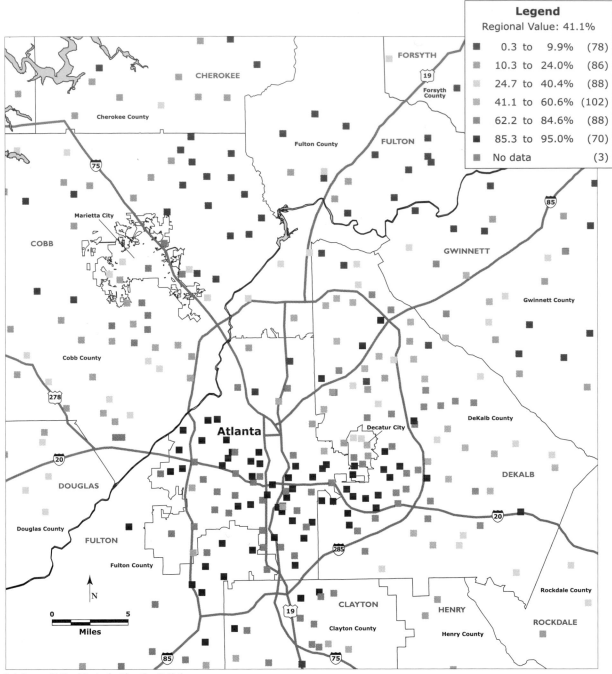

Legend

Regional Value: 41.1%

■	0.3 to 9.9%	(78)
■	10.3 to 24.0%	(86)
■	24.7 to 40.4%	(88)
■	41.1 to 60.6%	(102)
■	62.2 to 84.6%	(88)
■	85.3 to 95.0%	(70)
■	No data	(3)

Data Source: National Center for Education Statistics.

MAP 1-2. ATLANTA REGION (CENTRAL AREA)
Change in Percentage of Elementary Students Eligible for Free Lunch, by School, 1992–97

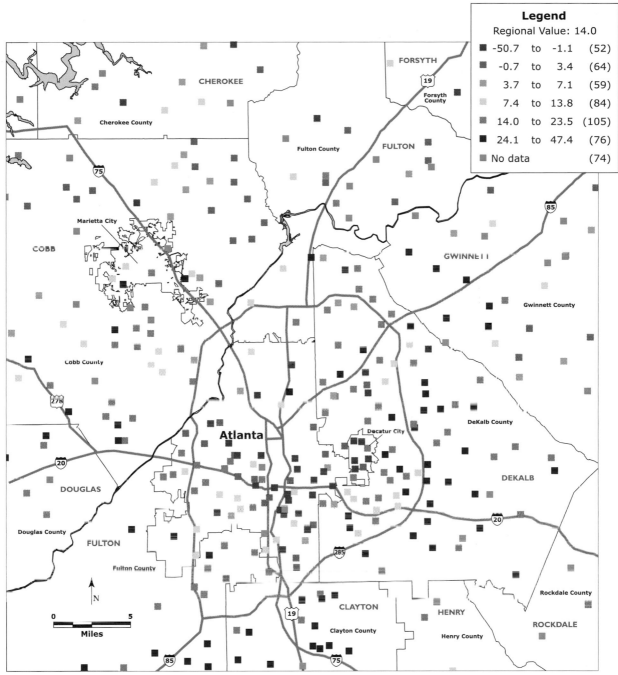

Legend
Regional Value: 14.0

■	-50.7 to -1.1	(52)
■	-0.7 to 3.4	(64)
■	3.7 to 7.1	(59)
■	7.4 to 13.8	(84)
■	14.0 to 23.5	(105)
■	24.1 to 47.4	(76)
■	No data	(74)

Data Source: National Center for Education Statistics.

MAP 1-3. DENVER REGION (CENTRAL AREA)
Percentage of Elementary Students Eligible for Free Lunch, by School, 1997

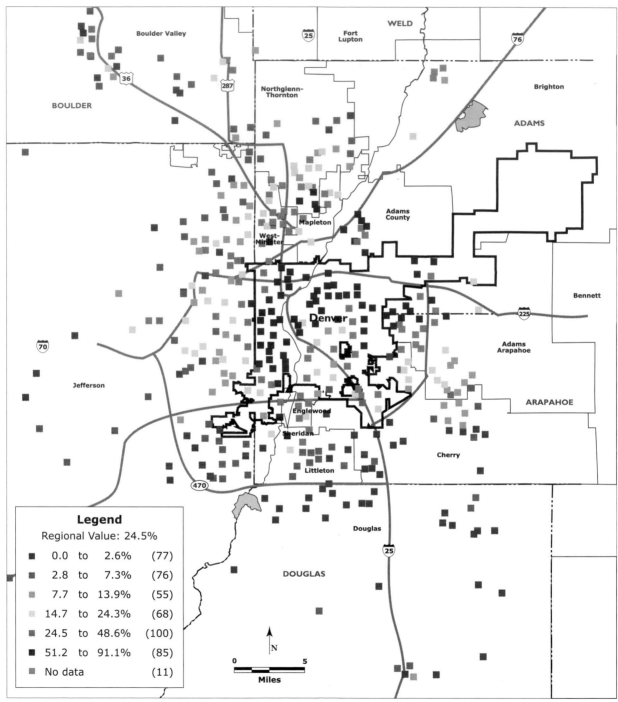

Legend

Regional Value: 24.5%

■	0.0 to 2.6%	(77)
■	2.8 to 7.3%	(76)
■	7.7 to 13.9%	(55)
■	14.7 to 24.3%	(68)
■	24.5 to 48.6%	(100)
■	51.2 to 91.1%	(85)
■	No data	(11)

Data Source: National Center for Educational Statistics.

MAP 1-4. DENVER REGION (CENTRAL AREA)
Change in Percentage of Elementary Students Eligible for Free Lunch, by School, 1992–97

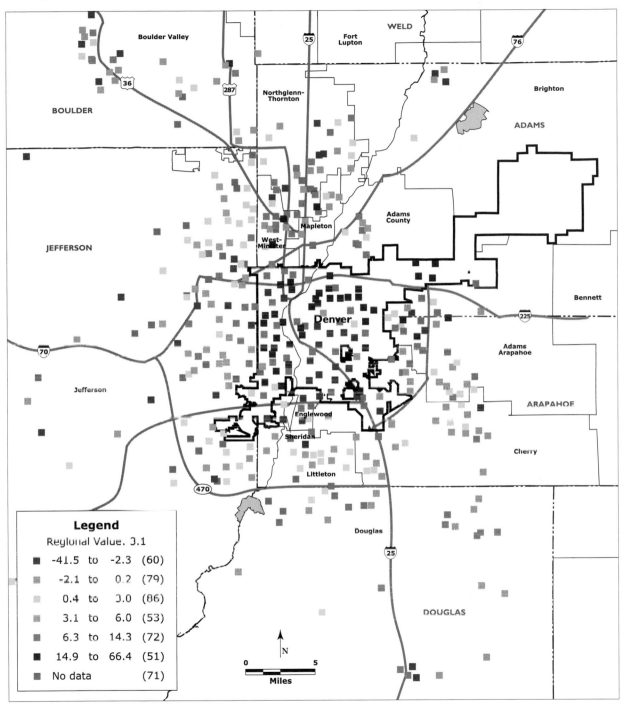

Legend

Regional Value: 3.1

■	-41.5 to -2.3	(60)
■	-2.1 to 0.2	(79)
■	0.4 to 3.0	(86)
■	3.1 to 6.0	(53)
■	6.3 to 14.3	(72)
■	14.9 to 66.4	(51)
■	No data	(71)

0 — 5 Miles

N

Data Source: National Center for Educational Statistics.

MAP 1-5. MINNEAPOLIS–ST. PAUL REGION (CENTRAL AREA)
Percentage of Elementary Students Eligible for Free Lunch, by School, 1997

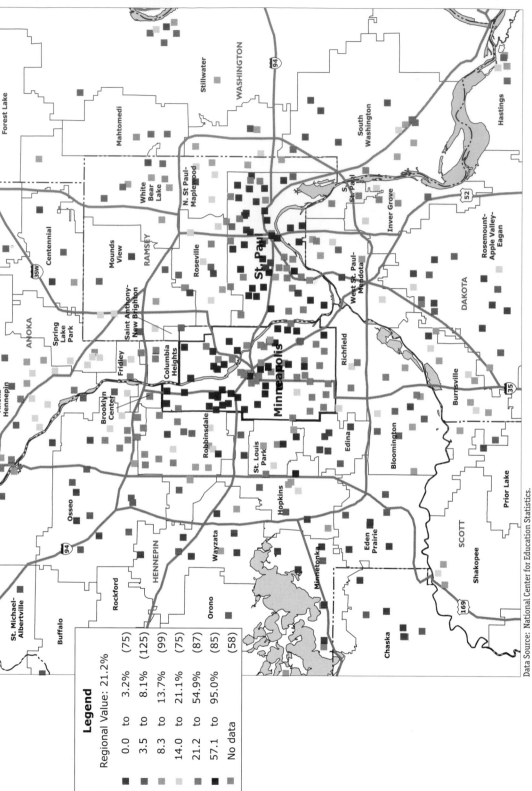

Legend

Regional Value: 21.2%

0.0	to	3.2%	(75)
3.5	to	8.1%	(125)
8.3	to	13.7%	(99)
14.0	to	21.1%	(75)
21.2	to	54.9%	(87)
57.1	to	95.0%	(85)
No data			(58)

Data Source: National Center for Education Statistics.

MAP 1-6. MINNEAPOLIS–ST. PAUL REGION (CENTRAL AREA)
Change in Percentage of Elementary Students Eligible for Free Lunch, by School, 1992–97

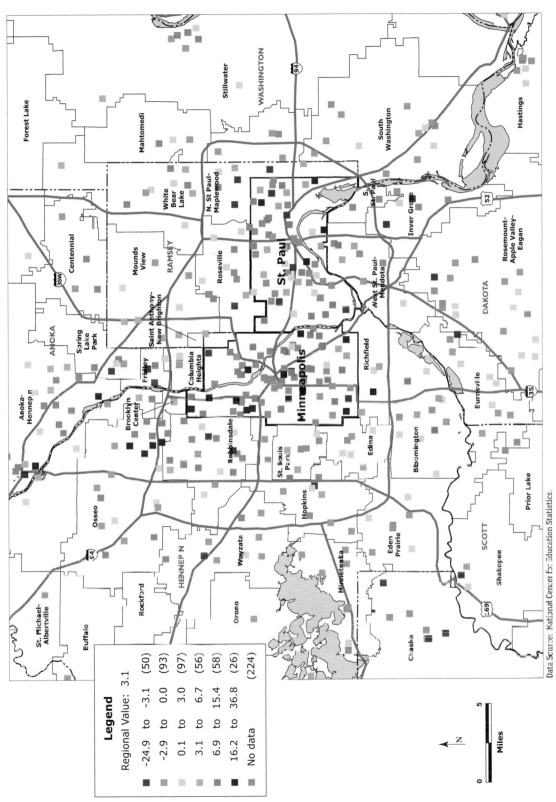

Legend

Regional Value: 3.1

-24.9 to -3.1	(50)
-2.9 to 0.0	(93)
0.1 to 3.0	(97)
3.1 to 6.7	(56)
6.9 to 15.4	(58)
16.2 to 36.8	(26)
No data	(224)

N

0 5
Miles

Data Source: National Center for Education Statistics.

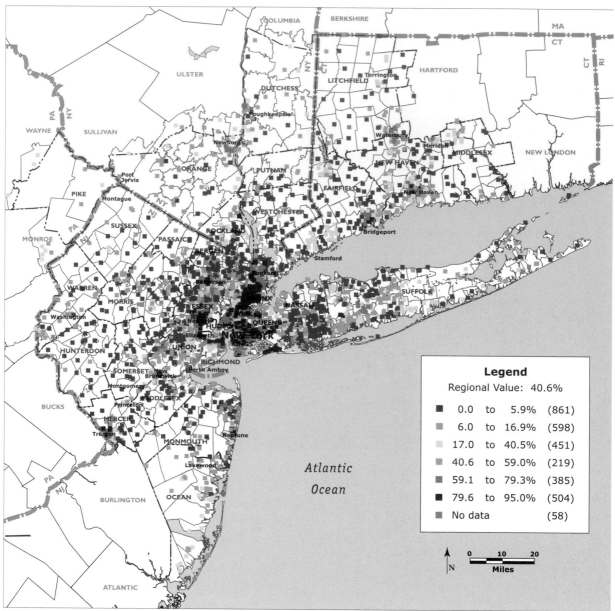

Legend

Regional Value: 40.6%

■	0.0 to 5.9%	(861)
■	6.0 to 16.9%	(598)
■	17.0 to 40.5%	(451)
■	40.6 to 59.0%	(219)
■	59.1 to 79.3%	(385)
■	79.6 to 95.0%	(504)
■	No data	(58)

0 10 20
Miles

Data Source: National Center for Education Statistics.

MAP 1-8. NEW YORK REGION (CENTRAL AREA)
Percentage of Elementary Students Eligible for Free Lunch, by School, 1997

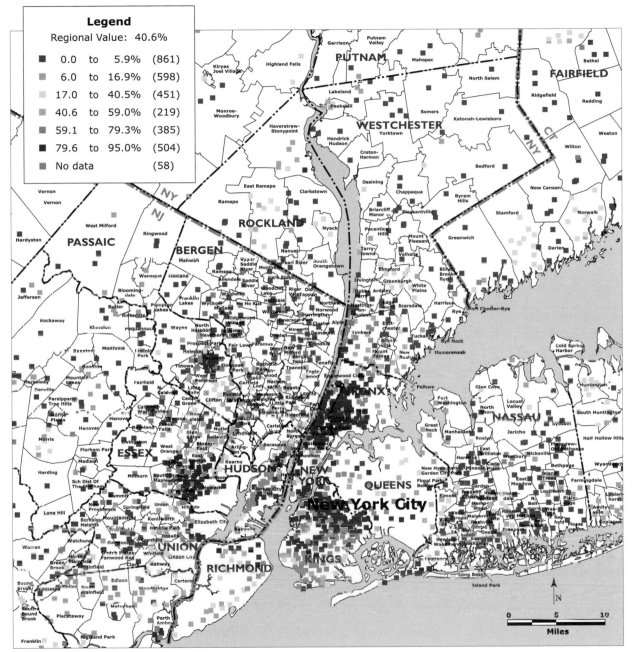

Legend

Regional Value: 40.6%

■	0.0	to	5.9%	(861)
■	6.0	to	16.9%	(598)
■	17.0	to	40.5%	(451)
■	40.6	to	59.0%	(219)
■	59.1	to	79.3%	(385)
■	79.6	to	95.0%	(504)
■	No data			(58)

Data Source: National Center for Education Statistics.

MAP 1-9. NEW YORK REGION
Change in Percentage of Elementary Students Eligible for Free Lunch, by School, 1993–97

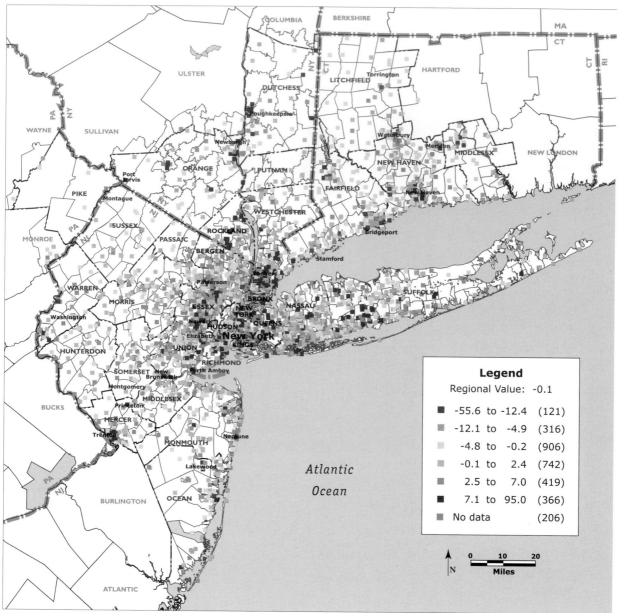

Legend

Regional Value: -0.1

■	-55.6 to -12.4	(121)
■	-12.1 to -4.9	(316)
■	-4.8 to -0.2	(906)
■	-0.1 to 2.4	(742)
■	2.5 to 7.0	(419)
■	7.1 to 95.0	(366)
■	No data	(206)

0   10   20
Miles

N

Data Sources: National Center for Education Statistics; New York State Education Department.

MAP 1-10. NEW YORK REGION (CENTRAL AREA)
Change in Percentage of Elementary Students Eligible for Free Lunch, by School, 1993–97

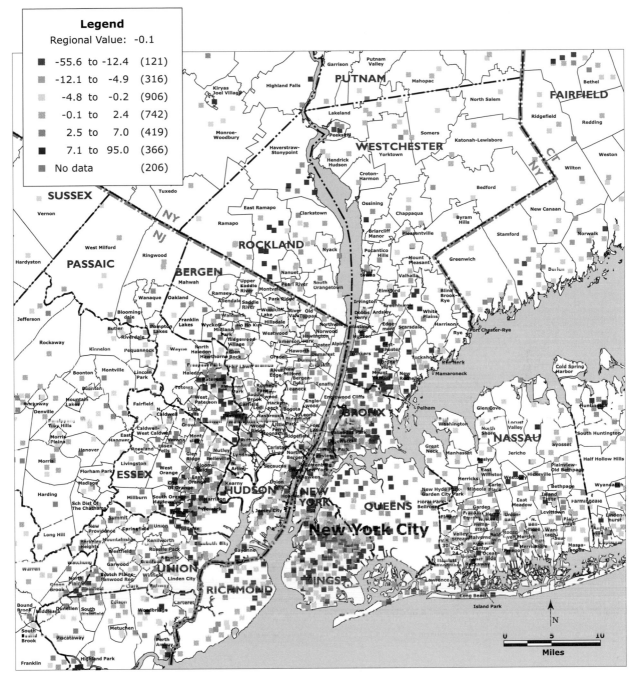

Legend

Regional Value: -0.1

■	-55.6 to -12.4	(121)
■	-12.1 to -4.9	(316)
■	-4.8 to -0.2	(906)
■	-0.1 to 2.4	(742)
■	2.5 to 7.0	(419)
■	7.1 to 95.0	(366)
■	No data	(206)

Data Sources: National Center for Education Statistics; New York State Education Department.

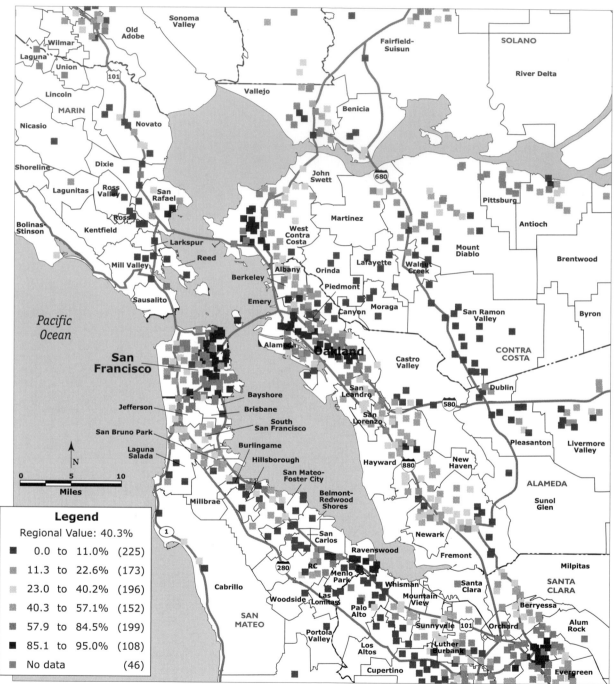

Legend
Regional Value: 40.3%

■	0.0 to 11.0%	(225)
■	11.3 to 22.6%	(173)
■	23.0 to 40.2%	(196)
■	40.3 to 57.1%	(152)
■	57.9 to 84.5%	(199)
■	85.1 to 95.0%	(108)
■	No data	(46)

Data Source: National Center for Education Statistics.

MAP 1-12. SAN FRANCISCO REGION (CENTRAL AREA)
Change in Percentage of Elementary Students Eligible for Free Lunch, by School, 1992–97

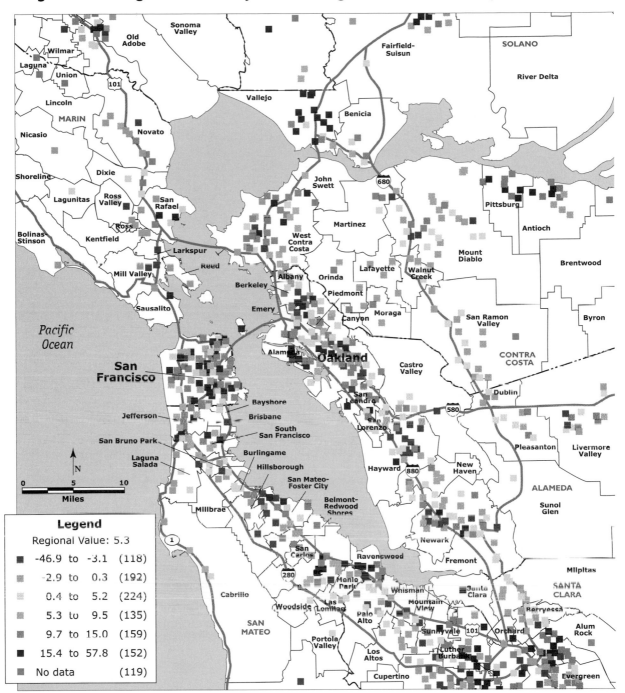

Legend

Regional Value: 5.3

■	-46.9 to -3.1	(118)
▨	-2.9 to 0.3	(192)
▫	0.4 to 5.2	(224)
▨	5.3 to 9.5	(135)
▨	9.7 to 15.0	(159)
■	15.4 to 57.8	(152)
▪	No data	(119)

Data Source: National Center for Education Statistics.

MAP 1-13. ATLANTA REGION (CENTRAL AREA)
Percentage of Non-Asian Minority Elementary Students, by School, 1997

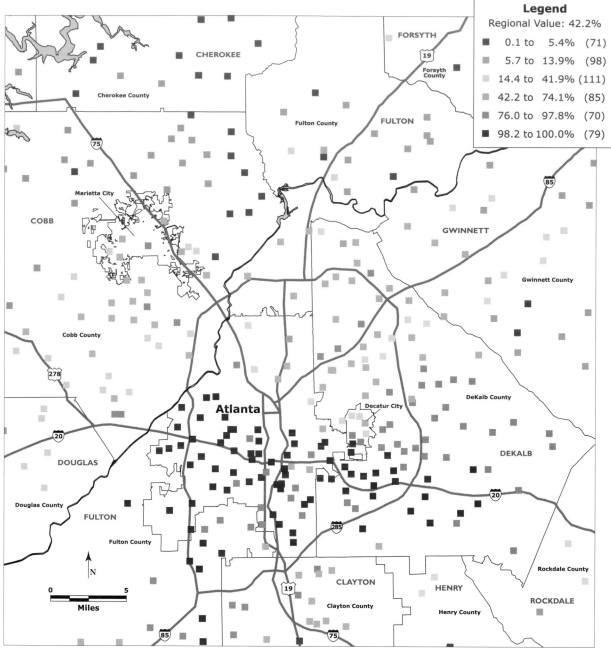

Legend
Regional Value: 42.2%

- 0.1 to 5.4% (71)
- 5.7 to 13.9% (98)
- 14.4 to 41.9% (111)
- 42.2 to 74.1% (85)
- 76.0 to 97.8% (70)
- 98.2 to 100.0% (79)

Data Source: National Center for Education Statistics.

MAP 1-14. ATLANTA REGION (CENTRAL AREA)
Change in Percentage of Non-Asian Minority Elementary Students, by School, 1992–97

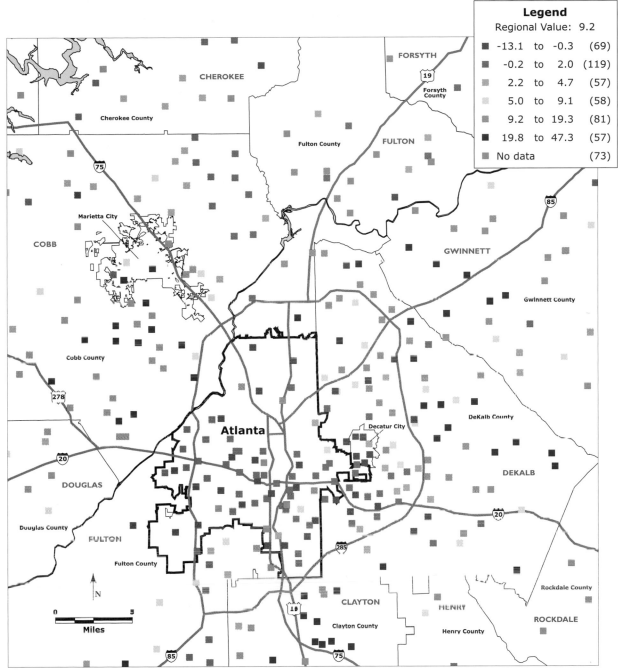

Legend
Regional Value: 9.2

■	-13.1 to -0.3	(69)
■	-0.2 to 2.0	(119)
■	2.2 to 4.7	(57)
■	5.0 to 9.1	(58)
■	9.2 to 19.3	(81)
■	19.8 to 47.3	(57)
■	No data	(73)

Data Source: National Center for Education Statistics.

MAP 1-15. CHICAGO REGION (CENTRAL AREA)
Percentage of Non-Asian Minority Elementary Students, by School, 1997

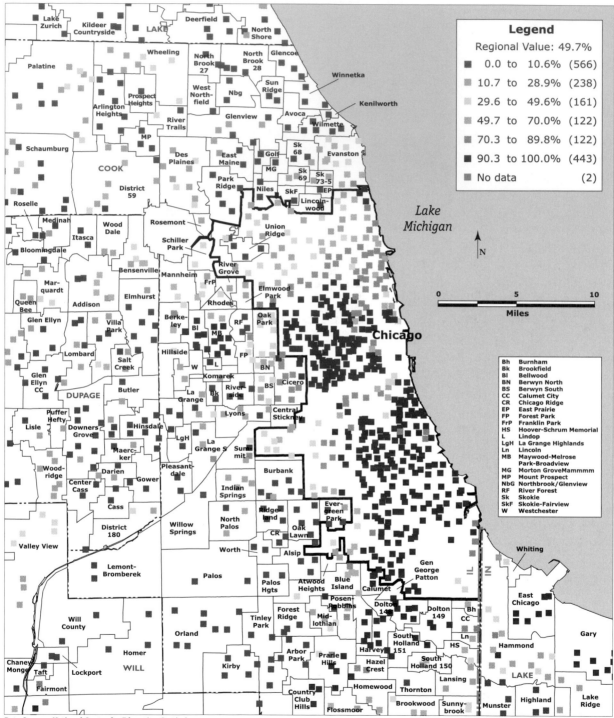

Legend

Regional Value: 49.7%

■	0.0 to 10.6%	(566)
■	10.7 to 28.9%	(238)
■	29.6 to 49.6%	(161)
■	49.7 to 70.0%	(122)
■	70.3 to 89.8%	(122)
■	90.3 to 100.0%	(443)
■	No data	(2)

Bh Burnham
Bk Brookfield
Bl Bellwood
BN Berwyn North
BS Berwyn South
CC Calumet City
CR Chicago Ridge
EP East Prairie
FP Forest Park
FrP Franklin Park
HS Hoover-Schrum Memorial
L Lindop
LgH La Grange Highlands
Ln Lincoln
MB Maywood-Melrose
     Park-Broadview
MG Morton Grove Mammmm
MP Mount Prospect
NbG Northbrook/Glenview
RF River Forest
Sk Skokie
SkF Skokie-Fairview
W Westchester

Lake Michigan

Data Source: National Center for Education Statistics.

MAP 1-16. CHICAGO REGION (CENTRAL AREA)
Change in Percentage of Non-Asian Minority Elementary Students, by School, 1992–97

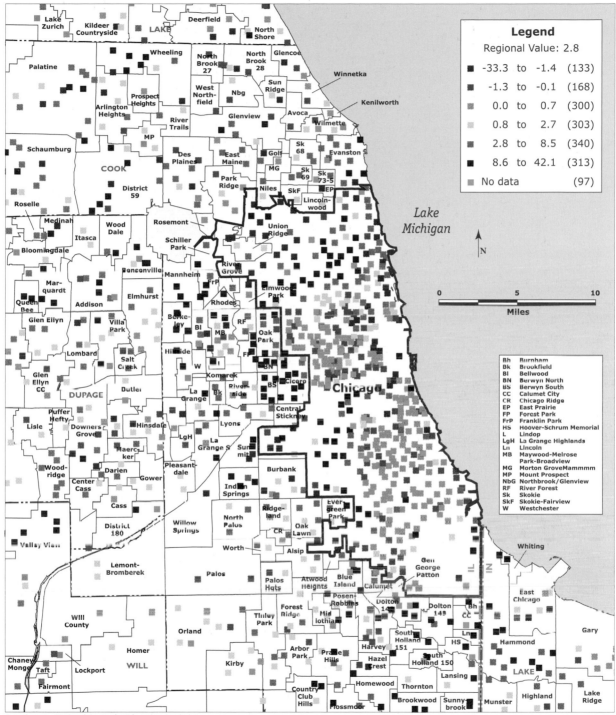

Legend

Regional Value: 2.8

■	-33.3 to -1.4	(133)
■	-1.3 to -0.1	(168)
▨	0.0 to 0.7	(300)
▨	0.8 to 2.7	(303)
▨	2.8 to 8.5	(340)
■	8.6 to 42.1	(313)
▨	No data	(97)

Bh	Burnham
Bk	Brookfield
Bl	Bellwood
BN	Berwyn North
BS	Berwyn South
CC	Calumet City
CR	Chicago Ridge
EP	East Prairie
FP	Forest Park
FrP	Franklin Park
HS	Hoover-Schrum Memorial
L	Lindop
LgH	La Grange Highlands
Ln	Lincoln
MB	Maywood-Melrose Park-Broadview
MG	Morton GroveMammmm
MP	Mount Prospect
NbG	Northbrook/Glenview
RF	River Forest
Sk	Skokie
SkF	Skokie-Fairview
W	Westchester

Data Source: National Center for Education Statistics.

MAP 1-17. DENVER REGION (CENTRAL AREA)
Percentage of Non-Asian Minority Elementary Students, by School, 1997

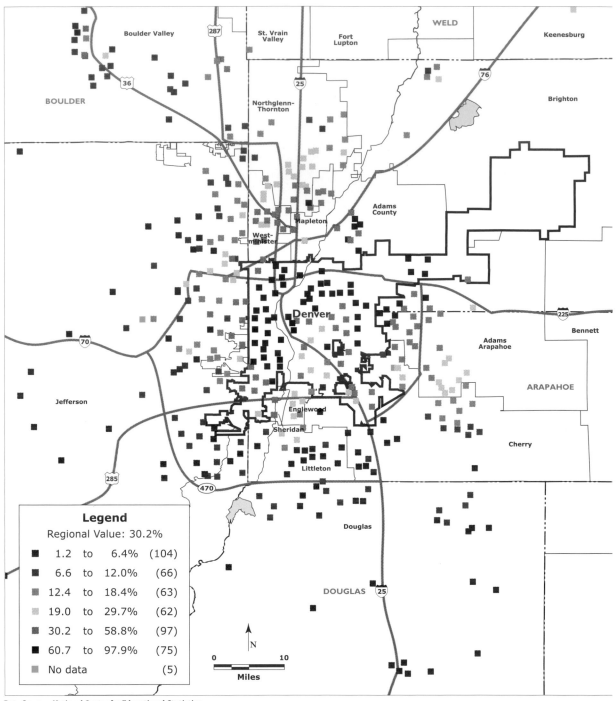

Legend

Regional Value: 30.2%

- ■ 1.2 to 6.4% (104)
- ■ 6.6 to 12.0% (66)
- ■ 12.4 to 18.4% (63)
- ■ 19.0 to 29.7% (62)
- ■ 30.2 to 58.8% (97)
- ■ 60.7 to 97.9% (75)
- ■ No data (5)

N

0   10

Miles

Data Source: National Center for Educational Statistics.

MAP 1-18. DENVER REGION (CENTRAL AREA)
Change in Percentage of Non-Asian Minority Elementary Students, by School, 1992–97

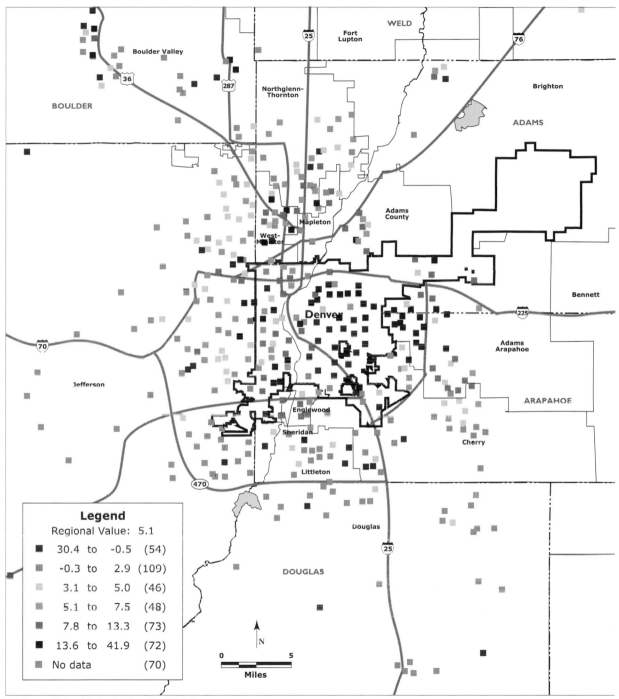

Legend

Regional Value: 5.1

■	30.4 to −0.5	(54)
■	−0.3 to 2.9	(109)
■	3.1 to 5.0	(46)
■	5.1 to 7.5	(48)
■	7.8 to 13.3	(73)
■	13.6 to 41.9	(72)
■	No data	(70)

0   5
Miles

Data Source: National Center for Educational Statistics.

MAP 1-19. MINNEAPOLIS–ST. PAUL REGION (CENTRAL AREA)
Percentage of Non-Asian Minority Elementary Students, by School, 1997

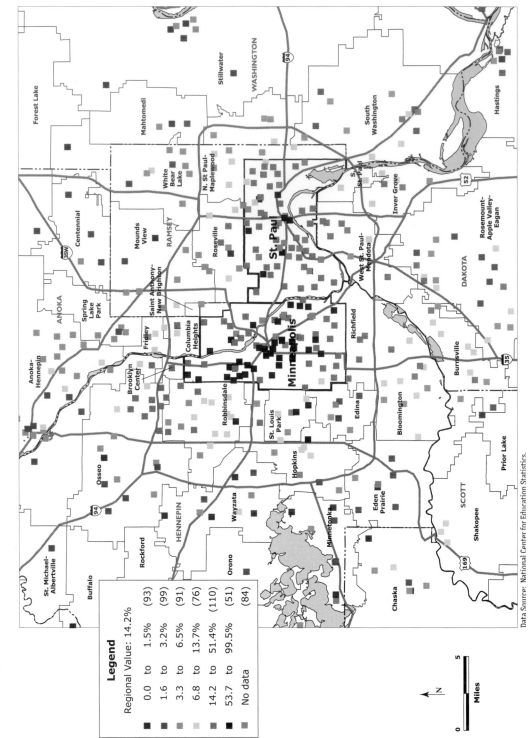

Legend

Regional Value: 14.2%

0.0	to	1.5%	(93)	
1.6	to	3.2%	(99)	
3.3	to	6.5%	(91)	
6.8	to	13.7%	(76)	
14.2	to	51.4%	(110)	
53.7	to	99.5%	(51)	
No data			(84)	

Data Source: National Center for Education Statistics.

MAP 1-20. MINNEAPOLIS-ST. PAUL REGION (CENTRAL AREA)
Change in Percentage of Non-Asian Minority Elementary Students, by School, 1992–97

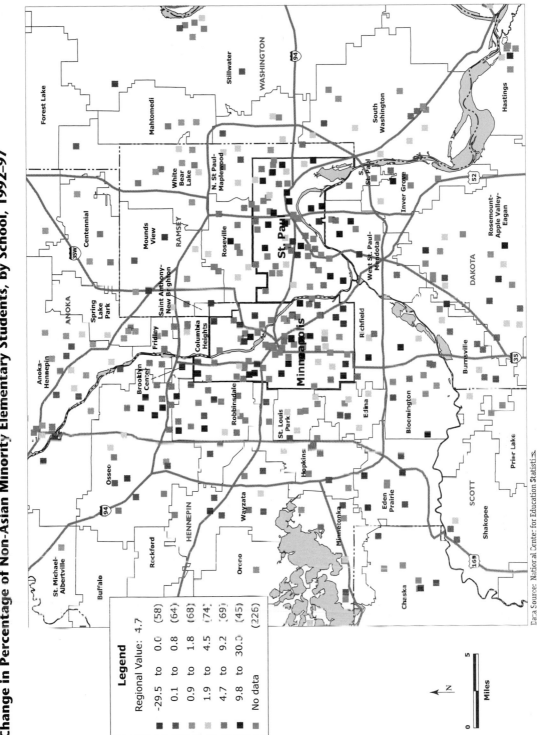

Legend

Regional Value: 4.7

-29.5 to 0.0	(58)
0.1 to 0.8	(64)
0.9 to 1.8	(68)
1.9 to 4.5	(74)
4.7 to 9.2	(69)
9.8 to 30.0	(45)
No data	(226)

N

0 ___ 5

Miles

Data Source: National Center for Education Statistics

MAP 1-21. NEW YORK REGION (CENTRAL AREA)
Percentage of Non-Asian Minority Elementary Students, by School, 1997

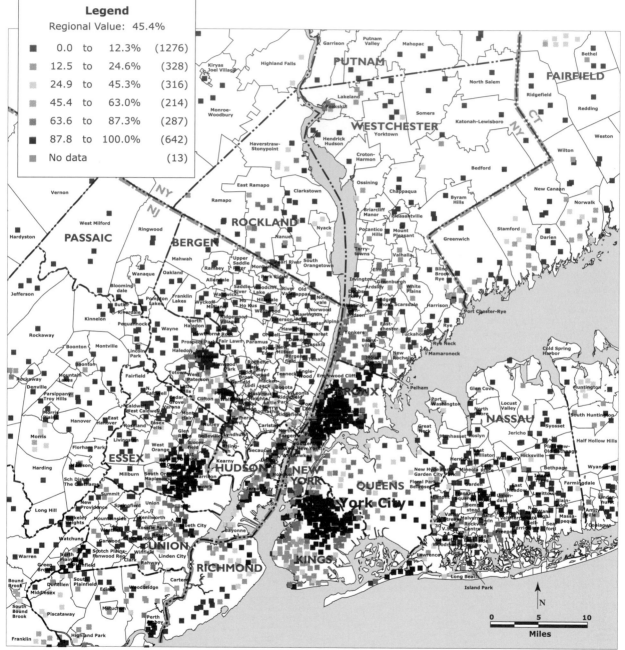

Legend

Regional Value: 45.4%

■	0.0	to	12.3%	(1276)
■	12.5	to	24.6%	(328)
■	24.9	to	45.3%	(316)
■	45.4	to	63.0%	(214)
■	63.6	to	87.3%	(287)
■	87.8	to	100.0%	(642)
■	No data			(13)

Data Source: National Center for Education Statistics.

MAP 1-22. NEW YORK REGION (CENTRAL AREA)
Change in Percentage of Non-Asian Minority Elementary Students, by School, 1992–97

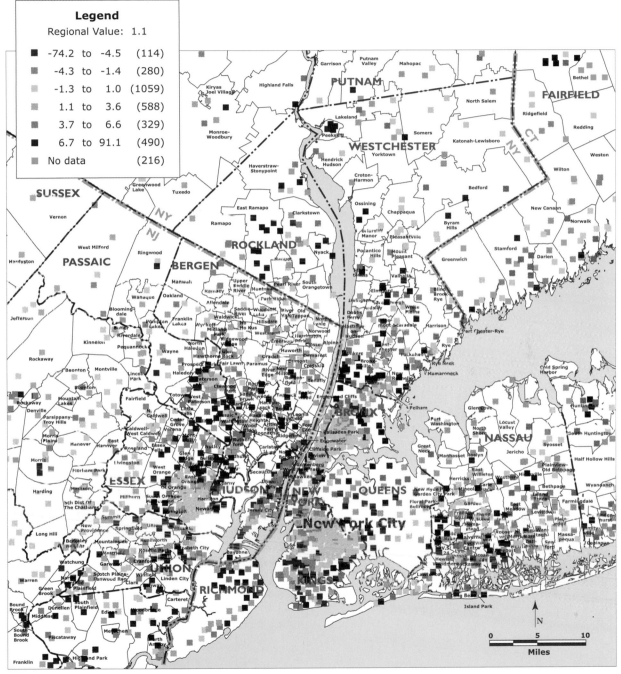

Legend

Regional Value: 1.1

■	-74.2 to -4.5	(114)
■	-4.3 to -1.4	(280)
▨	-1.3 to 1.0	(1059)
▨	1.1 to 3.6	(588)
▨	3.7 to 6.6	(329)
■	6.7 to 91.1	(490)
▨	No data	(216)

Data Source: National Center for Education Statistics.

MAP 1-23. SAN FRANCISCO REGION (CENTRAL AREA)
Percentage of Non-Asian Minority Elementary Students, by School, 1997

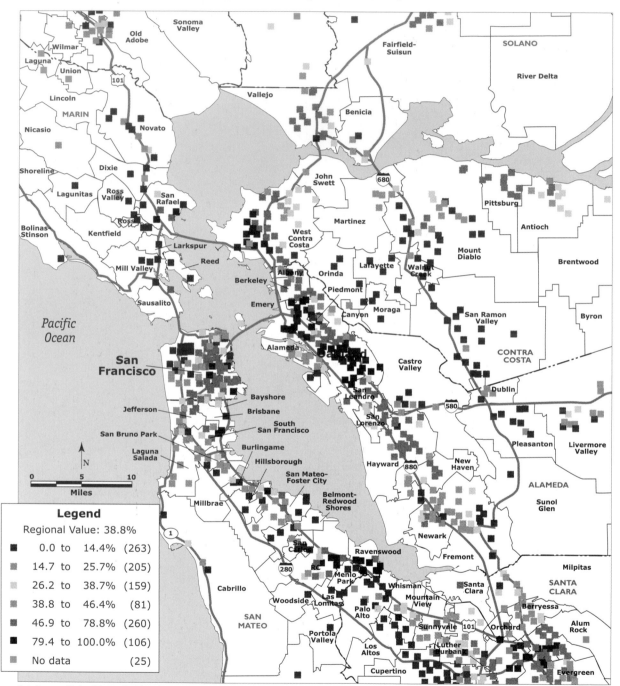

Legend

Regional Value: 38.8%

■	0.0 to 14.4%	(263)
■	14.7 to 25.7%	(205)
■	26.2 to 38.7%	(159)
■	38.8 to 46.4%	(81)
■	46.9 to 78.8%	(260)
■	79.4 to 100.0%	(106)
■	No data	(25)

Data Source: National Center for Education Statistics.

MAP 1-24. SAN FRANCISCO REGION (CENTRAL AREA)
Change in Percentage of Non-Asian Minority Elementary Students, by School, 1992–97

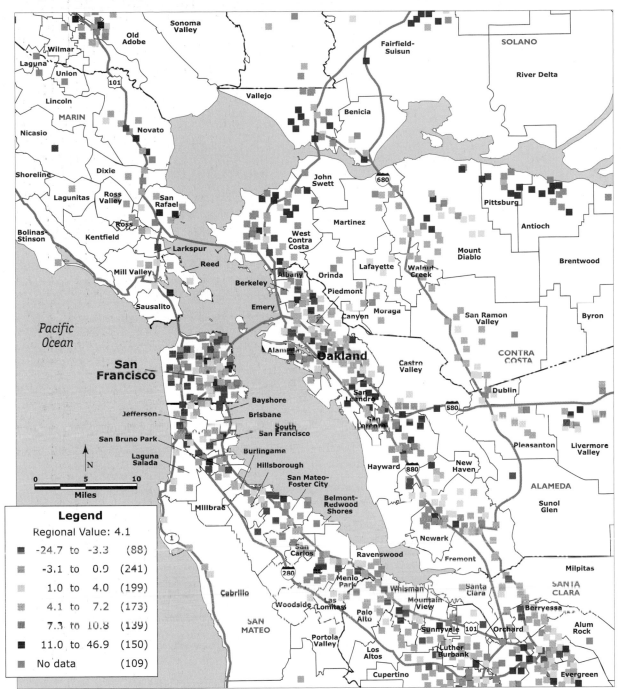

Legend

Regional Value: 4.1

■	-24.7 to -3.3	(88)
■	-3.1 to 0.9	(241)
■	1.0 to 4.0	(199)
■	4.1 to 7.2	(173)
■	7.3 to 10.8	(139)
■	11.0 to 46.9	(150)
■	No data	(109)

Data Source: National Center for Education Statistics.

MAP 1-25. ATLANTA REGION
Tax Capacity per Household, by Municipality and County Unincorporated Area, 1998

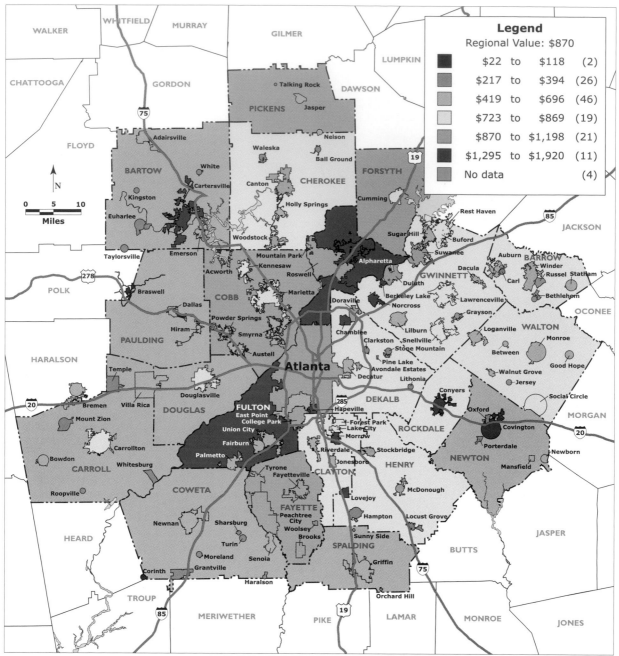

Legend

Regional Value: $870

$22	to	$118	(2)
$217	to	$394	(26)
$419	to	$696	(46)
$723	to	$869	(19)
$870	to	$1,198	(21)
$1,295	to	$1,920	(11)
No data			(4)

Data Sources: Georgia Department of Revenue (property tax data); MARC (household estimates).

MAP 1-26. ATLANTA REGION
Percentage Change in Tax Capacity per Household, by Municipality and County Unincorporated Area, 1993–98

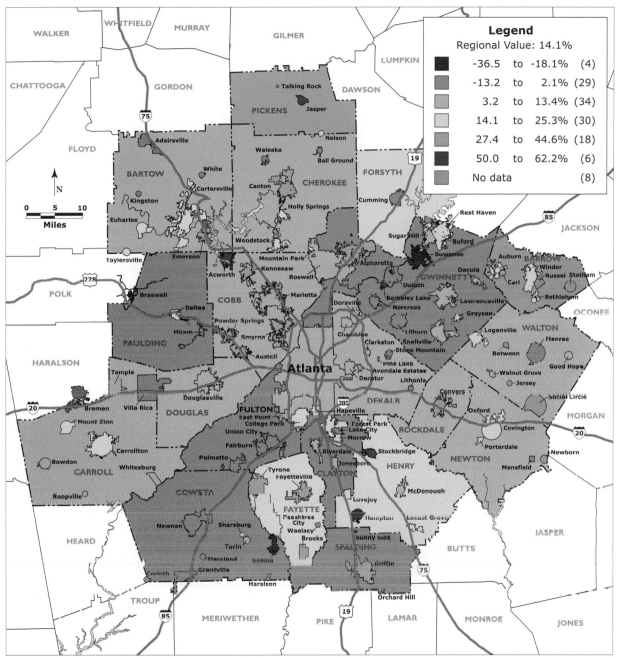

Data Sources: Georgia Department of Revenue (property tax data); MARC (household estimates).

MAP 1-27. CHICAGO REGION
Tax Capacity per Household, by Municipality and County Unincorporated Area, 1998

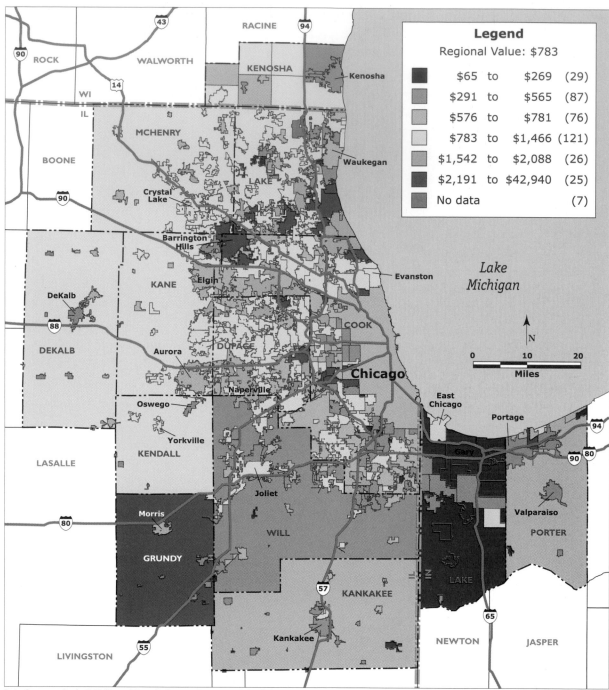

Legend

Regional Value: $783

	$65	to	$269	(29)
	$291	to	$565	(87)
	$576	to	$781	(76)
	$783	to	$1,466	(121)
	$1,542	to	$2,088	(26)
	$2,191	to	$42,940	(25)
	No data			(7)

Data Sources: Cook, DeKalb, and Grundy County Assessors; Lake (IL), Kane, DuPage, Will, McHenry, Kendall, and Kankakee County Clerks (property tax data); Wisconsin and Illinois Departments of Revenue (property and sales tax data); Indiana State Board of Tax Commissioners (property and sales tax data); MARC (household estimates).

MAP 1-28. CHICAGO REGION
Percentage Change in Tax Capacity per Household, by Municipality and County Unincorporated Area, 1993–98

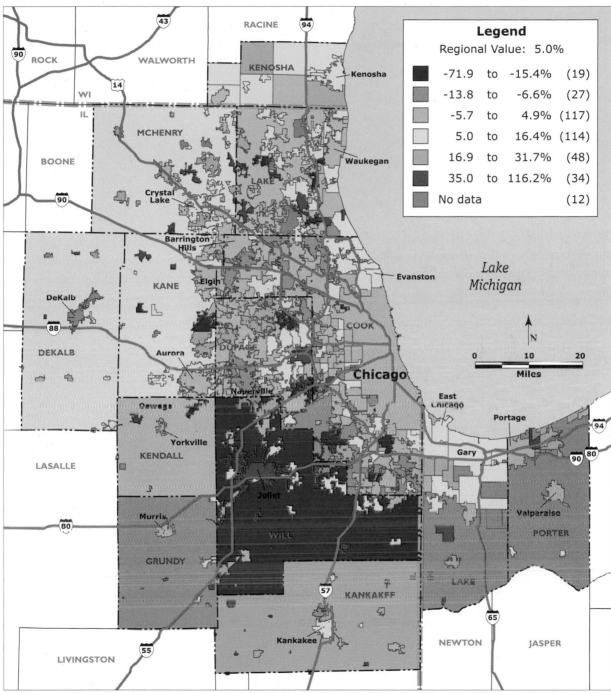

Legend

Regional Value: 5.0%

-71.9	to	-15.4%	(19)
-13.8	to	-6.6%	(27)
-5.7	to	4.9%	(117)
5.0	to	16.4%	(114)
16.9	to	31.7%	(48)
35.0	to	116.2%	(34)
No data			(12)

Data Sources: Cook, DeKalb, and Grundy County Assessors; Lake (IL), Kane, DuPage, Will, McHenry, Kendall, and Kankakee County Clerks (property tax data); Wisconsin and Illinois Departments of Revenue (property and sales tax data); Indiana State Board of Tax Commissioners (property and sales tax data); MARC (household estimates).

MAP 1-29. DENVER REGION
Tax Capacity per Household, by Municipality and County Unincorporated Area, 1998

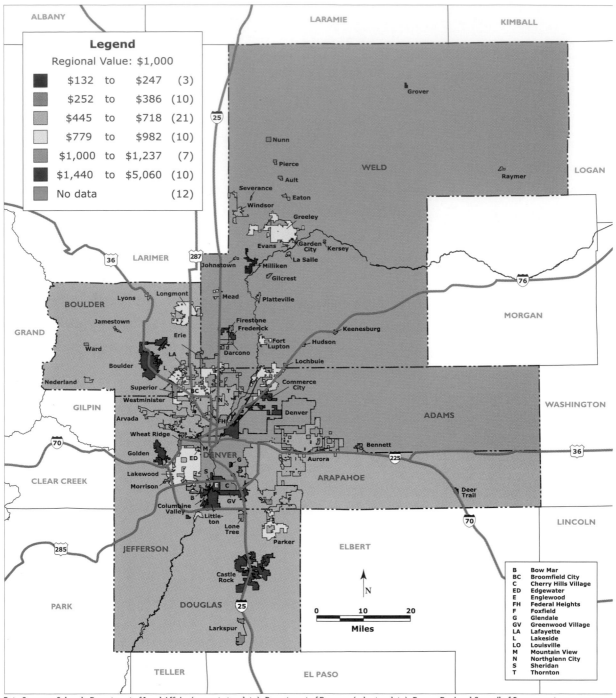

Legend
Regional Value: $1,000

$132	to	$247	(3)
$252	to	$386	(10)
$445	to	$718	(21)
$779	to	$982	(10)
$1,000	to	$1,237	(7)
$1,440	to	$5,060	(10)
No data			(12)

B   Bow Mar
BC   Broomfield City
C   Cherry Hills Village
ED   Edgewater
E   Englewood
FH   Federal Heights
F   Foxfield
G   Glendale
GV   Greenwood Village
LA   Lafayette
L   Lakeside
LO   Louisville
M   Mountain View
N   Northglenn City
S   Sheridan
T   Thornton

N

0   10   20
Miles

Data Sources: Colorado Department of Local Affairs (property tax data); Department of Revenue (sales tax data); Denver Regional Council of Governments (household estimates).

MAP 1-30. DENVER REGION
Percentage Change in Tax Capacity per Household, by Municipality and County Unincorporated Area, 1993–98

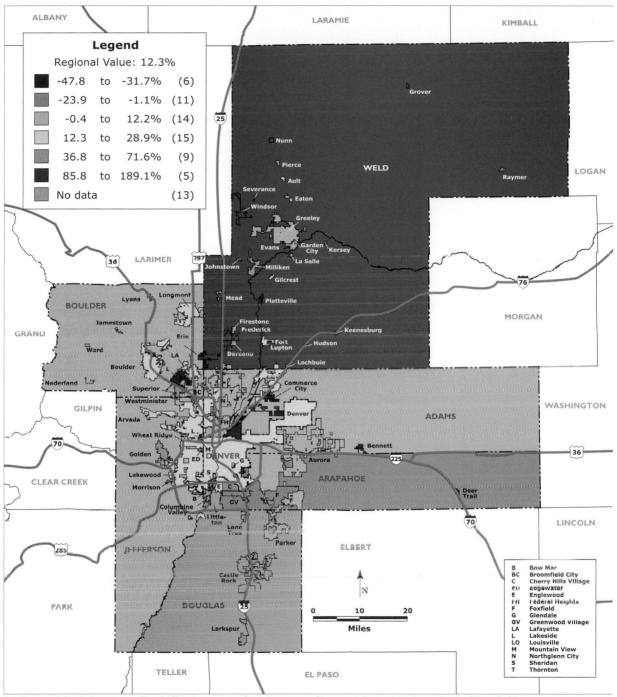

Legend

Regional Value: 12.3%

■	-47.8	to	-31.7%	(6)
■	-23.9	to	-1.1%	(11)
■	-0.4	to	12.2%	(14)
■	12.3	to	28.9%	(15)
■	36.8	to	71.6%	(9)
■	85.8	to	189.1%	(5)
■	No data			(13)

B	Bow Mar
BC	Broomfield City
C	Cherry Hills Village
ED	Edgewater
E	Englewood
FH	Federal Heights
F	Foxfield
G	Glendale
GV	Greenwood Village
LA	Lafayette
L	Lakeside
LO	Louisville
M	Mountain View
N	Northglenn City
S	Sheridan
T	Thornton

Data Sources: Colorado Department of Local Affairs (property tax data); Department of Revenue (sales tax data); Denver Regional Council of Governments (household estimates).

MAP 1-31. MINNEAPOLIS–ST. PAUL REGION
Tax Capacity per Household, by Municipality, 1998

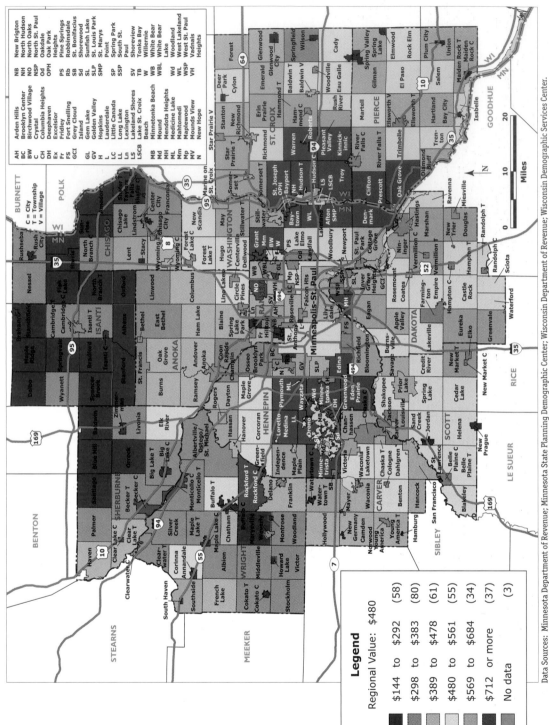

Legend

Regional Value: $480

$144 to $292	(58)
$298 to $383	(80)
$389 to $478	(61)
$480 to $561	(55)
$569 to $684	(34)
$712 or more	(37)
No data	(3)

Data Sources: Minnesota Department of Revenue; Minnesota State Planning Demographic Center; Wisconsin Department of Revenue; Wisconsin Demographic Services Center.

MAP 1-32. MINNEAPOLIS–ST. PAUL REGION (CENTRAL AREA)
Percentage Change in Tax Capacity per Household, by Municipality, 1993–98

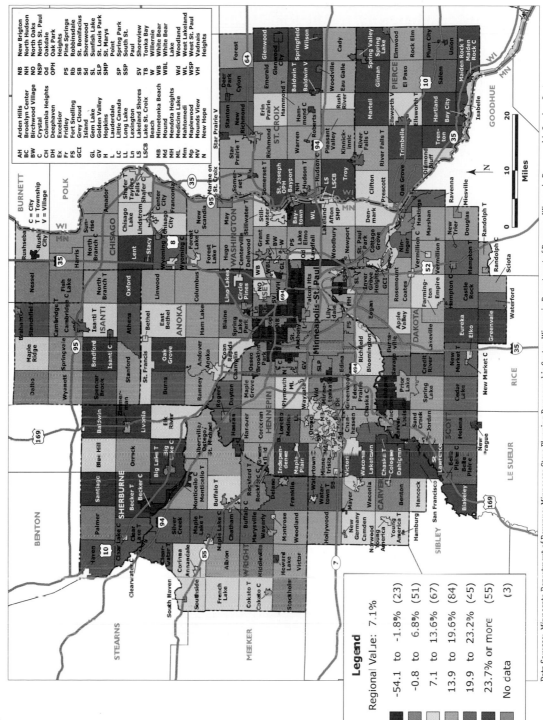

Legend

Regional Value: 7.1%

-54.1 to -1.8% (23)
-0.8 to 6.8% (51)
7.1 to 13.6% (67)
13.9 to 19.6% (84)
19.9 to 23.2% (<5)
23.7% or more (55)
No data (3)

Data Sources: Minnesota Department of Revenue; Minnesota State Planning Demographic Center; Wisconsin Department of Revenue; Wisconsin Demographic Services Center.

MAP 1-33. NEW YORK REGION
Tax Capacity per Household, by Municipality, 1998

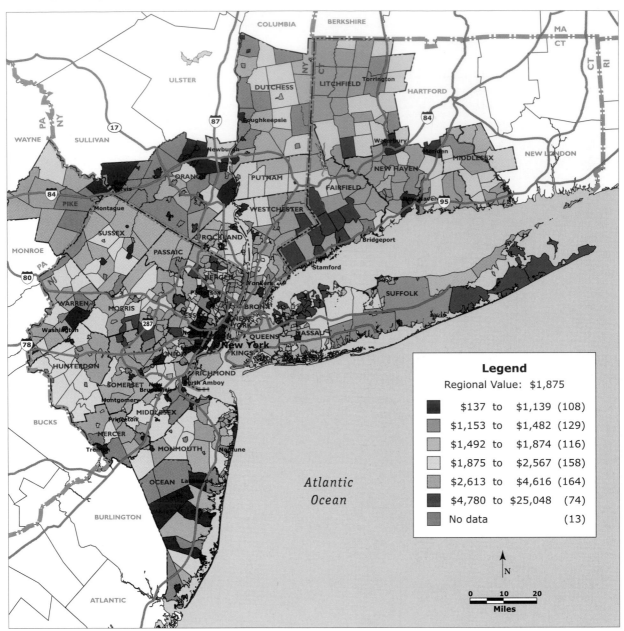

Legend

Regional Value: $1,875

$137 to $1,139 (108)
$1,153 to $1,482 (129)
$1,492 to $1,874 (116)
$1,875 to $2,567 (158)
$2,613 to $4,616 (164)
$4,780 to $25,048 (74)
No data (13)

N

0 10 20
Miles

Data Sources: Connecticut Office of Property and Management; New Jersey Department of the Treasury; New Jersey Department of Community Affairs, Division of Local Government Services; New York State Comptroller; Pennsylvania State Tax Equalization Board; Pennsylvania Department of Community and Economic Development.

MAP 1-34. NEW YORK REGION (CENTRAL AREA)
Tax Capacity per Household, by Municipality, 1998

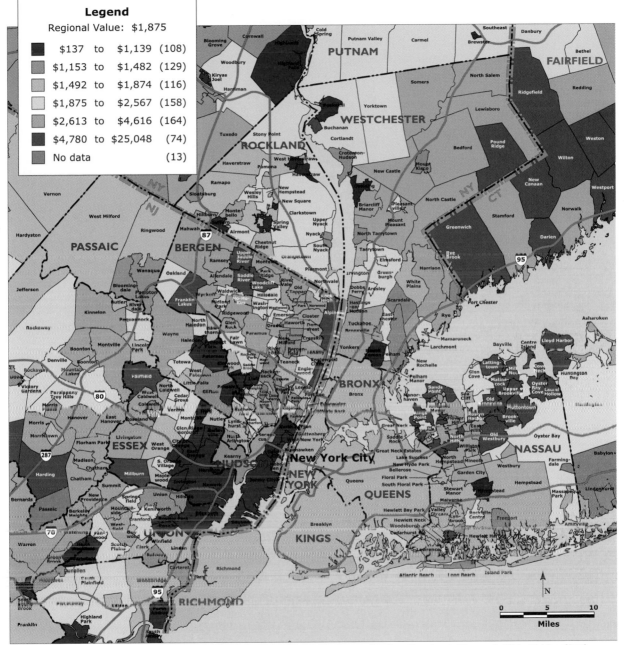

Legend

Regional Value: $1,875

$137	to	$1,139	(108)
$1,153	to	$1,482	(129)
$1,492	to	$1,874	(116)
$1,875	to	$2,567	(158)
$2,613	to	$4,616	(164)
$4,780	to	$25,048	(74)
No data			(13)

Data Sources: Connecticut Office of Property and Management; New Jersey Department of the Treasury; New Jersey Department of Community Affairs, Division of Local Government Services; New York State Comptroller; Pennsylvania State Tax Equalization Board; Pennsylvania Department of Community and Economic Development.

MAP 1-35. NEW YORK REGION
Percentage Change in Tax Capacity per Household, by Municipality, 1993–98

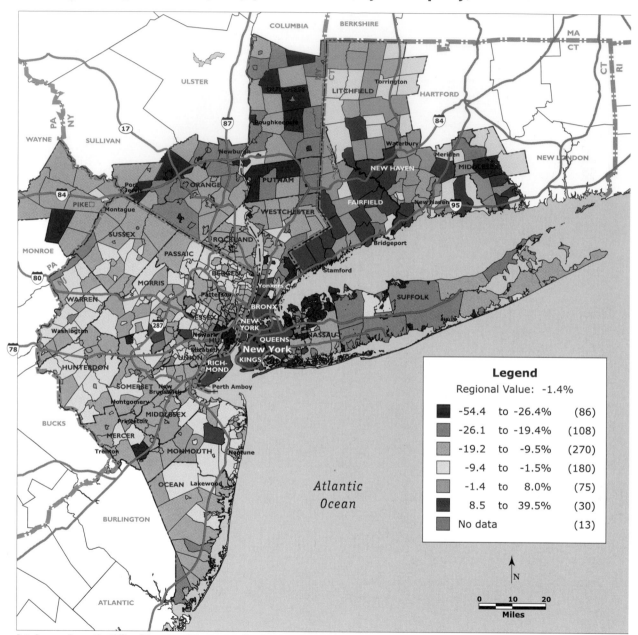

Legend

Regional Value: -1.4%

■	-54.4 to -26.4%	(86)
■	-26.1 to -19.4%	(108)
■	-19.2 to -9.5%	(270)
□	-9.4 to -1.5%	(180)
■	-1.4 to 8.0%	(75)
■	8.5 to 39.5%	(30)
■	No data	(13)

N

0   10   20
Miles

Data Sources: Connecticut Office of Property and Management; New Jersey Department of the Treasury; New Jersey Department of Community Affairs, Division of Local Government Services; New York State Comptroller; Pennsylvania State Tax Equalization Board; Pennsylvania Department of Community and Economic Development; MARC.

MAP 1-36. NEW YORK REGION (CENTRAL AREA)
Percentage Change in Tax Capacity per Household, by Municipality, 1993–98

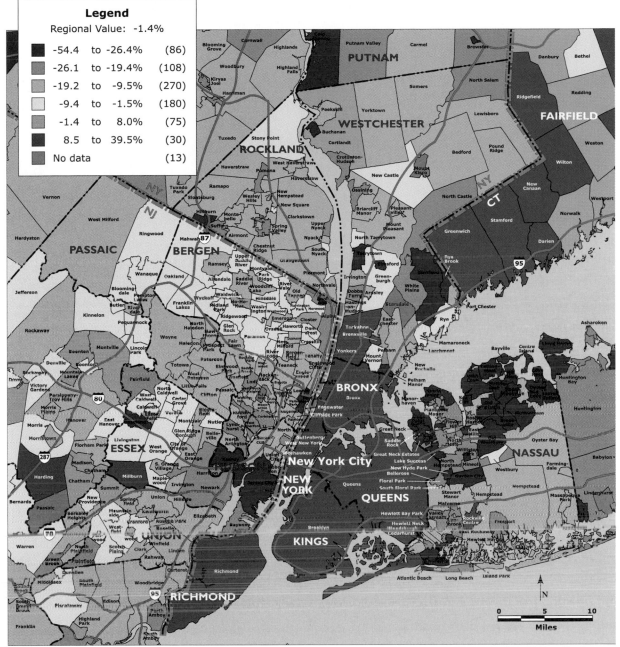

Legend

Regional Value: -1.4%

	-54.4 to -26.4%	(86)
	-26.1 to -19.4%	(108)
	-19.2 to -9.5%	(270)
	-9.4 to -1.5%	(180)
	-1.4 to 8.0%	(75)
	8.5 to 39.5%	(30)
	No data	(13)

Data Sources: Connecticut Office of Property and Management; New Jersey Department of the Treasury; New Jersey Department of Community Affairs, Division of Local Government Services; New York State Comptroller; Pennsylvania State Tax Equalization Board; Pennsylvania Department of Community and Economic Development; MARC.

MAP 1-37. SAN FRANCISCO REGION
Tax Capacity per Household, by Municipality and County Unincorporated Area, 1998

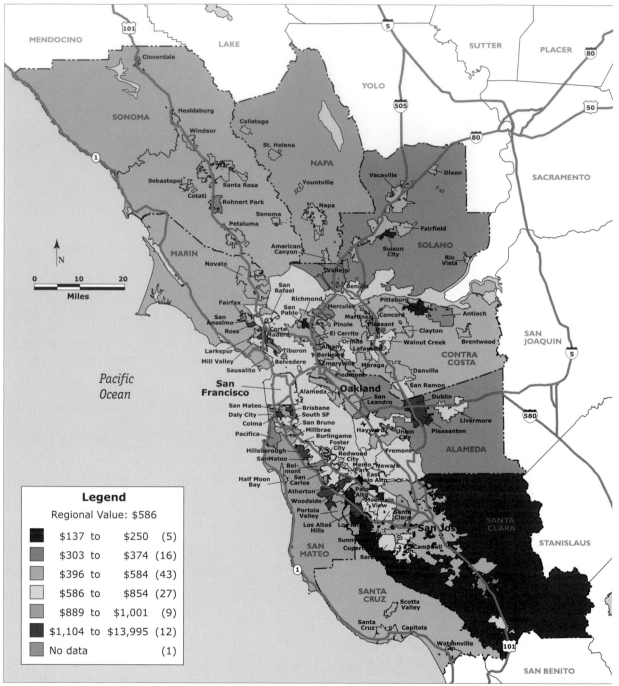

Legend

Regional Value: $586

■	$137 to $250	(5)
■	$303 to $374	(16)
■	$396 to $584	(43)
■	$586 to $854	(27)
■	$889 to $1,001	(9)
■	$1,104 to $13,995	(12)
■	No data	(1)

Data Sources: California State Controller's Office (property and sales tax data); MARC (household estimates).

MAP 1-38. SAN FRANCISCO REGION
Percentage Change in Tax Capacity per Household, by Municipality and County Unincorporated Area, 1993–98

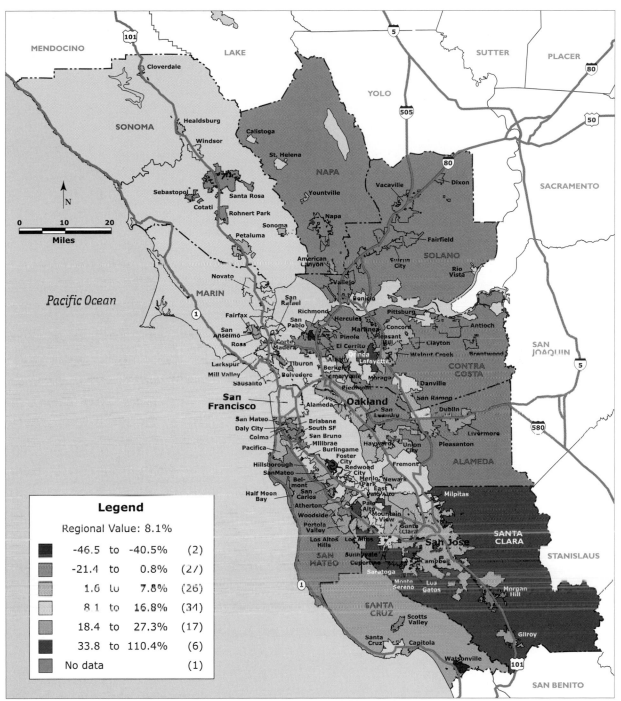

Legend

Regional Value: 8.1%

■	-46.5 to -40.5%	(2)
▨	-21.4 to 0.8%	(27)
▨	1.6 to 7.8%	(26)
▨	8.1 to 16.8%	(34)
▨	18.4 to 27.3%	(17)
■	33.8 to 110.4%	(6)
▨	No data	(1)

Data Sources: California State Controller's Office (property and sales tax data); MARC (household estimates).

if local governments are fiscally conscious—if they are alert—they will necessarily seek to zone for the most expensive homes that the market will bear and the most valuable commercial/industrial property that they can capture. This system sets them into competition against each other. The local governments have no choice about it. As noted in the next section, there are few winners in this game, and the region as a whole is definitely a loser.

MEASURING FISCAL CAPACITY

A municipality's general fiscal condition is determined by two factors: its ability to raise resources (*revenue capacity*) and the costs of providing local services (*expenditure needs*). The interplay of those factors determines whether the municipality can provide the services its households and businesses want at a tax rate that is competitive within the regional economy. Here is described the procedure that will be used throughout the book for measuring the fiscal capacity of localities and exploring variations in capacities within the 25 largest U.S. metropolitan areas.

Revenue capacity is determined by several characteristics of the locality and its economic and institutional operating environment. First, the robustness of the local tax base determines how high the local tax rate must be to raise adequate revenues. Second, state law determines the mix of local taxes and other revenue instruments available to localities. Third, in many states, local tax rates are regulated (or limited) by state law. And fourth, most state governments share their tax revenues with localities.

The measure of local revenue capacity used in this book accounts for the first three factors by projecting the amount of revenue a locality would have if average local tax rates within the locality's metropolitan area were applied to its actual local tax base. Three local taxes are considered: property, sales, and income taxes. Together those taxes made up 84 percent of all local tax revenues in the United States in 1996.[9]

---

9. U.S. Bureau of the Census (2000). The tax-capacity measure does not include fees and charges. Although these are important local revenue sources in many states (representing about one third of local government general revenues nationwide in 1996), how to measure a place's capacity to raise revenues in these ways is problematic. Income is one possible measure, and the inclusion of poverty rate in the clustering procedure partly controls for this issue. Local tax capacity is a useful measure for comparing the tax capacity of localities within a given metropolitan area, but it allows for only limited comparisons across metropolitan areas. One can compare the tax capacities of the city of Los Angeles and its suburbs, say, regardless of whether

The final element of local revenue capacity, state aid to local governments, is an important policy instrument in many states. Direct measures of that component of local revenues are available for most states. Of particular interest is the degree to which aid systems target localities with limited local resources and the extent to which they equalize the localities' overall capacity to provide public services.[10]

Table 1-1 shows the number of jurisdictions and the taxes available to them (and therefore included in the capacity calculation) in each of the metropolitan areas. All local governments in the 25 metropolitan areas had access to the property tax in 1998. In 5 of the 25 areas, the property tax was the only local tax. Localities in 11 areas used both local sales and property taxes; those in 4 other areas could use both local income and property taxes. In 2 multistate metropolitan areas, only jurisdictions in one state in the area could use the sales tax, and in 3 multistate areas only those in one of the included states could use the income tax. In addition, a few jurisdictions (mainly large cities) in several metropolitan areas had special access to one or more taxes not available to all municipalities in their state. The most notable examples were Washington, D.C., Kansas City, and St. Louis, Missouri, the only cities in their regions with access to a local income tax; Detroit and New York City, which (together with a very few other municipalities in their regions) can assess income taxes; Minneapolis–St. Paul and New York City, which (together with a very few other municipalities) can assess a local sales tax; and Philadelphia, the only jurisdiction in Pennsylvania empowered to tax the earnings of nonresidents who work in the city.

---

all localities in the comparison group employ the full range of taxes available to them under state law (property and sales taxes in California). However, the measure cannot be used to compare the tax capacities of the Los Angeles metropolitan area and the Atlanta metropolitan area for two reasons. First, the only local tax available to localities in Atlanta is the property tax, and adequate tax-base data are available only for that tax. Second, because Georgia and California differ in the division of responsibilities for expenditures among state, regional, county, and local governments, average tax rates will differ in the two metropolitan areas. See appendix A for a full discussion of the procedures used in computing tax capacities.

10. Tax capacities were calculated for nearly all of the 4,977 general-purpose municipalities in the 25 largest metropolitan areas in the United States. Of those, 371 municipalities were eliminated either because they were too small to generate reliable data (places with fewer than 50 households in 1998) or because adequate fiscal data were not available. Estimates of tax capacity were generated for the remaining 4,606 municipalities and for the unincorporated portions of 135 of the 151 counties in the sample that were not fully incorporated.

TABLE 1-1. **Local Taxes Available in the 25 Largest Metropolitan Areas, 1998**

| Metropolitan area | Number of municipalities | Taxes available to local governments | | |
		Property	Sales	Income
Atlanta	101	X		
Boston	394	X		
Chicago	340	X	X (Illinois only)	
Cincinnati	104	X		X (Ohio and Kentucky only)
Cleveland	145	X		X
Dallas	154	X	X	
Denver	54	X	X	
Detroit	276	X		X (5 cities only)
Houston	88	X	X	
Kansas City	116	X	X	X (Kansas City, Mo. only)
Los Angeles	171	X	X	
Miami	40	X		
Milwaukee	107	X		
Minneapolis–St. Paul	324	X	X (Minneapolis and St. Paul only)	
New York	725	X	X (5 NY cities)	X (2 New York cities and 2 Pennsylvania towns)
Philadelphia	415	X		X (Pennsylvania and Wilmington, Del. only)
Phoenix	22	X	X	
Pittsburgh	397	X		X
Portland	78	X	X (Washington only)	
San Diego	18	X	X	
San Francisco	102	X	X	
Seattle	79	X	X	
St. Louis	213	X	X	X (St. Louis only)
Tampa	32	X		
Washington, D.C.	111	X	X (7 Virginia cities and Washington, D.C.)	X (Washington, D.C. only)
Total	**4,606**	**25**	**15**	**9**

Maps 1-25 through 1-38 also show the geography of tax capacities and tax capacity changes in six representative metropolitan areas. The tax-capacity patterns in Denver and Atlanta are typical of one group of metropolitan areas that have relatively strong central cities. The inner portions of both areas contain groups of relatively low-capacity suburbs, many of them islands of pink in a sea of blue: moderately low-capacity incorporated towns surrounded by unincorporated areas with higher-than-average capacity. Most of the lowest-capacity localities are farther from the core of the region—scattered in the case of Atlanta and concentrated largely in the north in Denver. Both areas show another common phenomenon: a few relatively high-capacity outer suburbs surrounded by relatively low-capacity unincorporated areas. In Atlanta, they lie largely to the east (in Rockdale and Newton Counties) and northwest (Cherokee and Bartow Counties), while in Denver they lie to the northwest (Boulder County) and south (Douglas County) of the central city. Other metropolitan areas with similar patterns are Kansas City, Phoenix, Portland, San Diego, Seattle, Tampa, and Washington, D.C.

San Francisco and Chicago display a different pattern. In both areas, two of the three central cities show lower-than-average capacity, and the suburbs exhibit very clear geographic patterns. In San Francisco, most of the highest-capacity suburbs are south of San Francisco, with lower capacities clustered to the east. In Chicago, most of the lower-capacity suburbs are in the south and east, with higher capacities in the west and north. Some of the other areas with geographic clusters are Cincinnati, Cleveland, Dallas, Houston, Los Angeles, Miami, and St. Louis.

New York and Minneapolis–St. Paul are fairly typical of the fully incorporated metropolitan areas of the Northeast and North-Central regions (including Boston, Detroit, Milwaukee, Philadelphia, and Pittsburgh). In that group, low-capacity suburbs tend to fit into two categories: high-density inner-ring suburbs and lower-density outer-ring "exurbs." The tax capacity of the central cities varies. Two-thirds of the large cities have below-average capacity (Boston, Milwaukee, New York, Newark, Philadelphia, and St. Paul), while a third have above-average capacity (Detroit, Minneapolis, and Pittsburgh). Most of these metropolitan areas also show significant clustering of affluent communities. In New York, clustering occurs in the second-ring suburbs to the west, northeast, and east in parts of Long Island. Minneapolis–St. Paul and other areas have even more distinct corridors of affluence, often parallel to ring roads—to the south and southwest of the central cities in Minneapolis–St. Paul; to the west in Boston; to the north and northwest in Detroit; and to the west and northwest in Pittsburgh.

Tax base per household increased by greater than regional averages in four of the eight central cities in our representative metropolitan areas (Denver, New York, San Francisco, and St. Paul) and increased in absolute terms in the other four (Atlanta, Chicago, Minneapolis, and Oakland). The declining (or slowest-growing) tax bases tend to be in inner suburbs and outlying exurbs—places likely to be facing increasing social needs or rapid population growth.

CHAPTER 2

THE NEW SUBURBAN TYPOLOGY

As mentioned earlier, the formal clustering or grouping of the suburbs of the 25 largest U.S. metropolitan areas proposed in this volume is based on a wide range of indicators, including schools, taxes, the cost of aging infrastructure in older places, racial make up, and physical growth. Although *American Metropolitics* is predominantly about U.S. suburbs, it is important to say a word about the central cities surrounded by these suburbs. Just as the suburbs are not a monolith, neither are their central cities.

POVERTY AND RACE IN THE CENTRAL CITIES

The central cities and some of their suburbs, despite their different degrees of stress, have one common characteristic: they lack the resources to meet their social and physical needs. Table 2-1 compares three aspects of the study sample's 30 central cities and 25 metropolitan regions: poverty and racial diversity in the public schools, spatial concentration of poverty, and the relative tax burdens on city residents and suburbanites. As table 2-1 shows, Denver, Minneapolis–St. Paul, Phoenix, Portland, San Diego, San Francisco, Seattle, and Tampa are all consistently less stressed than the average of the 30 cities. The percentage of school children eligible for the free-lunch program in those cities is about 50 percent, relatively small percentages of the population (below 10 percent) live in high-poverty census tracts, and city tax rates do not exceed suburban averages by exorbitant amounts (about 25 percent on average).

Not even in such relatively well-off cities, however, is the picture all positive. Elementary school populations have become poorer in each of

TABLE 2-1. **Central City Characteristics, Selected Years[a]**

Percent

Central cities	City elementary students free lunch eligible		City elementary students non-Asian minority		Central city population in high poverty census tracts		Tax rate as percentage of suburban average	
	1992	1997	1992	1997	1980	1990	1993	1998
Atlanta	73	77	89	91	21.6	21.9	n.a.	113
Boston	n.a.	72	71	77	3.4	4.5	128	124
Chicago	n.a.	n.a.	86	87	12.3	13.7	156	141
Cincinnati	48	53	54	60	15.1	18.3	134	135
Cleveland	82	82	76	78	12.4	19.8	101	118
Dallas	73	66	78	85	4.1	8.1	108	95
Fort Worth	55	55	62	66	3.2	6.3	154	138
Denver	44	57	65	73	3.4	4.9	79	91
Detroit	73	70	91	96	9.4	36.6	275	176
Houston	64	64	76	81	2.9	9.7	109	103
Kansas City	53	65	52	58	3.1	5.6	66	112
Los Angeles	79	79	79	82	2.9	6.3	177	150
Miami	78	76	96	96	10.0	23.8	141	165
Milwaukee	68	64	70	76	4.6	22.1	57	133
Minneapolis	50	62	45	56	4.6	15.1	152	161
St. Paul	55	58	25	34	1.1	6.6	166	149
New York	74	74	74	75	14.3	12.6	131	135
Newark	80	82	89	91	32.1	17.5	152	170
Philadelphia	n.a.	52	72	77	12.7	11.8	133	163
Phoenix	n.a.	n.a.	42	52	4.2	5.4	143	102
Pittsburgh	58	63	56	60	7.9	15.2	255	238
Portland	46	39	20	23	1.3	3.4	124	126
San Diego	53	59	49	55	0.5	3.6	111	103
San Francisco	61	68	41	42	1.7	1.7	166	167
Oakland	68	75	73	76	2.7	5.0	246	211
Seattle	52	49	34	36	1.1	2.7	110	114
St. Louis	78	78	80	83	10.9	15.1	62	118
Tampa	54	60	51	60	11.5	10.4	107	109
Washington, D.C.	71	67	94	94	4.4	3.4	104	95
Baltimore	69	70	81	85	15.4	14.2	107	118
Average	**64**	**66**	**66**	**70**	**7.8**	**11.5**	**136**	**136**

Sources: National Center for Education Statistics, Bureau of the Census, and various state and local government agencies (fiscal data).

a. Tax rates were computed as the weighted average for property, sales, and income taxes. Washington D.C., Kansas City, Mo., and St. Louis estimates exclude the city income tax. Minneapolis and St. Paul exclude the city sales tax.

n.a. = Not available.

them except Portland and Seattle, and the geographic concentration of poverty has increased in each. All of these cities have neighborhoods where public schools retain the confidence of middle-class parents—for now. However, even in Portland, the strongest of these central cities, the middle class is growing concerned about the schools.[1]

At the other end of the scale are cities such as Chicago, Cleveland, Detroit, Miami, New York, Newark, Oakland, and St. Louis. They show higher-than-average values of the negative indicators of school composition, concentrated poverty, and tax burdens almost across the board. The majority of students in their schools (between 70 and 95 percent in most schools) are poor and minority children, high proportions of the population (from 13 to 24 percent) live in high-poverty tracts, and tax rates exceed suburban averages by large amounts in most (by more than 50 percent on average). Many of these cities have large poverty-stricken and segregated neighborhoods and few middle-class neighborhoods (chapter 1). These central cities have few public schools attractive to middle-class families. Detroit stands out in particular: most of its central city is blighted by countless abandoned structures and empty industrial plants.

TAX CAPACITY, NEEDS, AND COSTS IN THE CENTRAL CITIES

The fiscal condition of the large cities in this sample is determined by both their capacity to raise revenues and their expenditure needs and costs. Table 2-2 shows where they stand in relation to their metropolitan areas in tax capacity, tax-capacity growth, *total revenue capacity* (tax capacity plus state aid), and four indicators of local service needs.

The large cities in this sample compare relatively well with their regions in their ability to raise revenues. In 1998 average tax capacity per household in the 30 cities was 102 percent of regional average tax capacity. Tax capacity ranges from just 29 percent of the regional average (Newark) to 209 percent (St. Louis). Of the 30 cities, 13 show a tax capacity below the regional average; 17 show a tax capacity above the regional average. In 5 of the 17 cities with a tax capacity above the regional average, however, much of the "extra" capacity results from special access to taxes not available to most (or all) of their suburbs. That extra capacity is a mixed blessing. There is a great deal of evidence to

1. Betsy Hammond, "Expected Enrollment Boom Busts," *The Oregonian*, October 9, 1997, p. D1.

TABLE 2-2. Central City Characteristics as Percentages of
Metropolitan Area Averages, Selected Years

Percent

Central cities	Tax capacity per household, 1998	Change in tax capacity per household, 1993–98	Total capacity per household, 1998	Children eligible for free lunch, 1997	Population density, 1998	Age of housing stock, 1990	Population growth, 1993–98
Atlanta	104	94	106	188	195	128	87
Boston	97	107	132	294	1,733	123	98
Chicago	74	96	78	n.a.	334	124	97
Cincinnati	110	88	123	190	207	116	93
Cleveland	112	99	120	240	277	126	96
Dallas	118	98	n.a.	174	183	118	93
Fort Worth	80	101	n.a.	144	96	129	95
Denver	110	102	114	322	136	135	89
Detroit	112	104	151	214	826	137	93
Houston	107	102	n.a.	142	159	102	95
Kansas City	146	73	138	163	103	121	95
Los Angeles	96	94	99	133	182	120	98
Miami	96	94	98	146	183	134	94
Milwaukee	56	92	95	204	673	117	94
Minneapolis	101	95	139	291	1,590	154	91
St. Paul	82	107	126	269	1,143	145	92
New York	94	120	102	182	1,376	112	99
Newark	29	78	71	202	552	107	96
Philadelphia	98	108	84	164	1,028	127	93
Phoenix	106	106	106	n.a.	147	119	96
Pittsburgh	103	95	153	200	1,262	121	96
Portland	97	103	97	178	119	132	92
San Diego	104	97	101	113	104	110	100
San Francisco	112	101	115	172	417	152	97
Oakland	69	95	80	190	161	137	98
Seattle	155	95	152	148	131	133	94
St. Louis	209	103	143	291	233	132	89
Tampa	117	102	119	139	82	114	97
Washington, D.C.	126	94	108	130	159	112	87
Baltimore	50	100	69	136	137	116	87
30 City average	**102**	**98**	**112**	**191**	**464**	**125**	**94**

Sources: National Center for Education Statistics and Bureau of the Census.

a. All variables are expressed as percentages of metropolitan area averages. Population growth and change in tax capacity were calculated as the ratio of 1998 levels to 1993 levels.

show that such special taxing powers can impair the ability of these cities to compete for economic activity against other jurisdictions in the metropolitan area.[2]

The 30 cities' average growth in tax capacity was 98 percent of the regional average growth in tax capacity, which implies that central city capacity growth lagged behind regional growth by roughly 2 percentage points between 1993 and 1998. Of the 30 cities, 13 show greater tax-capacity growth (measured as the ratio of 1998 tax capacity to 1993 capacity) than the regional average, but most trail their regional counterparts on that measure. Overall, the relative position of cities in this sample worsened between 1993 and 1998.

According to the total revenue capacity data, most of the large cities benefit more from state aid than do their suburban counterparts. The relative positions of 21 of the 27 cities for which aid data are available improve when state aid is added to the calculation. Four of the six cities that lose ground—Washington, D.C., St. Louis, Kansas City (Missouri), and Philadelphia—are among the cities that benefit the most (in terms of tax capacity) from access to special local taxes. "Institutional" aid to these cities is apparently offset by lower state aid flows than might otherwise occur, another reason special access to a tax base may be less advantageous than it seems.[3] On average, the big cities' total revenue capacity is 12 percent higher than that of their suburban counterparts.

That relatively small advantage on the capacity side of the ledger is more than offset by the cities' higher costs. Poverty, which is almost uniformly higher in cities than in the suburbs, dramatically raises the cost of providing local public services.[4] Similarly, population grew by more than the regional average in only 1 of the cities and declined in 12 between 1993 and 1998. Very low population growth or outright population decline is likely to increase the per-person cost of providing many local public services.[5]

In 29 of the 30 metropolitan areas, the difference in the percentage of elementary school children eligible for free lunch in the city and its

On average, big cities' total revenue capacity is 12% higher than their suburbs'—but that small advantage is more than offset by their higher costs.

---

2. For a review of this evidence, see Bartik (1991).

3. The average improvement in the relative position of the eight cities with special access to tax bases (Washington, D.C., Detroit, Kansas City, Missouri, Minneapolis–St. Paul, New York, Philadelphia, and St. Louis) is just 3.8 percentage points compared with 12.1 percentage points for the remainder of the group. This is consistent with findings of Ladd and Yinger (1989, p. 277), that states that provide fairly high institutional aid to large cities also tend to provide relatively little in monetary aid.

4. Ladd and Yinger (1989); Pack (1995).

5. Ladd (1994a).

Many suburbs and older satellite cities are experiencing rapid social changes, particularly in their schools, but lack the local resources to deal with them.

suburbs is higher than the difference in total revenue capacity. Similar patterns are apparent for the other cost factors included in table 2-2. In 23 of the 30 metropolitan areas, the difference in the age of the cities' housing stock versus the region's housing stock is higher than the difference in revenue capacity.[6] The higher density in cities also outweighs the greater comparative revenue capacity in 28 of the 30 metropolitan areas studied. Thus the cost disadvantages for the 30 cities far outweigh any small advantage they may possess in revenue capacity. The cities' proportionate disadvantages for each of the four indicators exceed their proportionate capacity advantage by large margins.

Given that their disadvantages are so great, it is not surprising that most of the cities tax their residents at higher rates than surrounding suburbs do. This is reflected in the tax rate comparisons in table 2-1. Detroit exemplifies the situation of many central cities. It has 112 percent of the regional average tax capacity, owing to its very low property tax wealth (one-third of the regional average) and special access to a local income tax (also the case in four other cities in the region). Even with its greater-than-average capacity, however, Detroit still has to tax its residents and businesses heavily to meet its needs (the depths of which are evident from the figures in tables 2-1 and 2-2). Its average overall tax rate exceeds suburban averages by nearly 2 to 1. Tax differentials of that magnitude are a serious disincentive to investment in the city, a problem for most of the 30 cities in the study sample.

THE MYTH OF THE SUBURBAN MONOLITH

The suburbs contain more than half of the U.S. population, an even higher percentage of voters, and an overwhelming majority of elites. The perceived power of the supposed suburban monolith shapes American domestic policy and politics but, in truth, this power is fragmented. To judge from some 18 commissioned regional reports, different types of suburbs are emerging in U.S. metropolitan regions.[7]

Many suburbs and older satellite cities are beginning to experience rapid social changes, particularly in their school systems, but they lack the local resources to deal with these changes. Some places are more troubled than the central cities they surround. Another large and im-

6. The age of housing stock is a measure commonly used as a proxy for the age of the infrastructure.
7. See Orfield (1997, appendix C).

portant group of fast-growing communities lacks adequate local resources for schools and infrastructure. Finally, a smaller, very affluent group of cities enjoys all the benefits of a regional economy without having to pay the costs. Ironically, this group often appears to be least happy with the status quo of America's suburban development patterns.

The balance between a locality's ability to raise revenues and the range and depth of needs those revenues must meet determines how high local taxes must be to provide local services of acceptable quality. So far, this chapter has concentrated on the relative tax capacities and needs of the 30 large cities within the 25 largest U.S. metropolitan areas. The same methods can be used to examine the revenue-raising capacity of suburban jurisdictions, and these data and other socioeconomic characteristics of particular suburbs can be used to develop a typology of suburban jurisdictions. Because there are more than 4,600 suburban jurisdictions in the 25 metropolitan areas, it is impossible to measure each one individually against other suburbs. Instead, this book uses *cluster analysis* to group suburban areas according to several measures of their *fiscal characteristics* (revenue capacity and expenditure needs) and *sociopolitical environments.*[8]

Fiscal characteristics comprise several factors. First, the way public service responsibilities are divided among the various levels of government (state, regional, county, and local) determines the mix of services that a locality must (or can) provide. Second, the characteristics and preferences of local residents and businesses affect the amount and mix of services. Third, population density, terrain, poverty concentrations, and other features of a jurisdiction affect the cost of providing services.

Ideally, expenditure needs should be estimated place by place, using a standard measure that accounts for all the factors that contribute to demand and costs. That measure could then be compared with a standard measure of revenue capacity to generate a "need-capacity gap."[9]

8. Cluster analysis is a procedure that divides observations in a data set (municipalities, in this case) into homogeneous groups, according to specified characteristics (here, the two capacity variables, four cost variables, and one race variable).

9. For a full description of the need–capacity gap approach, see Ladd and Yinger (1989). In the context of that discussion, the tax-capacity measure employed here is a variant of the Representative Tax System (RTS) developed by the Advisory Commission on Intergovernmental Relations (ACIR). The primary difference is that *American Metropolitics* uses metropolitan-level average tax rates instead of the national averages used by ACIR in its interstate comparisons. This procedure avoids the pitfalls of applying the RTS to places with access to different mixes of tax bases (discussed by Ladd and Yinger) but limits the ability to make intermetropolitan comparisons.

However, data limitations preclude full modeling of local expenditure needs.[10] Instead, a set of local characteristics that heavily influence local costs is used, together with the tax-capacity measure, to group jurisdictions according to both their capacity and service costs.

Cost differences among localities are not solely determined by the price of inputs needed to produce public goods and services. The cost of inputs is not likely to vary much from place to place within a single metropolitan area. More important are the costs associated with the *service environment*—the environment in which a locality provides services like police and fire protection, schools, sanitation, streets, and transit. Service environments, which vary from place to place within a metropolitan area, affect the way activities like police patrols, teaching, infrastructure construction and maintenance, and transit systems translate into public goods—such as freedom from crime, educational opportunities, mobility, and a healthy living environment. This analysis relies on a set of local characteristics that shows up consistently in discussions and empirical analyses of service environment costs: population density, poverty rate, age of the housing stock, and population growth.[11]

Poverty and older housing stock mean that jurisdictions must pay a higher cost per person to provide a wide range of public goods. For instance, neighborhoods of concentrated poverty have extreme crime rates, often many times the regional average. The costs of limiting crime are therefore likely to be higher in high-poverty environments. Similarly, older housing stock is likely to be associated with aging public infrastructure that is costly to maintain.

Determining the relation of public service costs to density and population growth is more complicated. In terms of regional planning, moderate-density, medium- to small-lot development with apartment buildings and clustered commercial development can create a more efficient use of public space than low-density development. In this context, higher governmental costs are likely to be associated with both

10. Primary among these is the lack of current data on local socioeconomic conditions. When 2000 census estimates become available, expenditure needs can be modeled more rigorously.

11. Other variables often mentioned in this context are total population and job densities (or jobs per capita). Population was not used in *American Metropolitics* because it shows such wide variations within metropolitan areas that it would overwhelm any effects of the other variables in the cluster analysis. In addition, six of the seven variables included in the analysis (all but tax capacity) are significantly correlated with population at the 95 percent confidence level. Job density was not included in the analysis because adequate local data are not available in most of the 25 metropolitan areas.

very low densities and very high densities. Very low densities can increase per-person costs for public goods involving transportation (schools, police and fire protection) and for infrastructure (roads, sewerage). Although high-density urban cores can create strong and necessary agglomeration effects, very high densities generate congestion. Similarly, population decline tends to increase the per-person cost of long-lived public goods such as infrastructure (streets and sewerage) because, in the short run, the number of users declines while the supply remains fixed. Very large increases in population tend to increase per-person costs of the same goods because, for a variety of reasons, the cost of new infrastructure is likely to fall disproportionately on current residents, not future residents. In short, moderate densities and growth rates are likely to be associated with lower governmental costs while extremely low or high values are associated with higher costs.

The characteristics of the service environment used in this analysis also capture a good cross section of the socioeconomic characteristics that often define political character or logical political coalitions. Poverty, density, housing age, growth characteristics, and wealth are also among the characteristics people examine when deciding whether a place is "their kind of place." Racial composition, which is not captured by the characteristics of the service environment, is also critical, and therefore a measure of racial diversity is included in the following analysis.

Poverty, density, housing age, growth characteristics, and wealth are among the factors people examine to decide if it is "their kind of place."

CLUSTER ANALYSIS OF SUBURBS

The 4,606 incorporated municipalities and 135 unincorporated areas in the 25 metropolitan regions were grouped according to two broad categories: tax capacity and costs. Two tax-capacity measures were included: 1998 tax capacity per household and growth in tax capacity from 1993 to 1998. Four characteristics of the service environment were used for the cost measures: percentage of elementary students eligible for the free- or reduced-price lunch program in 1997; 1998 population density; population growth from 1993 to 1998; and the age of the housing stock in 1990. The proportion of elementary students who were non-Asian minorities in 1997 was also included. That characteristic was not included as a cost variable per se but rather as a reflection of factors that depress growth prospects and housing prices in communities with many minority residents (for example, racial discrimination in housing markets and white flight).

The variables for each municipality were computed as a percentage of the average value for the metropolitan area. All the suburban communities were then divided into groups using cluster analysis. Central cities were put into their own cluster, which was not included in the cluster analysis.[12]

Six types of suburban communities emerge from the analysis. Three types of communities under significant fiscal or social stress are designated *at-risk communities*. One group, made up of fast-growing communities with only modest fiscal resources at their disposal, is designated *bedroom-developing communities*. Finally, two groups of very affluent communities under little stress from either low tax capacity or high costs are labeled *affluent job centers*.

Office development— one of the few sources of tax base that more than pays its way—is often a key to local fiscal well-being.

Tables 2-3 and 2-4 present the results of the clustering procedure. Table 2-3 shows the characteristics of the different community types that emerged from the analysis, and table 2-4 shows how population, poverty, tax capacity, and population growth were distributed across the clusters in the 1990s. One of the most important characteristics that distinguishes one community type from another is tax capacity. Four of the six groups—the three at-risk categories and the bedroom-developing communities—each command relatively low levels of local resources; their tax capacities vary from 66 to 90 percent of their regional averages. Only in the bedroom-developing communities were capacities keeping up with regional averages in terms of change in tax capacity. The at-risk communities were falling further behind.

What leads to these kinds of disparities in local resources? Unbalanced regional development patterns—unequal distribution of high-end housing and commercial-industrial development—are the likely source. This can be seen very clearly from the distribution of office space across the different types of communities. In a modern service economy, office development is often a key to local fiscal well-being. It is one of the few sources of tax base that more than "pays its way."

CB Richard Ellis, a large real estate firm, provided parcel-level, office location data for 16 of the 25 largest regions in the study. Matching

12. The procedure used for the grouping was the K-means clustering procedure in SPSS. The K-means procedure is designed to handle large numbers of observations, but the number of clusters must be specified. Alternative groupings for five, six, and seven clusters were compared. The six-cluster run was chosen because it generated groups that could most easily be identified by geographic location within metropolitan areas. In particular, the step from five to six clusters made it possible to separate outer-ring suburbs with low tax capacity from inner-ring suburbs with low capacity (on the basis of the density measure).

TABLE 2-3. **Characteristics of the Community Types**[a]

Percent

Municipality type	Number of munici- palities	Tax capacity	Change in tax capacity	Eligible for free lunch	Density	Popu- lation growth	Age of housing	Minority percentage
At-risk, segregated	348	66	93	175	369	97	108	209
At-risk, older	391	74	96	59	735	98	110	35
At-risk, low-density	1,104	66	96	103	104	102	97	65
Bedroom-developing	2,152	90	100	32	83	106	85	16
Affluent job center	625	212	105	27	97	105	88	26
Very affluent job center	91	525	102	39	46	101	91	38
Central cities	30	101	97	193	452	94	125	207
All suburban	**4,711**	**106**	**99**	**61**	**164**	**104**	**92**	**45**

Sources: See table 2-1.

a. All variables except number of municipalities are expressed as percentages of metropolitan area averages. Population growth and change in tax capacity were calculated as the ratio of 1998 levels to 1993 levels.

these data with the community types shows that office space, representing jobs and fiscal capacity, is very unequally distributed across metropolitan regions. Table 2-5 shows the distribution of office space and population across the community types. Not surprisingly, the central cities contain a large portion of regional office space: 51 percent of the total in the 16 metropolitan areas with data, a percentage that far exceeds their share of households (24 percent). However, the distribution in suburban areas is highly skewed. The three at-risk categories and the bedroom-developing communities together contain 34 percent of office space, which is less than half their share of the region's households, while the proportion of office space in the two affluent job center categories is more than twice their share of population. These two job center categories also contain disproportionate shares of the "best" office space: roughly 70 percent of their office space is rated "A" or "B," compared with just 52 percent for central cities and 55 to 60 percent for all the other categories combined. In short, households in the affluent job center communities benefit disproportionately from the fiscal dividends generated by office development.

At-Risk Communities

The myth of urban deterioration and suburban prosperity suggests that social and economic decline stops neatly at the borders of central cities.

33

TABLE 2-4. **Distribution of Community Types within Metropolitan Areas in the 1990s**

Percent of regional total unless otherwise indicated

Metropolitan area	Central cities	At-risk, segregated	At-risk, older	At-risk, low-density	Bedroom-developing	Affluent job center	Very affluent job center
All							
Number of municipalities	30	348	391	1,104	2,152	625	91
Population	28	8	6	26	26	7	0
Poverty population	49	12	3	24	10	2	0
Tax capacity	29	6	5	16	28	14	2
State aid	40	12	6	17	20	5	0
Total capacity	31	7	5	16	26	13	2
Population growth	3	2	0	27	56	11	0
Atlanta							
Number of municipalities	1	21	0	64	34	4	0
Population	12	22	0	17	42	7	0
Poverty population	35	26	0	21	18	0	0
Tax capacity	12	20	0	14	42	12	0
State aid	54	7	0	17	9	13	0
Total capacity	13	19	0	14	42	12	0
Population growth	1	5	0	15	68	11	0
Chicago							
Number of municipalities	1	20	3	56	208	63	7
Population	33	5	2	11	40	10	0
Poverty population	64	10	1	10	13	2	0
Tax capacity	25	3	1	9	40	21	2
State aid	38	9	1	14	30	8	1
Total capacity	29	5	1	10	37	17	2
Population growth	3	−4	−2	12	75	16	0
Denver							
Number of municipalities	1	18	0	32	5	4	1
Population	23	21	0	42	11	3	0
Poverty population	40	25	0	23	9	3	0
Tax capacity	28	19	0	30	14	9	0
State aid	44	18	0	27	7	4	0
Total capacity	30	19	0	30	13	8	0
Population growth	4	17	0	55	20	4	0

TABLE 2-4. Distribution of Community Types within Metropolitan Areas in the 1990s *(continued)*

Percent of regional total unless otherwise indicated

Metropolitan area	Central cities	At-risk, segregated	At-risk, older	At-risk, low-density	Bedroom-developing	Affluent job center	Very affluent job center
Minneapolis–St. Paul							
Number of municipalities	2	3	63	41	188	28	1
Population	25	2	33	6	28	7	0
Poverty population	55	2	21	5	14	3	0
Tax capacity	24	2	30	5	28	12	0
State aid	47	2	26	4	18	3	0
Total capacity	34	2	28	4	24	8	0
Population growth	–1	1	25	8	56	11	0
New York							
Number of municipalities	2	38	65	64	366	156	36
Population	39	9	5	9	29	8	1
Poverty population	66	13	2	6	10	2	0
Tax capacity	36	5	4	7	29	16	4
State aid	52	14	4	7	18	5	0
Total capacity	39	7	4	7	27	13	3
Population growth	23	0	2	5	55	16	1
San Francisco							
Number of municipalities	2	11	1	47	32	17	0
Population	19	8	0	49	17	6	0
Poverty population	31	13	0	45	8	3	0
Tax capacity	19	8	0	43	17	12	0
State aid	25	11	0	43	16	6	0
Total capacity	21	9	0	43	17	10	0
Population growth	5	6	0	60	23	7	0

Sources: See table 2-1.

Nothing could be farther from the truth. Once poverty and social instability permeate communities just outside the central city and begin to grow in older satellite cities, decline accelerates and intensifies. About 40 percent of the population in this sample (56 percent of the suburban population) lives in at-risk suburbs—communities that have high social needs but relatively limited, and often declining, local resources. These

**TABLE 2-5. Distribution of Office Space in 16 of the
25 Largest Metropolitan Areas**[a]

Municipality type	Office space per household (square feet)	Share of total regional office space (%)	Share of total regional households (%)	Office space share/ household share	"A" and "B" office space share of total space
At-risk, segregated	41	4	8	0.5	54
At-risk, older communities	36	3	7	0.4	53
At-risk, low-density	36	13	29	0.4	56
Bedroom-developing	44	14	26	0.5	63
Affluent job centers	167	14	7	2.0	70
Very affluent job centers	570	2	0	7.1	68
Central cities	173	51	24	2.1	52
Total	**81**	**100**	**100**	**1.0**	**58**

Sources: C. B. Richard Ellis and the Bureau of the Census.

a. Metropolitan areas: Chicago, Cincinnati, Cleveland, Denver, Detroit, Kansas City, Miami, Minneapolis-St. Paul, Philadelphia, Phoenix, Pittsburgh, Portland, San Francisco, Seattle, St. Louis, and Tampa.

communities include older suburbs, satellite cities and newer, lower-density communities with relatively high poverty rates. They have only about two-thirds of the fiscal capacity of the central cities, and their fiscal capacity is growing more slowly. Many at-risk communities lack the central cities' strong business district, vitality, resources, high-end housing, parks, cultural attractions, amenities, and public infrastructure (for example, police and social service agencies experienced in coping with social stress). As a result, these communities often become poor *faster* and lose local business activity even more rapidly than the cities they surround. In terms of 1990 median incomes, incomes in the at-risk suburbs (between $27,000 and $30,000) were below the regional median income and closer to the central city ($29,000) than to the affluent job centers (between $59,000 and $69,000). Similarly, the median 1990 home values in the at-risk suburbs were close to the median value for central cities and about half the median value of homes in the affluent job centers. Finally, as noted, this group's share of regional office space was less than half its share of households (in the 16 metropolitan areas where office space data were available). There are three kinds of at-risk municipalities: segregated communities, older communities, and low-density communities.

At-Risk Segregated Communities. Of the at-risk communities, 347 had very low tax capacity, slow tax-capacity growth, high municipal costs, and high concentrations of minority children in the public schools. In these 347 places, tax capacity per household was just 66 percent of the regional average; and the change in tax base per household from 1993 to 1998 was roughly seven points lower than the regional average. (The ratio of the 1998 tax base per household to the 1993 tax base was just 93 percent of the average.) On the cost side, this group had very high poverty rates (nearly twice the regional average), lower-than-average population growth, old housing stock, a population density more than three times the regional average, and very high concentrations of minority students in the schools. This group's average 1990 median income (at $27,862) was slightly below the central city average ($29,949). Its average home value ($83,387) was only 65 percent of the cities' average ($126,970). Eight percent of the population in the 25 metropolitan areas in the sample lived in this kind of community, but only 4 percent of the office market space was there.

Racial transition, rather than stable racial integration, is the norm in suburban America.

On average, the non-Asian minority proportion of these communities' school-age population exceeds even the central-city average. These at-risk segregated communities include many of the inner suburban areas of Fulton, DeKalb, and Clayton Counties outside Atlanta; Chicago's southern and western inner suburbs and satellite cities; Denver's northern and western suburbs; two relatively small northern suburbs of Minneapolis; large contiguous areas in New Jersey, inner Long Island, and Yonkers in Westchester, all in the New York region; and, in California's Bay Area, several communities in the East Bay surrounding Oakland. In short, virtually every region in the nation with a significant black or Latino population has a number of suburbs in this category. The average minority percentages for different categories of municipalities shown in the last column of table 2-3 imply an all-or-nothing quality to suburban racial patterns. The numbers suggest that racial transition, rather than stable racial integration, is the norm in suburban America.

The at-risk segregated communities—often experiencing dramatic social and fiscal change—are some of metropolitan America's worst places to live. Poor and segregated, they have a fraction of the resources of the central cities they surround. In 1994, the taxes on a $100,000 house in the at-risk segregated suburb of Maywood, Illinois, were $4,672. This level of taxation would support local school spending of $3,350 per pupil. In Kenilworth, an affluent suburb to the north, the taxes would be $2,688, yet this lower rate, applied to the whole tax base

37

would support almost three times the level of spending per pupil. Similarly, business taxes on a 100,000-square-foot office building in booming DuPage County were $212,639, compared with $468,000 in south suburban Cook County.[13] In the mid-1990s, many of these at-risk segregated suburbs looked as if they had been hit by a neutron bomb: there were few residents, and only dilapidated structures remained standing. Tall grass grew between cracks in the pavement in parking lots in empty malls, and drug dealers worked the street corners.

Although at-risk older communities are much less racially diverse than the at-risk segregated suburbs they often border, many are in the beginning stages of rapid racial change.

At-Risk Older Communities. The second group of at-risk communities included 391 very high-density suburbs that had relatively low poverty rates, low tax capacity, slower-than-average growth in fiscal capacity, and slow population growth. In 1998 average tax capacity for this group was just 74 percent of the regional average, and tax-base growth was below average. Averages for population density, population growth, and age of housing stock each implied higher-than-average costs. Poverty and minority school population rates were 59 and 35 percent of the regional averages, respectively—significantly lower than rates in the at-risk segregated suburbs but often much higher than in the other groups of suburbs. As noted, school change in terms of race begins to accelerate dramatically when the percentage of minority school children is low, often between 10 and 25 percent. In this respect, although at-risk older communities are much less racially diverse than at-risk segregated communities, they are often at the beginning stages of rapid racial change. These places often stand cheek by jowl with the at-risk segregated suburbs. There is a heavily defended racial line between many of them. This line, however, can quickly recede in a process of flight and resegregation.

This class of communities, which includes about 6 percent of the population of the 25 metropolitan area sample, is found largely in the fully incorporated metropolitan areas of the Northeast and North-Central states. This group had an average 1990 median household income of $33,753, which was about 110 percent of the city average and about half of the affluent job centers' average. It had an average 1990 median home price of $102,701, about 80 percent of central cities' average price and half the affluent suburbs' average.

The group comprises mostly older, inner-ring suburbs and small, outlying cities that have been swallowed up by metropolitan growth.

13. The tax capacities of Harvey, Ford Heights, and Robbins in 1998 were, respectively, 60, 21, and 19 percent of the regional average, and the proportion of non-Asian minority students in their elementary schools was, respectively, 98, 100, and 100 percent.

Examples of the first type include Conshohocken, Lansdowne, and Cheltenham in the Philadelphia metropolitan area; Brooklyn Park, Burnsville, and Bloomington in the Twin Cities; and Brookline and Everett in Boston. The second type includes Media and Gloucester City in the Philadelphia area; Anoka and Center City in the Twin Cities metropolis; and Ann Arbor and Dearborn in the Detroit area.

The at-risk segregated and older communities have many common concerns. Both groups have slow population growth or (decline), relatively meager local resources, and struggling commercial districts. Their main street corridors and commercial districts cannot attract new, big businesses that could easily build on greenfield sites. As described in more detail in the "Metropolicy" and "Metropolitics" sections, both of these groups stand to gain from state-level school equity programs that redistribute tax resources from other communities in order to reduce their local tax rates and increase their local spending. They are also likely to benefit from state and regional land-use planning to curb urban sprawl and spread affordable housing to newer communities. Furthermore, both are likely to benefit from transportation policies that support rebuilding existing infrastructure rather than building new highways and that provide more flexible resources for transit. Despite these commonalities, segregated and older at-risk suburbs have not formed a cohesive political whole, probably because they are often divided on the issue of race.

Many at-risk segregated communities resemble segregated or deeply poor urban neighborhoods. Fear about what is happening to their neighbors often leads those in at-risk older communities to try to distance themselves from people in at-risk segregated communities. The at-risk older communities often struggle with lawsuits alleging housing discrimination against black and Latino homeowners or renters attempting to move from the at-risk segregated communities. This does not help relations on either side.

In anonymous interviews conducted in relation to my Chicago study in 1995, a city manger in an at-risk older suburb of Chicago, after speaking for 10 minutes on the need for school equity reform stated: "While we have common issues with Harvey [an at-risk segregated community], in the end, we identify more with communities like Orland Park and Tinley Park [bedroom-developing communities]. We may have some issues, but we are struggling to make something of ourselves here. Places like Robbins, Harvey, and Maywood are lazy and don't care."

Another city manager in an at-risk older community stated: "You should see the white homeowners in this city. Whether they have kids or not, they are constantly monitoring the test scores at the school. At the first hint of change, everybody will be out of there. People paid big money for these houses—they have a lot of their saving tied up in them, and if they were threatened in this investment, they would be gone."

A third city manager in a gradually changing at-risk older community told me, while a school aid bill was slowly moving through the Illinois legislature, that "even if you were talking about revenue issues in which both types of suburbs would gain, the race factor would play into it. Everything is racial." Many of the officials interviewed complained that real estate agents, the county, or the at-risk segregated communities directed minorities seeking housing to look in these communities and also complained about policies that disproportionately sent Section 8 certificates (public housing) to their areas.

The futility of such attitudes is seen in a comparison of East Cleveland and Cleveland Heights.[14] East Cleveland, which denied it was experiencing social and racial change while it went from working class to poor and segregated in a matter of a few years, commanded just 35 percent of the Cleveland average school district tax capacity in 1998. Students in its elementary schools were 99.8 percent non-Asian minority, and 76 percent were eligible for free and reduced-cost lunch. On the other hand, Cleveland Heights (another suburb in this sample) embraced its diversity but also moved to stabilize its potential social problems and thus is combating the dual challenges of economic decline and resegregation with some success. In 1998 its school tax capacity was 9 percent above the regional average. Students in its elementary schools were 68 percent non-Asian minority (up a bit from 62 percent in 1992), and only a third qualified for the free-lunch program. The conscious, successful effort of Cleveland Heights is discussed in the "Metropolicy" section.

A case of rapid transition and decline can be seen in the Gateway Cities southeast of Los Angeles, a massive agglomeration of declining industrial cities in an area that once had the industrial capacity of Germany's Ruhr Valley.[15] The Gateway Cities include 27 municipalities, 10 of them at-risk segregated communities. Among these 10, average 1998 tax capacity was 61 percent of the regional average and growing at a rate well below the average, and the average percentage of elementary school children eligible for the free-lunch program exceeded 85 percent. The cities "Latinized" between the mid-1970s and the late 1980s. By

14. See Keating (1994).
15. Fulton (1997).

1990, Latinos constituted more than 88 percent of the population and Anglos less than 10 percent, a change of about twenty percentage points in just 10 years.[16] After Latino leaders wrested political power from white politicians they believed were unresponsive to the interests of the community, the new leaders found that they had few financial resources and no real tools to address the wave of social, racial, and fiscal change moving through their communities. Much like their predecessors, they found themselves seeking out gambling facilities, waste storage, and other low-amenity industries to help pay the bills. One author termed these communities "cities of extraction."[17]

Once the middle class begins to leave an area, whether suburb or central city, and particularly when most of the middle class is gone, voter participation and oversight decline. The caliber of people running for election diminishes. Civic watchfulness disappears, and corruption sets in. This is another one of social separation's devastating effects. During my study of Chicago, corruption and scandals were brewing in 4 of the 16 cities in which interviews took place. The last mayor of Chicago Heights was in prison on corruption charges. A middle class is necessary not only for tax base and good schools, but also for a functioning democracy.

At-Risk Low-Density Communities. The final group of at-risk communities comprises 1,104 relatively low-density localities with low tax capacities that are growing more slowly than their regions and with higher-than-average poverty and population growth rates. These communities, home to about a fourth of the population in the 25 metropolitan areas, are typically located in the metropolitan areas' outer portions. Many of them are exurbs that still contain some pockets of rural poverty, but they are changing as they become integrated into the metropolitan area. Their average tax capacity, 66 percent of the regional average in 1998, is growing slowly, so the gap is widening. As they make the transition from rural to suburban, these localities must cope with the costs of greater-than-average population growth, relatively high poverty, and older-than-average housing stock. This group had a 1990 average median income of $30,106 and a median home price of $89,331, about 70 percent of the central city average home value. With about 25 percent of the regional population, they had just 13 percent of total office space.

16. Fulton (1997, pp. 82–83).
17. Fulton (1997, pp. 67–98).

The Twin Cities, Atlanta, and San Francisco each have a band of at-risk low-density communities on the outermost fringes of the metropolitan area. In Atlanta and San Francisco, the band is in the unincorporated areas in the outermost counties. In the fully incorporated Twin Cities metropolitan area, it consists of a nearly continuous belt of semirural townships in the north and west.

Bedroom-Developing Communities

While bedroom-developing communities had one-fourth of the population in the study areas in 1998, they captured 60% of the population growth between 1993 and 1998.

The fourth classification of suburbs comprises what many would regard as the prototypical suburb. The population—mostly white—is growing more quickly in the suburbs in this group than in any other. Density is low, housing is new, and tax capacity is just below average and growing at an average rate. All those characteristics suggest the typical bedroom suburb. Although this group contained about a fourth of the population in the study areas in 1998, it had captured nearly 60 percent of the population growth in those areas between 1993 and 1998. It had only 13 percent of the regional office market, about half its share of households. Of the six clusters, this one had the most school-age children per household. Though not experiencing the social stress of the at-risk communities, these localities must manage the costs of a high rate of population growth with only average (or below-average) local resources. How well they manage new growth will largely determine whether they experience fiscal stress. If new development is at a cost-effective density and coincides with the provision of adequate infrastructure, they may benefit from growth. If growth is scattered, low in density, and poorly coordinated with infrastructure provision, they may face significant fiscal stress as a result of excessive infrastructure costs. This group had an average 1990 median household income of $40,000 and an average median home value of $121,009—about the same as the central city average.

Schools and Infrastructure in At-Risk Low-Density, and Bedroom-Developing Suburbs

Both the at-risk low-density and the bedroom-developing suburbs share fiscal pressures arising from school and infrastructure finance. In all the large regions, the student-to-household ratio in at-risk low-density and bedroom-developing suburbs is much higher than the regional average. In Minneapolis–St. Paul, these two kinds of suburbs have a 25 percent higher ratio of children per household than the central city. In Portland, it is 26 percent higher; in Denver, 21 percent higher; and in Seattle, an astonishing 42 percent higher. In the mid-1990s in Cherokee County,

Georgia, students often attended schools set up in trailers, as their communities had neither the tax base nor resources to build new schools for a growing population. Since schools account for the largest share of local expenditure, these sizable differences in the ratio of children per household are very important fiscally. Because of this ratio and their (at best) average tax base, these two kinds of suburbs have the lowest per-pupil spending in metropolitan America. In states without a significant aid system for equalizing the resources available to school districts, such as Illinois, Pennsylvania, and Ohio, these districts have extremely low spending, high school taxes, or both.

Developmental infrastructure such as roads and sewerage can also present large challenges for the at-risk and bedroom-developing suburbs. In the Detroit region, moderate-income workers, often in the automobile or related industries, seek out their bit of paradise in the rapidly developing northern quadrant of Macomb County, northeast of Detroit, where they can afford a lot of land and enjoy low taxes. But this package deal does not include sewer systems or roads. Although the Macomb communities included a combination of all the suburban types, at-risk low-density and bedroom-developing suburbs predominated. The Southeast Michigan Council of Governments found that, with their low fiscal capacity and the federal government's declining commitment to finance suburban sewer improvements, these suburbs had no way to pay for the 3,172 to 4,560 miles of sewers needed, estimated to cost between $2 billion and $4 billion ($4 billion and $8 billion, factoring in inflation and interest on debt).[18]

The communities of Macomb County present a powerful example of the downside of unplanned growth from a base of low fiscal capacity. Throughout the 1990s, Lake St. Clair, a large freshwater lake on the county's eastern border, was becoming unsafe for swimming. Of the eight public beaches monitored on Macomb County's web page, all were closed several days during the summer of 2001 because of *E. coli* from untreated sewage. At least one of the lake's large public beaches was closed for the entire summer. Failed septic systems caused much of this problem, but several of the cities have recently admitted to dumping raw sewage into the waterways feeding Lake St. Clair.[19]

This may seem outrageous, but Macomb is by no means unique. In 2000 the Natural Resources Defense Council reported 11,270 beach

18. "Investing in Michigan's Quality of Life" (April 2000) (http:www.semcog.org/products/pdfs/sewerneeds2.pdf).
19. See Ben Schmitt and Emilia Askari, "A Tide of Pollution; State Presses Cities to Stop Overflow," *Detroit Free Press*, April 5, 2001.

closings in the United States, 85 percent of them caused by bacteria from improperly treated sewage and only spotty monitoring of beach safety and water quality.[20] Faulty sewage treatment is emerging as a major public health concern, not only in recreational areas but also in many bedroom-developing suburbs of regions in the Midwest, Northeast, and South.

Residents of these communities are also skeptical that their local elected officials will handle growth appropriately. Consequently, there has been an explosion in local ballot initiatives in the bedroom-developing suburbs. An analysis conducted in 2000 of a national database of ballot initiatives, separating the initiatives that could be identified with a specific city rather than a larger, more diverse county, suggests that bedroom-developing communities often drive local ballot initiatives. In Los Angeles, this group of suburbs put forward 3 of the 10 ballot initiatives proposed that year; in the Bay Area, 8 of 16; in Chicago, 11 of 14; in Philadelphia, 10 of 14; and in New York, 23 of 41.

Affluent Job Centers

Many suburbs have moved well beyond their traditional role as bedroom communities for large cities and are now major players in their regional economy.[21] "Edge cities"—suburban communities with more than 5 million square feet of office space and more jobs than bedrooms—are the major winners in the decentralization of U.S. metropolitan areas. They reap the benefits of extraordinary tax bases, while paying only a fraction of the costs of the central cities that once monopolized the office market. Although congestion and rapid loss of open space are among the costs they cannot escape, most of these communities have developed in ways (sometimes market driven, sometimes planned) that enable them to evade the social costs associated with poverty. Edge cities in this study include the Route 128 Corridor in Boston, the Schaumburg area west of O'Hare International Airport in Chicago, the Perimeter Center north of Atlanta, the Irvine area south of Los Angeles, several areas in New York (Stamford-Greenwich, Great Neck–Lake Success, and the Garden City area), and Pleasanton-Dublin in San Francisco, to name just a few.

The municipalities in these edge cities represent a significant proportion of the last two clusters in our analysis: "affluent job centers" and "very affluent job centers" (containing 625 and 91 municipalities,

20. NRDC (2001).
21. Garreau (1992).

respectively). For example, along Route 128 in Massachusetts, from south to north, are Westwood, Dover, Needham, Wellesley, Newton, Weston, Waltham, Lincoln, Lexington, Concord, and Bedford. Of those localities, only Waltham is not in one of the affluent job center clusters. Among the others, 1998 tax capacities ranged from 172 percent of the regional average (Bedford) to 383 percent (Weston), and those capacities were growing faster than the regional average in all but one (Bedford). Poverty among elementary school-age children ranged from just 4 percent of the regional average (Dover) to 22 percent of the average (Newton).

Similar patterns can be seen in the edge cities of other metropolitan areas. Barrington Hills, Inverness Village, Itasca, Schaumberg Village, and South Barrington Village (the Schaumberg area in Chicago) had an average 1998 tax capacity of 282 percent of the Chicago regional average and an average free-lunch-eligible rate of just 14 percent of the regional average. Costa Mesa, Irvine, and Newport Beach (the Irvine area of Los Angeles) had corresponding averages of 186 percent and 41 percent; Pleasanton and Dublin (San Francisco) had rates of 197 percent and 25 percent; and Stamford and Greenwich (New York) had rates of 319 percent and 43 percent.

What is most striking about these kinds of suburbs is their enormous concentration of office space. Home to 7 percent of the population, these places have 17 percent of the office space—nearly 2.5 times their fair share. They have more than four times the office space per household of any other group of suburbs, more even than central cities. Concentration of commercial capacity is their distinguishing feature. Although many residents of other municipalities benefit from the employment opportunities and commercial activities in these areas, only a few can enjoy the tax (and resulting public service) benefits.

As might be expected, the political and business leaders in these affluent job centers work hard to maintain the quality of life of the community, and, of all types of suburbs, they are the ones that have revolted most successfully against growth and sprawl.[22] Their residents are highly educated and quite willing to stand up for themselves. Some of the highest-profile, local antigrowth controversies have taken place in America's wealthiest suburban areas: the anti-Disney theme park battle in Loudoun County, Virginia; the adoption of growth boundaries in Ventura County in 1998; and the growth moratoriums and slow-growth regulations in San Francisco's South Bay and eastern Contra

Affluent job centers have more than 4 times the office space per household of any other group of suburbs— more even than central cities.

22. Myers and Puentes (2000).

Costa County. Affluent Bellevue and Redmond, Washington (home of Microsoft Corporation), contain powerful pockets of resistance to sprawl. Residents of Silicon Forest (in the western suburbs of Portland) have worked hard to hold Portland's urban growth boundary constant, constraining further growth in their direction. The lovely Saint Croix River Valley of the Twin Cities is home to strong opponents of growth—recent polls put growth above education and taxes as a key election issue. Antigrowth ballot measures were disproportionately found on the ballots in the affluent job centers of Los Angeles (4 of 10 of the region's initiatives), Chicago (3 of 14), New York (16 of 41), and Cleveland (7 of 21), although most antigrowth initiatives were on ballots in the bedroom-developing suburbs.[23]

These places might seem to have it all: affluent people, a high tax base, an average load of children, and very low poverty. However, the mass of jobs and commercial activity also has its downside. First, because many workers cannot afford the local housing, these beehives of local activity generally have bad traffic congestion. Second, because land becomes so valuable it is often difficult to maintain open space.

DISTRIBUTION OF COMMUNITY TYPES WITHIN METROPOLITAN AREAS

Table 2-4 shows the distribution of population, tax capacity, aid, poor populations, and population growth among the central cities and the six types of suburban communities in the full sample of 25 metropolitan areas and in the 6 representative areas used in chapter 1. In the full sample, 68 percent of the population lived in a community experiencing fiscal stress of some sort: 28 percent were in central cities; 14 percent in the two high-density, at-risk groups; and 26 percent in the low-density, at-risk group. Localities in some kind of fiscal stress housed 88 percent of the people living in poverty in the sample metropolitan areas, but they controlled only 56 percent of local tax capacity. Although they received greater-than-average amounts of state aid, their share of total fiscal capacity (59 percent) was still well below their shares of total population and extremely poor people.

Another quarter of the population in the 25 metropolitan areas was in the bedroom-developing suburbs. Those localities controlled roughly average shares of tax capacity, state aid, and total capacity, but they captured 56 percent of total population growth in the metropolitan areas

23. Fulton and others (2000).

between 1993 and 1998. That growth and its management are important issues not only for the municipalities themselves but also for their metropolitan areas as a whole.

Just 7 percent of the population in the 25 metropolitan areas lived in communities in the two affluent job center categories. Those localities controlled 13 percent of total local fiscal capacity, but they were home to only 2 percent of people living in poverty. Although they captured more than their proportionate share of growth, they were not the hothouses of growth that the bedroom-developing suburbs were between 1993 and 1998. They thus enjoy a disproportionate share of the benefits of regional growth patterns with very few of the costs.

The six metropolitan areas in the comparison group have distinctly different mixes of community types. In the regions in which large shares of the population are in unincorporated areas (Atlanta, Chicago, Denver, and San Francisco), low-density communities are the most common type of at-risk community. In regions that are fully incorporated (Minneapolis–St. Paul and New York), at-risk communities are much more likely to be segregated or older. Atlanta and Chicago have the smallest number of residents—only 51 percent of the regional population—in at-risk communities and central cities. In Atlanta, that reflects the fact that nearly 70 percent of the region's total population lives in unincorporated areas, most of which are classified as bedroom-developing communities. In the other four regions, the proportion of the population in communities in the at-risk categories and central cities ranges from 62 to 85 percent.

There is much less variation, however, in the extent to which poor populations tend to cluster in the at-risk communities and central cities. The share of the total poor population in at-risk communities ranges from 83 percent (Minneapolis–St. Paul) to 89 percent (San Francisco). Similarly, the percentage of the poor population living in communities in the two affluent job center categories was very low everywhere, ranging from just 3 percent in Denver to 10 percent in Chicago.

Maps 2-1 through 2-6 show the geographic pattern of community types in the six metropolitan areas. The fully incorporated metropolitan areas (Minneapolis–St. Paul and New York) have the most distinctive patterns. Each has a distinct ring of at-risk suburbs surrounding the central cities; a mix of affluent job center and bedroom-developing suburbs in the second ring from the center; and a mix of at-risk, low-density, and bedroom-developing communities in the outermost parts of the regions. Atlanta shows a similar pattern, but large tracts of unincorporated areas predominate. Fulton County shows great variety, containing

47

Atlanta, a set of at-risk segregated suburbs south of Atlanta, and a relatively affluent unincorporated area. By contrast, the entire county of DeKalb, just east of Atlanta, is in the at-risk, segregated category. Another set of at-risk, segregated municipalities (including Marietta and Smyrna) lie to the northwest of Atlanta. The outermost counties tend to fall into the at-risk low-density category; the remainder, in the bedroom-developing category.

The San Francisco map is dominated by large expanses of at-risk low-density unincorporated areas. The inner suburbs include a group of at-risk segregated municipalities northwest and southeast of Oakland (including Hayward and Richmond) and farther south in the Menlo Park area. The more affluent suburbs, including places like Palo Alto, Portola Valley, Woodside, Santa Clara, and Milpitas, form a ring to the south.

Overall, inner suburbs tend to fall into the at-risk segregated or at-risk older categories. The middle ring of suburbs usually contains a mix of bedroom-developing and affluent job centers. Most outermost areas contain a mix of at-risk low-density and bedroom-developing suburbs.

MAP 2-1. ATLANTA REGION
Community Classification

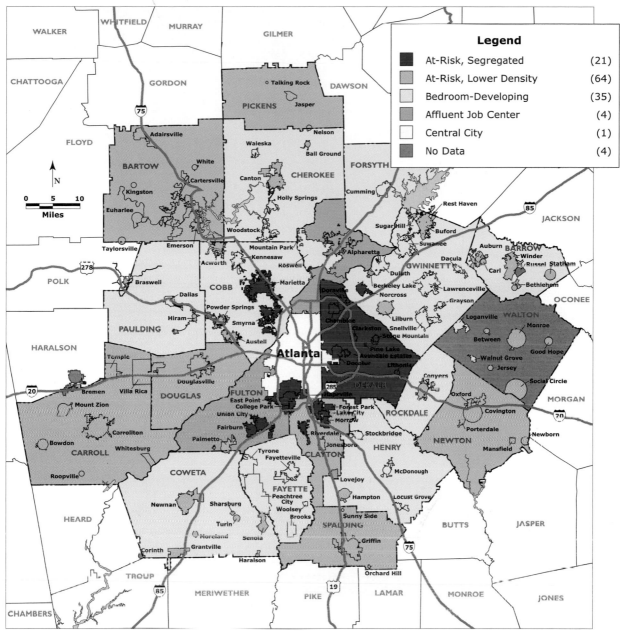

Legend

■	At-Risk, Segregated	(21)
■	At-Risk, Lower Density	(64)
■	Bedroom-Developing	(35)
■	Affluent Job Center	(4)
□	Central City	(1)
■	No Data	(4)

Data Source: Metropolitan Area Research Corporation.

MAP 2-2. CHICAGO REGION
Community Classification

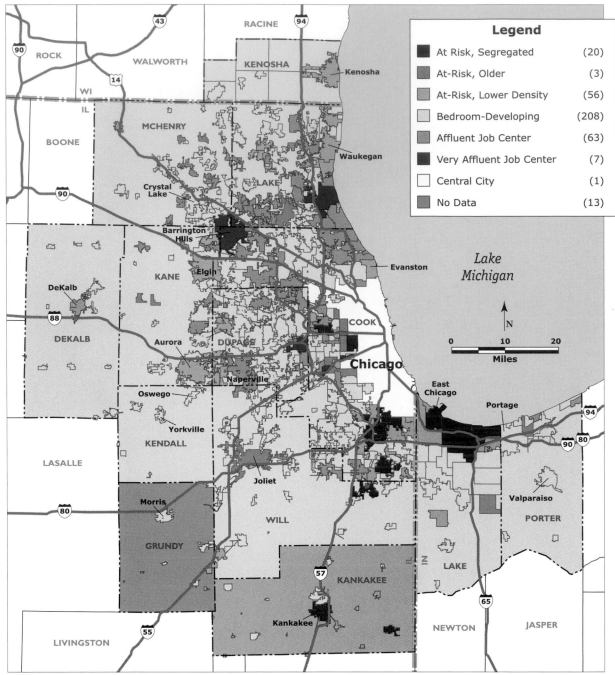

Legend

■	At Risk, Segregated	(20)
■	At-Risk, Older	(3)
■	At-Risk, Lower Density	(56)
■	Bedroom-Developing	(208)
■	Affluent Job Center	(63)
■	Very Affluent Job Center	(7)
☐	Central City	(1)
■	No Data	(13)

Lake Michigan

0   10   20
Miles

N

Data Source: Metropolitan Area Research Corporation.

MAP 2-3. CHICAGO REGION (CENTRAL AREA)
Community Classification

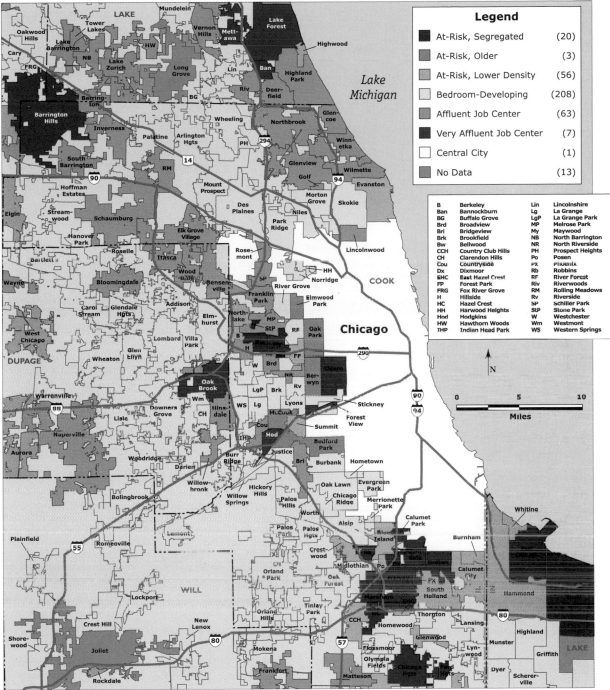

Legend

■	At-Risk, Segregated	(20)
■	At-Risk, Older	(3)
■	At-Risk, Lower Density	(56)
□	Bedroom-Developing	(208)
■	Affluent Job Center	(63)
■	Very Affluent Job Center	(7)
□	Central City	(1)
■	No Data	(13)

B	Berkeley	Lin	Lincolnshire
Ban	Bannockburn	Lg	La Grange
BG	Buffalo Grove	LgP	La Grange Park
Brd	Broadview	MP	Melrose Park
Bri	Bridgeview	My	Maywood
Brk	Brookfield	NB	North Barrington
Bw	Bellwood	NR	North Riverside
CCH	Country Club Hills	PH	Prospect Heights
CH	Clarendon Hills	Po	Posen
Cou	Countryside	Px	Phoenix
Dx	Dixmoor	Rb	Robbins
EHC	East Hazel Crest	RF	River Forest
FP	Forest Park	Riv	Riverwoods
FRG	Fox River Grove	RM	Rolling Meadows
H	Hillside	Rv	Riverside
HC	Hazel Crest	SP	Schiller Park
HH	Harwood Heights	StP	Stone Park
Hod	Hodgkins	W	Westchester
HW	Hawthorn Woods	Wm	Westmont
THP	Indian Head Park	WS	Western Springs

0   5   10
Miles

N

Data Source: Metropolitan Area Research Corporation.

MAP 2-4. DENVER REGION
Community Classification

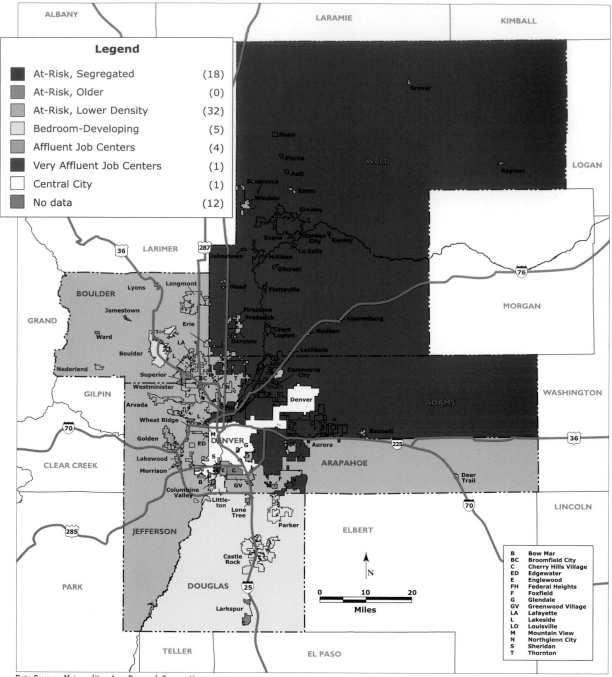

Legend

■	At-Risk, Segregated	(18)
■	At-Risk, Older	(0)
■	At-Risk, Lower Density	(32)
■	Bedroom-Developing	(5)
■	Affluent Job Centers	(4)
■	Very Affluent Job Centers	(1)
□	Central City	(1)
■	No data	(12)

B	Bow Mar
BC	Broomfield City
C	Cherry Hills Village
ED	Edgewater
E	Englewood
FH	Federal Heights
F	Foxfield
G	Glendale
GV	Greenwood Village
LA	Lafayette
L	Lakeside
LO	Louisville
M	Mountain View
N	Northglenn City
S	Sheridan
T	Thornton

0   10   20
Miles

N

Data Source: Metropolitan Area Research Corporation.

MAP 2-5. MINNEAPOLIS–ST. PAUL REGION
Community Classification

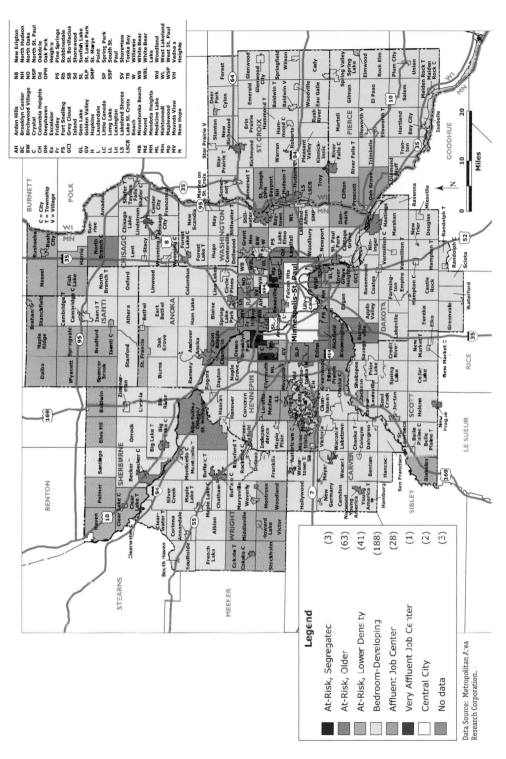

Legend

■ At-Risk, Segregated	(3)
■ At-Risk, Older	(63)
■ At-Risk, Lower Density	(41)
■ Bedroom-Developing	(188)
■ Affluent Job Center	(28)
■ Very Affluent Job Center	(1)
□ Central City	(2)
■ No data	(3)

Data Source: Metropolitan Area
Research Corporation.

MAP 2-6. NEW YORK REGION
Community Classification

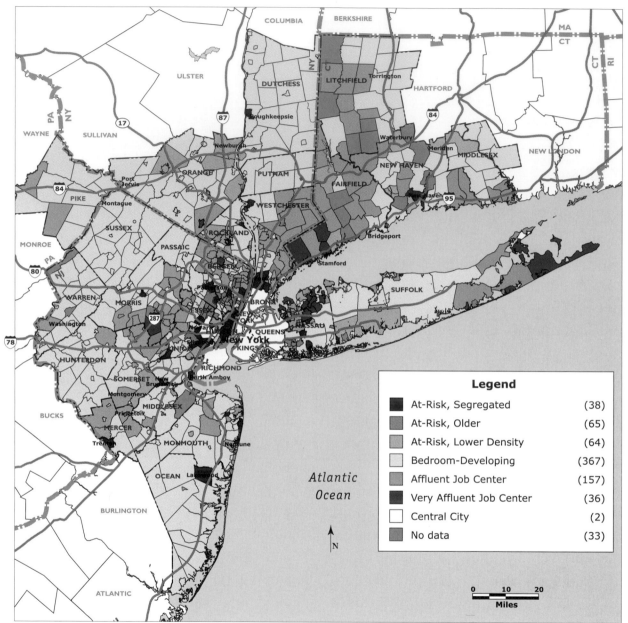

Legend

■	At-Risk, Segregated	(38)
■	At-Risk, Older	(65)
■	At-Risk, Lower Density	(64)
□	Bedroom-Developing	(367)
■	Affluent Job Center	(157)
■	Very Affluent Job Center	(36)
□	Central City	(2)
■	No data	(33)

Data Source: Metropolitan Area Research Corporation.

MAP 2-7. NEW YORK REGION (CENTRAL AREA)
Community Classification

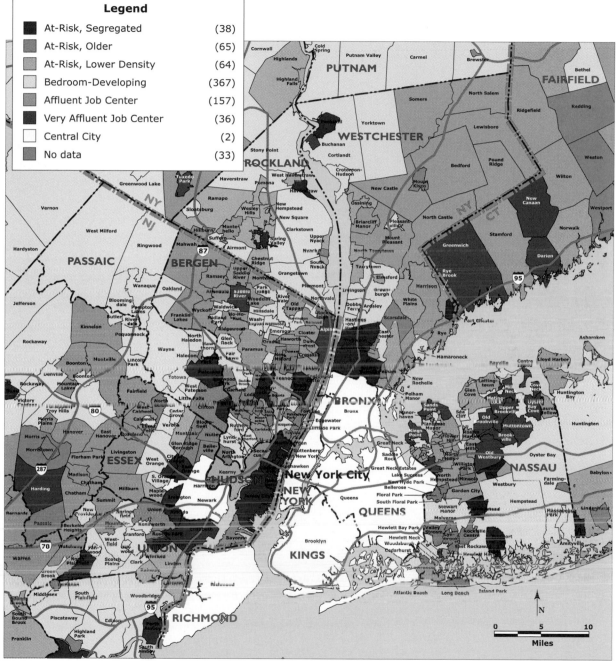

Legend

■	At-Risk, Segregated	(38)
■	At-Risk, Older	(65)
■	At-Risk, Lower Density	(64)
▢	Bedroom-Developing	(367)
■	Affluent Job Center	(157)
■	Very Affluent Job Center	(36)
□	Central City	(2)
■	No data	(33)

Data Source: Metropolitan Area Research Corporation.

MAP 2-8. SAN FRANCISCO REGION
Community Classification

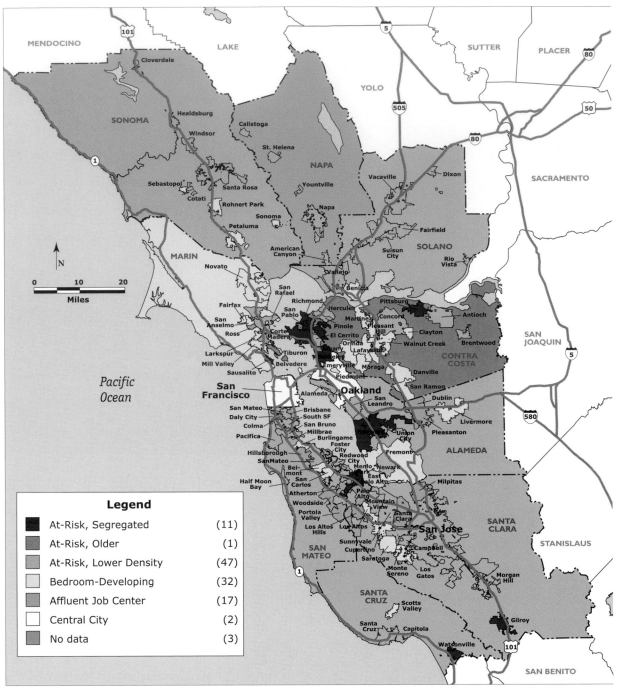

Legend

■	At-Risk, Segregated	(11)
■	At-Risk, Older	(1)
■	At-Risk, Lower Density	(47)
■	Bedroom-Developing	(32)
■	Affluent Job Center	(17)
☐	Central City	(2)
■	No data	(3)

Data Source: Metropolitan Area Research Corporation.

CHAPTER 3

A COMPARATIVE ANALYSIS OF SEGREGATION, FISCAL INEQUALITY, AND SPRAWL

Overall, school segregation in the United States—both socioeconomic and racial—is increasing, while neighborhood segregation remains high. Tax inequality among local governments is also very high and increasing. As a group, metropolitan areas are consuming new land much faster than they are gaining population.

However, the degree of segregation, inequality, and sprawl varies greatly among the 25 largest U.S. metropolitan areas, and in predictable ways. Metropolitan areas that are more segregated by income and race also tend to show more fiscal inequality. They tend to sprawl more. Sprawling metro areas—those that consume land at the fastest rates compared with their population growth—have growing suburbs with weaker resource bases and less growth in those resources than their counterparts in places that manage growth more efficiently.

RACIAL AND SOCIAL SEGREGATION

After a period of improvement, especially in the South, school segregation rose during the 1990s.[1] After an intensive effort and protracted court battles to integrate schools, the proportion of black students in majority white schools peaked in the early 1980s but declined to the level of the 1960s by the 1996–97 school year. Latino segregation has grown steadily throughout the last three decades. By 1980, Latinos were

1. Resegregation in America's Schools, The Civil Rights Project, Harvard University, June 1999, and www.law.harvard.edu/civilrights/publications/resegregation99.html.

more likely to attend predominantly nonwhite schools than blacks and, by the 1990s, slightly exceeded the proportion of blacks in intensely segregated schools (those with minority enrollments of 90 to 100 percent). In other words, the percentage of Latino students in predominantly nonwhite schools surpassed the percentage of black students in predominantly nonwhite schools and slightly exceeded the percentage of black students in almost entirely nonwhite schools. In 1968, 45 percent of Latino students attended majority white schools; by 1996 only 25 percent did. Although residential segregation is much less prevalent for Latinos than for blacks and their intermarriage rate with whites is higher, the school segregation rate is worse for Latinos—and worsening. As current patterns of Latino immigration and suburban migration continue, the challenges to the stability of the communities they move to will increase.[2]

Table 3-1 shows the degree of income segregation among elementary school students in each of the 25 metropolitan areas in 1992 and 1997. Dissimilarity indexes for students who are eligible for a free-lunch program are shown, together with the percentage change in the indexes. The *dissimilarity index* is a general measure of segregation that compares the spatial distribution of students eligible and ineligible for free lunch across different schools. It can be interpreted as the percentage of eligible students that would have to change schools to achieve an identical mix of students in each school. Higher values indicate greater degrees of income segregation.

Segregation of poor students in the 25 metropolitan areas worsened overall between 1992 and 1997. The dissimilarity index increased (worsened) in 12 areas; it was constant in 4; and it improved in only 5 of the 21 areas for which free-lunch eligibility data were available for both years. Segregation increased most markedly in the metropolitan areas that were least segregated at the beginning of the period (Portland, St. Louis, and Minneapolis–St. Paul). The most segregated areas (Chicago, Milwaukee, Cleveland, and Detroit) showed little change.

Table 3-2 shows similar measures of racial segregation. Dissimilarity indexes are shown for elementary school students in 1992 and 1997 and for the total population in each of the metropolitan areas in 1990 and 2000. Students are more segregated by race than by poverty in the 25 metropolitan areas overall—on average, 61 percent of non-Asian minority students would have had to change schools in 1997 to achieve

2. Orfield and Yun (1999, tables 8 and 9).

TABLE 3-1. **Segregation by Income in Elementary Schools: Dissimilarity Indexes for 1992 and 1997**

Metropolitan area	Dissimilarity indexes		
	1992	1997	Percent change
Atlanta	50	52	4
Boston	n.a.	55	n.a.
Chicago	94	95	1
Cincinnati	59	57	–3
Cleveland	62	64	3
Dallas	51	51	0
Denver	48	55	15
Detroit	60	60	0
Houston	39	39	0
Kansas City	54	53	–2
Los Angeles	54	57	6
Miami	49	50	2
Milwaukee	66	63	–5
Minneapolis–St. Paul	42	48	14
New York	n.a.	66	n.a.
Philadelphia	n.a.	51	n.a.
Phoenix	n.a.	n.a.	n.a.
Pittsburgh	43	39	–9
Portland	36	50	39
St. Louis	46	60	30
San Diego	51	51	0
San Francisco	48	53	10
Seattle	34	38	12
Tampa	32	36	13
Washington, D.C.	53	51	–4
25 metropolitan area average	**51**	**54**	**6**

Source: National Center for Education Statistics.
n.a. = Not available.

an equal distribution of students by race as compared with 54 percent of free-lunch eligible students. Racial separation also increased on average during the period, but it increased more slowly than segregation of poor students. Overall, segregation by race increased in 12 of the 25 metropolitan areas; it remained constant in 4 and decreased in 9.

TABLE 3-2. **Racial Segregation in Metropolitan Populations and Elementary Schools: Dissimilarity Indexes, Selected Years**

	Elementary schools			Metropolitan population		
Metropolitan area	1992	1997	Percent change	1990	2000	Percent change
Atlanta	66	67	2	69	66	−4
Boston	67	66	−1	71	66	−7
Chicago	76	75	−1	85	81	−5
Cincinnati	76	77	1	77	75	−3
Cleveland	76	76	0	83	77	−7
Dallas	58	58	0	64	59	−8
Denver	53	55	4	65	62	−5
Detroit	81	82	1	88	85	−3
Houston	46	45	−2	68	68	0
Kansas City	67	70	4	73	69	−5
Los Angeles	56	57	2	74	68	−8
Miami	60	60	0	73	74	1
Milwaukee	65	69	6	83	82	−1
Minneapolis–St. Paul	54	53	−2	64	58	−9
New York	72	71	−1	82	82	0
Philadelphia	66	67	2	77	72	−6
Phoenix	53	56	6	52	44	−15
Pittsburgh	70	69	−1	71	67	−6
Portland	42	40	−5	66	48	−27
St. Louis	66	69	5	79	74	−6
San Diego	44	46	5	59	54	−8
San Francisco	45	48	7	65	61	−6
Seattle	40	39	−3	58	50	−14
Tampa	37	35	−5	71	64	−10
Washington, D.C.	65	65	0	66	57	−14
25 metropolitan area average	**60**	**61**	**1**	**71**	**67**	**−7**

Sources: National Center for Education Statistics and 2000 Census of Population, compiled by the Lewis Mumford Center, State University of New York at Albany.

The 2000 census data show that housing markets are even more segregated than schools: on average, 67 percent of black residents would have had to move in 2000 to achieve perfect racial balance in the 25 metropolitan areas. However, the trends are much more positive in the metropolitan areas overall than in elementary schools—the degree of racial segregation in housing actually declined in 21 of the 25 areas in the 1990s.

The differing patterns in the school and population data imply that much of the improvement in housing markets (represented by the census population data) reflects changes in the distribution of families with no children in the public school system: empty-nesters; young entrants to the labor force who do not yet have children in the school system; or families that settle in the city core of a metropolitan area for more convenient access to jobs, amenities, and transit and send their children to private schools.

WHY SHOULD WE CARE ABOUT THIS STRATIFICATION?

Since the country's founding, the ideal of an open society, where all citizens have opportunities for advancement, has been a part of the American dream. Implicit in this dream is the belief, borne out by generations of social research, that social mobility is inextricable from contact with people from a variety of social and economic classes—social mixing (see chapter 6, pages 122–23, for a discussion of the Gautreaux program). In most of our European immigrant pasts lies the story of a poor forebear in the same classroom or neighborhood as someone higher on the social or economic ladder, who inspired the poorer newcomer to succeed. Observing success within the boundaries of our own experience clarifies the possibilities and processes of social advance and stimulates healthy competition and ambition. It shows the way up.

Social separation leaves middle-class children in overcrowded, underfunded schools, but its more powerful harms accrue to the poor people of color left behind in communities of concentrated poverty in many American cities and some older suburbs. Neighborhoods of concentrated poverty destroy the lives of the people trapped in them and create a growing social and fiscal cancer in the midst of previously healthy communities.[3] In cities and older suburbs, as joblessness, racial segregation, and single-parent families come to dominate neighbor-

Neighborhoods of concentrated poverty destroy the lives of those trapped in them and create a growing social and fiscal cancer in the midst of once healthy communities.

3. See Lemann (1986, 1991); Wilson (1987); Massey and Denton (1993); Melton (1993).

53

hoods, residents are cut off from middle-class society and the private economy.[4] Individuals, particularly children, are deprived of successful local role models and connections to opportunities outside their neighborhood. A distinct society emerges with expectations and patterns of behavior at odds with middle-class norms, and the "exodus of middle and working-class families from ghetto neighborhoods removes an important social buffer."[5]

Whether poor or middle-class, young people who live amid concentrated poverty are far more likely to become pregnant as teenagers, drop out of high school, and remain jobless than their counterparts in socioeconomically mixed neighborhoods.[6] In the social isolation of concentrated poverty, distinctive speech patterns develop that make interaction with mainstream society difficult and complicate educational progress and employment success.[7] Many urban employers believe that the people who live in distressed neighborhoods are an unsuitable work force. In neighborhoods lacking successful middle-class role models, gang leaders, drug dealers, and other antisocial figures are often the only local residents with money and status.[8] Tightly knit gangs provide family structures where none existed before. These factors interact with anger, frustration, isolation, boredom, and hopelessness and create a synergy of disproportionate levels of crime, violence, and other antisocial behavior.[9] Crime increases dramatically in areas of concentrated poverty. The crime rate in U.S. cities is closely correlated with the percentage of the city that is ghettoized.[10]

As concentrated poverty rises in a region's central city and other older communities, middle-class flight, business disinvestment, and the decline in property values in surrounding areas intensify. Local retailers have fewer customers. In the poorest metropolitan neighborhoods, basic private services, even grocery stores, disappear.[11] Social needs and hence property taxes begin to increase on a declining base of values. Local governments in these communities struggle to provide more with less. In the

4. Galster (1992).

5. Wilson (1987).

6. Hogan and Kitawaga (1985); Furstenburg (1987); McLanahan and Garfinkel (1989); Anderson (1991); Crane (1991); Mayer (1991); Massey and Denton (1993).

7. On speech patterns, see Kirschman and Neckerman (1991); Shuy (1975). On obstacles to education and employment, see Labov (1972, 1975, 1980); Baugh 1983; Labov and Harris (1986).

8. Anderson (1989, 1994).

9. Taylor, Gottfredson, and Brower (1985); Skogan (1992); Massey and Denton (1993); Anderson (1994).

10. Orfield (1997).

11. Orfield (1985).

end, many of them have to choose between raising taxes or providing fewer services of poorer quality, thereby further burdening poor residents and alienating any remaining middle-class residents.[12] As local property taxes rise and the quality of services declines in the least desirable parts of the metropolitan area, the flight of the middle class and the private economy accelerates. Larger industrial and service businesses are disadvantaged by high taxes, deteriorating public infrastructure, crime, and falling property values.[13] Local governments' capacity to provide basic services declines along with the neighborhoods they serve.

FISCAL INEQUALITY

Table 3-3 shows the 1998 tax capacity per household for each metropolitan area and two measures of the relative equality of tax capacities among jurisdictions in each. The equity measures shown in the table are the Gini coefficient and the ratio of the tax capacity per household in the ninety-fifth percentile municipality (the municipality with a tax capacity per household greater than 95 percent of the municipalities in the region) to the tax capacity of the fifth percentile. The Gini coefficient is a general measure of inequality in tax bases. Lower values imply more equal distributions of tax capacity across the jurisdictions; higher values imply less equal distributions. The ratio of the ninety-fifth to the fifth percentile shows the degree of inequality between local governments at the very high end of the distribution and those at the low end.[14]

The Gini coefficients vary a great deal across the 25 metropolitan areas, ranging from 0.11 in San Diego (the metropolitan area with the most equal distribution) to 0.39 in St. Louis, a ratio of 3.5. That range of values is very significant. For comparison, in a recent study of income inequality in 182 metropolitan areas in the United States, the ratio of the highest to lowest Gini coefficients for income was just 1.4 in 1989.[15]

---

12. Sternlieb (1977).

13. Kasarda (1985, 1989).

14. The Gini coefficient measures the difference between the actual distribution of capacities and a perfectly equal distribution. It varies between 0 and 1, taking on a value of 0 if the distribution is perfectly equal (all jurisdictions in the region have the same tax capacity per household) and 1 if the distribution is perfectly unequal (all tax capacity is in a single community with only one household). The ninety-fifth and fifth percentile values are used in place of the highest and lowest to avoid using the very low or high outliers that occur in many metropolitan areas, values that are often the result of extraordinary circumstances that occur in only a very few places.

15. Madden (2000, p. 39).

TABLE 3-3. **Measures of Inequality in Tax Capacity per Household in the 25 Largest Metropolitan Areas, 1998**

Dollars unless otherwise indicated

Metropolitan area	Mean	Gini coefficient	5th percentile	95th percentile	95th to 5th ratio
Atlanta	870	0.17	257	1,452	5.6
Boston	1,666	0.25	863	3,662	4.2
Chicago	783	0.27	204	2,422	11.9
Cincinnati	1,097	0.36	102	3,223	31.6
Cleveland	1,117	0.24	286	4,786	16.7
Dallas	965	0.19	257	1,722	6.7
Denver	1,000	0.21	232	3,650	15.7
Detroit	939	0.21	426	1,853	4.4
Houston	911	0.15	185	3,198	17.3
Kansas City	804	0.25	106	1,213	11.4
Los Angeles	456	0.22	180	1,521	8.5
Miami	706	0.21	365	4,066	11.1
Milwaukee	1,548	0.27	1,141	3,757	3.3
Minneapolis–St. Paul	480	0.17	230	888	3.9
New York	1,871	0.23	829	7,302	8.8
Philadelphia	880	0.33	242	2,184	9.0
Phoenix	649	0.15	85	1,138	13.4
Pittsburgh	484	0.26	161	1,042	6.5
Portland	860	0.15	395	1,331	3.4
San Diego	480	0.11	168	964	5.7
San Francisco	586	0.17	312	1,333	4.3
Seattle	1,049	0.21	317	2,641	8.3
St. Louis	383	0.37	41	818	20.0
Tampa	507	0.13	253	8,016	31.7
Washington, D.C.	1,965	0.22	804	4,796	6.0

Sources: Various state and local government agencies.

The ratios of tax capacity in the ninety-fifth percentile to tax capacity in the fifth percentile—which vary from 3.3 to 31.7—show even greater diversity across metropolitan areas than the Gini coefficients. The implications are twofold. First, state-local fiscal systems allow wide variations at the extremes of the tax-capacity distributions. Second, even in the metropolitan area with the most equitable distribution of tax capacities, the top 5 percent of localities can generate more than 3 times the revenues of the lowest 5 percent when all apply the same tax rates. In 10 of the 25 metropolitan areas, the richest localities (in terms of their tax base) can generate more than 10 times the revenues of the poorest when all apply the same tax rates. Those tax bases provide more than half of local financing for services generally regarded as basic rights in the United States (public safety, streets, and sanitation services).

Comparing the tax-base inequality measures in table 3-3 to the income and racial inequality measures in tables 3-1 and 3-2 shows just how closely tax-base inequality in a metropolitan area correlates with income and racial segregation. There is a very strong tendency for the metropolitan areas with the greatest degrees of tax-base inequality to also show the greatest degrees of segregation by race and income. Seven of the 10 metropolitan areas with the most unequal tax-base distributions are also among the 10 areas with the greatest degrees of income segregation in schools (the second column of table 3-1) and 8 of the 10 are among the 10 areas showing the greatest degrees of racial segregation in housing markets (the fifth column of table 3-2).[16]

Table 3-4 shows how far systems of state aid to local governments in the 25 metropolitan areas actually went toward achieving equity in 1998. Gini coefficients and the ratios of the ninety-fifth to fifth percentiles change when state aid per household is added to local capacity per household. The potential for state-local fiscal systems to ease tax-base inequality clearly differs from place to place. Aid as a percentage of tax capacity varies from just 5 percent in Atlanta to 77 percent in Minneapolis–St. Paul. However, in most of the metropolitan areas, state aid systems do reduce overall inequality. The Gini coefficient declines in 21 of the 23 metropolitan areas for which aid data are available, and that decline is 17 percent, on average. At the same time, the magnitudes of the changes vary a great deal. The coefficient declines by more than 20 percent in 10 of the 21 areas, by 10 percent to 20 percent in 5 areas, and by less than 10 percent in 6 areas. It increases in 2 areas.

Aid systems have larger effects at the extremes of the tax-capacity distributions. On average, aid reduces the ratios of the ninety-fifth to

The metropolitan areas with the greatest tax base inequality are very likely also to show the greatest segregation by race and income.

16. The correlation is strongest between tax-base inequality and racial segregation. The simple correlation between the 1998 Gini coefficients (second column of table 3-3) and the racial dissimilarity indexes for schools in 1997 (second column, table 3-2) and population in 2000 (fifth column, table 3-2) are .69 and .57 (both statistically significant at the 99 percent confidence level). The correlation between the 1998 Gini coefficients and the 1997 free-lunch-eligibility dissimilarity indexes (second column of table 3-1) is .40 (significant at the 94 percent confidence level).

TABLE 3-4. **Revenue Capacity Equity before and after Aid from State Governments**

Metropolitan area	Gini coefficients: revenue capacity			95th to 5th percentile ratio			Aid as a percent of tax capacity
	Before aid	After aid	Percent change	Before aid	After aid	Percent change	
Atlanta	0.17	0.17	3	5.6	5.9	4	5
Boston	0.25	0.19	−22	4.2	3.2	−25	28
Chicago	0.27	0.17	−36	11.9	5.6	−53	48
Cincinnati	0.36	0.35	−2	31.6	24.7	−22	13
Cleveland	0.24	0.22	−9	16.7	11.5	−31	14
Dallas/Fort Worth	0.19	n.a	n.a	6.7	n.a	n.a.	n.a.
Denver	0.21	0.20	−7	15.7	9.8	−38	14
Detroit	0.21	0.24	11	4.4	5.1	18	41
Houston	0.15	n.a	n.a	17.3	n.a	n.a.	n.a.
Kansas City	0.25	0.22	−11	11.4	7.2	−37	14
Los Angeles	0.22	0.15	−33	8.5	4.7	−44	53
Miami	0.21	0.17	−18	11.1	7.6	−31	30
Milwaukee	0.27	0.10	−63	3.3	2.3	−31	51
Minneapolis–St. Paul	0.17	0.17	−3	3.9	4.4	15	77
New York	0.23	0.18	−22	8.8	6.0	−32	26
Philadelphia	0.33	0.26	−21	9.0	6.7	−26	26
Phoenix	0.15	0.09	−41	13.4	3.0	−77	61
Pittsburgh	0.26	0.25	−4	6.5	4.8	−26	35
Portland	0.15	0.13	−12	3.4	2.9	−14	12
San Diego	0.11	0.08	−20	5.7	3.1	−47	49
San Francisco	0.17	0.13	−27	4.3	3.1	−27	41
Seattle	0.21	0.20	−7	8.3	7.3	−12	16
St. Louis	0.37	0.24	−36	20.0	5.7	−71	39
Tampa	0.13	0.12	−14	31.7	17.7	−44	47
Washington, D.C.	0.22	0.17	−24	6.0	6.1	2	18
25 Metro area average	**0.22**	**0.18**	**−17**	**10.8**	**6.9**	**−36**	**32**

Sources: See table 3-3.

fifth percentile by larger percentages than the corresponding reductions in the Gini coefficients. The ratio declines in 19 of the 23 metropolitan areas and by 35 percent on average. Declines of more than 20 percent are seen in 17 metropolitan areas, and declines of 10 to 20 percent occur in 2 areas.

Table 3-5 shows the extent to which tax-base inequality changed in the 25 metropolitan areas during the middle 1990s. Inequality increased overall: the average Gini coefficient increased by about 8 percent, from 0.20 to 0.22, between 1993 and 1998.[17] The Gini coefficient improved in only 4 of the 25 metropolitan areas: Washington, D.C., Kansas City, Minneapolis–St. Paul, and New York. The most dramatic increases in inequality occurred in places that began the period with relatively equal distributions: Seattle, Phoenix, and Portland. However, several metropolitan areas that began the period with greater-than-average inequality also showed greater-than-average increases: these included Philadelphia, Boston, St. Louis, Cincinnati, and Cleveland.

Several broad observations emerge from the fiscal capacity analysis. First, the metropolitan areas in this study are diverse. Tax systems, the degree of inequality in tax bases within metropolitan areas, geographic patterns of inequality, and the extent to which aid systems ease inequality vary enormously from place to place. However, there are some important commonalities as well. Each metropolitan area shows very significant place-to-place differences in the ability of localities to finance local services from local taxes. Even in the metropolitan areas with the most equitable distributions of tax capacity, there are large differences between the richest and poorest localities.

Second, the degree of inequality in these metropolitan areas also shows very clear correlations with the measures of social separation described in tables 3-1 and 3-2. As one would expect, the degree of fiscal inequality within a metropolitan area is correlated with the degree of income segregation. Less expected, and more disturbing, is the even stronger correlation between fiscal inequality and racial segregation—there is a very strong tendency for more segregated metropolitan areas to show greater-than-average degrees of inequality in tax capacities as well.

Third, aid systems somewhat reduce tax-base inequities, but substantial differences remain between the richest and poorest places in all of the metropolitan areas even after aid is taken into account. Clearly,

17. Inequality also increased after accounting for state aid systems. The average Gini coefficient increased by 6 percent, from .17 to .18.

TABLE 3-5. Tax Capacity:
1993 and 1998 Gini Coefficients

Metropolitan area	Gini coefficient		
	1993 coefficient	1998 coefficient	Percent change
Atlanta	0.16	0.17	2
Boston	0.21	0.25	16
Chicago	0.26	0.27	2
Cincinnati	0.31	0.36	15
Cleveland	0.21	0.24	14
Dallas/Fort Worth	0.17	0.19	10
Denver	0.20	0.21	8
Detroit	0.23	0.21	−5
Houston	0.13	0.15	15
Kansas City	0.32	0.25	−22
Los Angeles	0.20	0.22	9
Miami	0.19	0.21	10
Milwaukee	0.25	0.27	6
Minneapolis–St. Paul	0.18	0.17	−1
New York	0.24	0.23	−5
Philadelphia	0.28	0.33	20
Phoenix	0.11	0.15	38
Pittsburgh	0.26	0.26	2
Portland	0.11	0.15	30
San Diego	0.10	0.11	1
San Francisco	0.15	0.17	15
Seattle	0.11	0.21	99
St. Louis	0.32	0.37	15
Tampa	0.13	0.13	2
Washington, D.C.	0.25	0.22	−12
25 metro area average	**0.20**	**0.22**	**8**

Sources: See table 3-3.

aid systems could do more to equalize the capacity of local governments to provide average service levels at reasonable tax rates.

Fourth, the wide intrametropolitan variations in tax capacity evident in tables 3-3 and 3-4 also indicate that fiscal difficulties do not end at the city's boundary—suburban areas are not immune to the forces that hurt central cities. The large cities in this sample actually fare reasonably well in city-suburb comparisons of tax capacity and aid. However, the large cities fare poorly in comparisons involving factors likely to add to the cost of providing local public goods. That is why factors besides tax capacity must be considered when evaluating overall local fiscal conditions.

SPRAWL

Although this book is primarily about the social and fiscal characteristics of U.S. regions, it is important to at least mention the relationship of these two factors to land use and urban sprawl. Table 3-6 shows 1970 and 1990 U.S. Census Bureau estimates of the urbanized land area and population in the urbanized area in each of the 25 metropolitan areas.[18] Comparing the change in population within urbanized areas with the change in the amount of urbanized land gives an indication of whether the area as a whole is becoming more compact or more sprawling as it develops. Overall, the rate of urbanization of land in the nation's largest regions was more than 2.5 times the rate of increase in population in the urbanized areas. The net result was an 18 percent overall decrease in population density in the urbanized areas, with densities declining by roughly one-third in some regions (St. Louis, Philadelphia, Pittsburgh, and Atlanta). Population densities in the urbanized areas decreased in 19 of the 25 metro areas.

Changes in population density also varied across the metropolitan areas. The slow-growth, highly fragmented Northeast is using land 5 times faster than the population is growing, with the highly fragmented, slow-growth Midwest close behind at 4.5 times. Land use in the new, high-growth South is increasing 2.6 times faster, and in the water-delimited West 1.5 times faster, than the population growth.[19] All six of the regions with increased population density in urbanized areas (Dallas, Los Angeles, Miami, Phoenix, San Diego, and Seattle) are places where terrain (seacoasts, hills, or wetlands) or lack of resources (water) limits the region's physical expansion.

Clear correlations are evident in a comparison of the sprawl indicators in table 3-6 and the measures of segregation and inequality in tables 3-1 through 3-5. Regions where population density in the ur-

In the nation's largest regions, the rate of urbanization of land was more than 2.5 times the rate of population increase in urbanized areas.

18. The Census Bureau defines *urbanized area* as the central city and its adjacent urban fringe, including all contiguous territory settled at a density of at least 1,000 persons per square mile. Also included are large concentrations of nonresidential urban areas, such as industrial parks, office parks, and airports.

19. Fulton and others (2000).

61

TABLE 3-6. Urbanized Area and Population in the 25 Largest Metropolitan Areas, 1970 and 1990

Metropolitan area	Urbanized land area (square miles)			Population in urbanized area			Percent change in urbanized area population density
	1970	1990	Percent change	1970	1990	Percent change	
Atlanta	435	1,137	161	1,172,778	2,157,806	84	–30
Boston	664	891	34	2,652,575	2,775,370	5	–22
Chicago	1,277	1,585	24	6,714,578	6,792,946	1	–18
Cincinnati	335	512	53	1,110,514	1,212,675	9	–28
Cleveland	646	636	–2	1,959,880	1,677,492	–14	–13
Dallas	1,071	1,443	35	2,015,628	3,198,259	59	18
Denver	293	459	57	1,047,311	1,517,977	45	–8
Detroit	872	1,119	28	3,970,584	3,697,529	–7	–27
Houston	539	1,177	119	1,677,863	2,901,851	73	–21
Kansas City	493	762	54	1,101,949	1,275,317	16	–25
Los Angeles	1,572	1,966	25	8,351,266	11,402,946	37	9
Miami	259	353	36	1,219,661	1,914,660	57	15
Milwaukee	457	512	12	1,252,457	1,226,293	–2	–13
Minneapolis– St. Paul	721	1,063	47	1,700,725	2,079,676	22	–17
New York	2,425	2,966	22	16,206,841	16,044,012	–1	–19
Philadelphia	752	1,164	55	4,021,042	4,222,211	5	–32
Phoenix	388	741	91	863,357	2,006,239	132	22
Pittsburgh	596	778	30	1,846,042	1,678,745	–9	–30
Portland	267	388	45	876,526	1,172,158	34	–8
San Diego	381	690	81	1,198,323	2,348,417	96	8
San Francisco	681	874	28	2,987,850	3,629,516	21	–5
Seattle	413	588	42	1,238,107	1,774,086	43	1
St. Louis	461	728	58	1,882,944	1,946,526	3	–35
Tampa	131	650	398	368,742	1,708,710	363	–7
Washington, D.C.	804	1,537	91	4,061,041	5,252,904	29	–32
	16,931	**24,719**	**46**	**71,498,584**	**85,614,321**	**20**	**–18**

Source: Census of Population, 1970 and 1990.

banized areas declined the most tend to show the greatest degrees of racial segregation and tax-base inequality. Six of the 10 metropolitan areas with the most tax-base inequality and 5 of the 10 with the greatest degree of racial segregation are also in the group of 10 metropolitan areas with the greatest decreases in population density in the urbanized area.[20]

Comparing the sprawl data with fiscal capacity data for different types of communities also shows that sprawl affects the fiscal health of sprawling communities. The fiscal capacities of at-risk, low-density suburbs and bedroom-developing suburbs are greater in relation to other municipalities in the same region in metropolitan areas that are controlling sprawl more effectively. The average fiscal capacity of at-risk, low-density suburbs in the 12 metropolitan areas with the greatest degrees of sprawl (measured by the change in population density in the urbanized area) is 60 percent of the regional average. In the 13 metropolitan areas with the least sprawl, the average capacity is 78 percent of the regional average. The equivalent capacities for bedroom-developing suburbs are 82 percent of the regional average (in sprawling metropolitan areas) and 101 percent of the average (in more contained areas).[21] Clearly, the suburban areas most directly affected by sprawl are fiscally stronger relative to the rest of their metropolitan areas in regions where growth is managed more effectively.

In the future, better data are likely to be available to compare regional urban development trends to factors such as social separation and fiscal inequality. This section hints that regions using land far in excess of population growth increase the level of stress not only on the communities left behind, but also on the communities developing at the edge. The future may show that unduly sprawling regions are "growing against themselves" and in the process are hurting all types of regional communities and all citizens.

20. The simple correlation between change in density in the urbanized area between 1970 and 1990 and the tax capacity Gini coefficient is –.55 while the correlation between density change and the 1990 dissimilarity index is –.52 (both significant at the 99 percent confidence level).

21. The correlation between change in population density in urbanized areas between 1970 and 1990 and 1998 tax capacity (as a percentage of the regional average) is .44 for at-risk low-density suburbs and .40 for bedroom-developing suburbs. Both coefficients are significant at the 95 percent confidence level.

CONCLUSIONS

U.S. suburbs are not a monolith with one set of common interests. Suburban areas are diverse, both in the overall pattern in the 25 metropolitan areas in the study sample and within individual metropolitan areas. Many of the problems so long confined to central cities are present in today's suburbs. Some rural areas are growing into suburbs with a resource base too weak to finance the infrastructure investments implicit in the transition. Still other communities must cope with growth rates that far outstrip their modest resources. Only a small minority of localities have accumulated a critical mass of commercial, office, or industrial development in combination with a strong residential tax base.

The implied distribution of fiscal stress is highly skewed, and flows of state resources reduce inequality only modestly. Can metropolitan areas ease suburban stresses by guiding development in ways that reduce the costs of growth without stunting growth altogether? Can they redistribute resources to the areas most in need without seriously damaging regional economies? These are the policy issues examined in part 2, "Metropolicy."

PART

2

METRO POLICY

METRO
POLICY

The many challenges facing America's metropolitan areas can be attacked effectively only through a coordinated, regional approach. Concentrated poverty and community disinvestments, among the most important of the countless factors feeding metropolitan sprawl, are related to incentives built into public policies for metropolitan development. These incentives include tax policies that promote wasteful competition among local governments, transportation and infrastructure investment patterns that subsidize sprawling development, and fragmented governance that makes thoughtful, efficient local land-use planning more difficult.

This section begins with a history of efforts to address America's persistent problems of concentrated poverty, racial segregation, and community disinvestments—strategies that need to be examined as a growing part of suburbia is affected by these trends. States, in many ways the most necessary and proper actors to address these regional problems, have abdicated their role to the local and federal governments. Although well-intentioned federal policies and programs have had some measure of success, they cannot succeed without acknowledging the regional nature of the issues they are trying to address. The rest of this section focuses on building a comprehensive, regional agenda for reform to confront metropolitan America's true challenges. These reforms focus on tax policy, land-use policy, and governance. The roots of regional tax reform, which involves some form of a more equitable fiscal relationship between the cities in our metropolitan areas, have close cousins in the state school aid systems that exist in virtually every state in the country. Land-use reform to combat sprawl is a growing issue in the nation, and 16 states have adopted comprehensive growth-management acts. Their number is growing. Federal law has required that regional governments coordinate hundreds of millions of transportation dollars in every region in the country. The challenge now is to make these existing regional governments more effective and more accountable to the people they serve.

CHAPTER 4

FEDERAL URBAN POLICY

Over time, the tenuous nature of the war on poverty faded from memory; it began to seem that the government had tried everything to help the ghettos, spending untold billions in the process, and that nothing had worked.[1]

As the problems common to central cities become deeply rooted in at-risk suburbs, it is more important to evaluate our national urban policy to see whether it can serve as the potential basis for a new national inner suburban policy. Evidence suggests that our urban policy, which does not respond to the regional nature of problems caused by social separation and sprawl, has not worked in cities, nor is it likely to work in the suburbs.

THE POLITICAL NATURE OF URBAN POLICY

The types of policies that win strong support among lawmakers are usually those backed by a broad segment of U.S. society, generally the middle class. During the tumultuous period of the late 1960s and early 1970s, many Americans wanted lawmakers to address crime, concentrated poverty, and racial segregation. As a result, urban policies received more federal funding than they had before—or have since. Beginning in the 1980s, however, federal financial support declined sharply, in response to growing middle- and working-class resentment toward high spending on urban programs.

1. Lemann (1991, p. 219).

69

FIGURE 4-1. Growth in Federal Spending for Selected Agencies and Total Federal Budget, 1980–99

1999 dollars

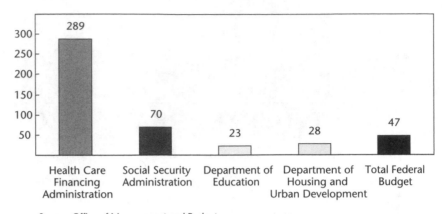

Source: Office of Management and Budget.

At the same time, programs that affect the broad U.S. middle class—Social Security and health care in particular—gradually widened their share of the federal budget, and they have seen large increases over the past 30 years (figure 4-1). What do these trends imply? The budgets of programs and policies with a broad base of support will increase; the budgets of those perceived to affect a small minority—no matter how severe their problems—will likely be cut. As long as urban problems are perceived to affect a small constituency outside the middle class, they are unlikely to receive much new funding or other support from any level of government—state, federal, or local. Perhaps as it becomes clear that these same problems are being felt in older suburban communities, support will grow. If this occurs, the next question becomes what to do.

LIMITATIONS OF FEDERAL URBAN PROGRAMS

The problems most often associated with large cities and increasingly with at-risk suburbs—concentrated poverty, racial segregation, crime, and community disinvestment—have become accepted as a natural feature of the metropolitan landscape. Government, philanthropic, and community-based programs to assist the poor and revitalize inner-city areas, though well intentioned and often attracting some of the nation's brightest and most dedicated people, have had limited success at best. Often, such programs unintentionally maintain the status quo, a politically comfortable arrangement that leaves the neediest people confined to the inner city.

Many U.S. urban efforts to address the decline of the metropolitan core have failed for four main reasons. First, antipoverty and urban revitalization initiatives have been largely symbolic and reactive. Second, those initiatives have been targeted at the localized symptoms of the problems, not the root causes—the structural systems operating at the metropolitan level. Third, policies that do address the metropolitan nature of the problems have lacked the political backing to move through the political process. Fourth, the effectiveness of antipoverty and urban revitalization programs is hard to judge because many lack explicit goals. As a result, no one has ever really argued that such strategies will turn the tide and restore the city or the urban poor to robust health.

Since the 1930s, U.S. policy on urban revitalization has followed a recurring pattern of sporadic government intervention and assistance that can be characterized only as a symbolic reaction to a national crisis. That pattern began as early as the 1930s, when the federally insured Federal Housing Administration (FHA) loan and public housing programs were created in reaction to the economic and social crisis of the Great Depression. Some people claim that the public housing program was enacted to jump-start the economy with new construction jobs more than to assist poor people.[2] Similarly, billions of dollars were poured into central cities during the 1960s, but only after racially charged riots in Los Angeles, Detroit, and many other U.S. cities forced Congress to take some sort of action. Proactive legislation that might prevent crises often sits for years until a new crisis forces Congress's hand. Then, under strong public pressure for action, legislation is rushed through before it can be properly formulated.[3]

Because urban policy has been reactionary instead of proactive in nature, its programs almost universally target the symptoms, not the root causes, of the poor people's segregation in blighted neighborhoods.

U.S. policy on urban revitalization since the 1930s can be characterized only as a symbolic reaction to a national crisis.

2. Marcuse (1998).

3. For instance, the nation's first Fair Housing Act was not passed until after the assassination of Martin Luther King Jr., in 1968, although it had been drafted for years. While symbolically significant, the final draft was a watered-down version of the original that lacked the enforcement powers necessary to make it a meaningful piece of racial discrimination legislation. A more recent example of the reactive nature of federal urban policy is the passage of empowerment zone legislation in 1993. This legislation had been around since the early 1980s, but only after the riots in Los Angeles following the Rodney King trial was the legislation dusted off and finally passed in 1993. See Davis (1993); Lemann (1994); Riposa (1996); and Zuckman (1992).

Thus, despite the billions of dollars spent and time and effort expended, the United States has failed to make meaningful progress in more than a half century. Today, with persistent concentrations of poverty in the inner cities and many older suburbs and widening disparity between rich and poor, there is little evidence of change in the lives of the urban poor or in the ongoing process of decline in the core of the nation's largest metropolitan areas.

The problem is that the nation's primary policies and programs for addressing urban problems are stuck in the same basic model. Empowerment zones are the beginning and end of federal urban revitalization policy, while philanthropic organizations and local activists are busy with community-development activities. Both kinds of initiatives have been referred to as "gilding-the-ghetto" strategies—in-place revitalization strategies that attempt to bring jobs, money, and human capital into the ghetto through tax breaks, physical rehabilitation of neighborhoods, and other economic incentives.

Yet there is little evidence such strategies work to revitalize communities. They may have lifted some individuals out of poverty, but those people usually move out of the ghetto, leaving a space quickly filled by another impoverished individual. As one political journalist and urban historian put it, "The standard model of progress for poor people living in urban slums . . . is to get a good job outside the neighborhood and then decamp for a nicer part of town."[4] In-place economic revitalization strategies run against the natural and powerful tide of upward mobility—something like running up a down escalator.[5]

In-place strategies are our only revitalization effort, when they should be part of a comprehensive national strategy to strike at the roots of urban decay. Central cities function within structural systems that operate across entire metropolitan areas, their housing and job markets, their transportation networks. Those structural systems must be altered before the spatial distribution of jobs, housing, and residents will shift. Until the problems of the cities are placed in their true, metropolitan geographical context, in-place initiatives will remain palliatives—a series of small, broken arrows in an increasingly empty quiver.

The intergenerational phenomena of poverty, the continuing and systematic exclusion of blacks and Latinos from opportunities to accumulate wealth, racial discrimination in housing and employment, and the growing concentration of poverty in the inner city are testament to

4. Lemann (1994).
5. Rusk (1999).

the failure of antipoverty and urban revitalization initiatives to make a real difference.[6] They have not succeeded in turning around urban neighborhoods, much less in restructuring the network of educational, employment, and other opportunities available to the urban poor.[7]

HISTORY OF MAJOR FEDERAL URBAN POLICIES

The urban renewal movement grew out of the "crisis of metropolitanization."[8] This crisis was brought on by several systematic trends throughout the prosperous post–World War II period: the out-migration of the middle class from the city; the massive in-migration of minorities; and industrial decentralization. These patterns had begun to exact their toll on the physical fabric of large cities' core areas. In most downtown areas, pockets of residential slums were pushing existing businesses out and deflecting new businesses. The developing suburbs were reaping the benefits of regional growth while avoiding growth-associated problems and the full costs of that growth. Unfavorable annexation laws prohibited most central cities from taxing outside their borders. Many people recognized this inequality at the time. Reorganizing governments along metropolitan lines was one answer briefly in vogue.[9]

Urban Renewal

The federal government, however, intervened with a more politically palatable alternative. In an effort to revitalize the declining inner cities, it took the path of urban renewal, as established in the Housing Act of 1949. Subsidies would be transferred to local agencies for slum clearance, housing construction, and economic development.

Urban renewal was touted as a vehicle for improving the lives of the urban poor and revitalizing the country's dying urban centers, but the

6. On opportunities to accumulate wealth, see Conley (1999); on poverty, Jargowsky (1997); and Massey and Denton (1993).

7. In a 1989 interview in the *Journal of Housing*, Charles L. Farris, a leading urban renewal administrator and community-development specialist, agreed that the limited set of economic and physical policy tools characteristic of revitalization initiatives are inadequate for combating widespread and powerful forces in a metropolitan area—such as racial discrimination and segregation in the housing and job markets, high inner-city crime rates, fragmented governance structure, and exclusionary zoning laws. To succeed at inner city revitalization, Farris believes it is crucial to design a sustained and comprehensive approach that addresses the metropolitan region as a whole.

8. O'Connor (1999).

9. O'Connor (1999).

projects undertaken during its first and most active phase, 1949 to 1967, were largely directed at physical and economic revitalization in the hope of regenerating a shrinking central city tax base. In some ways, that strategy pitted the economic needs of the city against the economic needs of its poorest citizens. It also foreshadowed the strategy—recognized or not—of "successful" cities such as San Francisco and Seattle that have maintained a comparatively strong tax base through the gentrification process. To regenerate the local tax base and better compete with surrounding suburbs, those cities have pushed out the poor and replaced them with middle- and upper-class residents.[10]

After federal program changes in 1967 redirected urban renewal efforts to the social goals originally intended, the character of urban renewal projects did change. The indiscriminate razing of blighted areas that characterized urban renewal programs was no longer pursued. There was a shift toward the preservation and rehabilitation of housing and historic structures, and local authorities became more responsive to the needs of residents in urban renewal areas. Those program changes, though significant, were short lived, lasting only until the program's demise in 1974 as political support evaporated. In terms of length of time and scope of activities, urban renewal's most enduring legacy dates from the first era, which lasted 18 years.

Urban renewal projects were individually approved and funded by the federal government to improve the physical environment. Through aggressive redevelopment of large tracts of razed slums, the projects were supposed to increase the tax base of dying central business districts and to improve the quality of housing for the poor families and individuals that were displaced. Those are tall orders for any geographically targeted program, especially one that was attempting to stem such sweeping forces as mass suburbanization and the transfer of social and economic resources out of the central city. In addition, federal guidelines for local urban renewal projects were inadequate, redevelopment experience at the local level was lacking, and there was an unswerving concentration on increasing the tax base—whatever the cost. As a result, most urban renewal projects had significant shortcomings and were ineffective in achieving the goals in the original legislation.[11]

Public Housing

The U.S. public housing program began in 1937 with the passage of the Wagner-Steagall Housing Act. Though seen today as housing of last re-

10. See powell (forthcoming); and Kennedy and Leonard (2001).
11. Anderson (1964); Kain (1969); and Sanders (1980).

sort, the program, as originally conceived, was to serve two goals. First, the construction of public housing throughout the nation was to assist in relieving unemployment and in reviving the economy. Second, public housing was to serve as temporary housing for the working and "deserving" poor. Under the original legislation, because rents were set in relation to the cost of other housing and not by household income, the very poor could not afford to live there.[12] By the end of 1962, the public housing program had put more than 2 million people in homes that were arguably much better than they would have had in the private market.[13] Only after structural changes in the program during the 1960s did public housing developments become synonymous with dilapidated inner-city environments, concentrated poverty, and high crime.

While the failure of the inner-city public housing program was not visible until almost 30 years after its inception, the terms of the original legislation guaranteed that public housing would be heavily concentrated in already very poor neighborhoods of the inner city. This only served to accelerate and institutionalize the ongoing process of poverty concentration, and thus, when the central city began to fall apart, inner-city neighborhoods and residents themselves would carry the responsibility for picking up the pieces.[14]

In the eyes of the middle and upper classes, such projects as Chicago's Cabrini-Green or St. Louis's Pruitt-Igoe became symbols of the way the urban poor lived.[15] Those monotonous, sterile, and often inhumane environments "became associated with the inner city, impoverished dependency, African Americans, and crime."[16] Instead of

By the end of 1962, the public housing program had put more than 2 million people into much better homes than they would have had in the private market.

12. Varady, Prieser, and Russel (1998).

13. Jackson (1985).

14. This occurred for several reasons. First, the program was voluntary and transferred federal funding for the capital costs of construction to municipalities that decided to provide such housing. Predictably, many suburban locations opted out of the program. Or if they did participate, they built public housing for the elderly. The second provision that further ensured concentration in central cities was the "one-for-one" rule. To construct one unit of public housing, one unit of substandard housing had to be demolished. Since the central cities had the bulk of "substandard" housing, they were active participants in the public housing program. In addition, the public housing that was built was confined to the slums where the substandard units were located. The argument that the replacement housing was of a higher quality than the housing it replaced is defensible. However, it is also true that, given the program's policy structure, public housing ultimately perpetuated the slum environment that was replaced.

15. These high-rise developments of concentrated poverty were the exception, rather than the norm. However, because of the media attention drawn by the illicit activities in these developments, they became the "poster child" of public housing.

16. Varady and others (1998); von Hoffman (1998).

attributing the failure of public housing to structural problems in policy design, the larger society came to view the failures of public housing as "due to cultural characteristics of the poor themselves, who were seen to be resisting improvement."[17] In reality, public housing failed because "the program by itself could not solve social problems, integrate society, or usher in a new high-rise urbanism."[18]

In 1992 Congress passed the Urban Revitalization Demonstration Program (HOPE VI) in an attempt to improve the poor condition of public housing. Local housing authorities were given funds to demolish high-rise structures in severe distress and replace them with low-rise, mixed-income developments on sites throughout a metropolitan area linking residents to a broad array of services. HOPE VI is an improvement over the public housing policy of the 1960s and 1970s because it recognizes the deleterious effects of confining large numbers of poor families within deteriorating central city neighborhoods.

Still, attempts to deconcentrate poverty by demolishing high-rise public housing projects are destined to fail unless affordable housing is made available throughout a metropolitan region.[19] Further, affordable housing must be a practical option: it must provide access to jobs, public transit, and the social services needed by families moving into the community. In most regions, practical, affordable housing can be found in only a few places, generally the central city and a few inner suburbs. As a result, an attempt to deconcentrate poverty in one area simply pushes low-income families into the already fragile communities surrounding them, creating further destabilization. HOPE VI highlights the need for comprehensive fair housing plans across metropolitan areas to avoid the further concentration of poverty.

Empowerment Zones

Federal empowerment zone/enterprise community legislation of 1993 was the first resuscitation of any semblance of a national urban policy

17. Jackson (1985).

18. Varady and others (1998).

19. For instance, under the HOPE VI program, for every 100 families displaced as a result of demolition, 30 families are offered housing in the rebuilt low rises, while the other 70 families are given Section 8 housing vouchers for use in the private rental market. This program has resulted in an absolute decline in public housing units available for the poorest families. While the deconcentration of poverty in public housing is a positive goal, many housing advocates worry that the increased reliance on Section 8 housing vouchers will perpetuate the concentration of poverty in areas that have lower-cost housing, namely the central cities.

in almost 20 years.[20] Many members of the Congress touted it as the "new urban policy," but it was not much different from the "gilding-the-ghetto" initiatives launched since the 1960s and President Lyndon B. Johnson's Model Cities program.[21] Though first introduced in Congress in 1980, the empowerment zone concept was not given a chance until the Los Angeles riots of 1992, which left the federal government scrambling to find a solution to the new urban crisis.[22] According to one government expert, it was "the only thing left on the shelf."[23] Initially vetoed by President George H. Bush in 1992, the legislation was reintroduced in 1993, with administration-supported additions, and signed by the newly elected President William Jefferson Clinton.

Offering tax breaks to businesses as a means of revitalizing depressed, low-income areas, the enterprise zone idea had been tried in England since 1978.[24] In the United States, it had been experimented

20. 26 USC 1391 *Omnibus Reconciliation Budget Act of 1993*. The empowerment zone legislation also included limited funding for enterprise communities, which have smaller populations, less social need, and are predominantly rural. In addition, both *urban* and *rural* empowerment zones are designated throughout the country. However, most of the resources flow into the urban empowerment zones. For the purpose of this discussion in the context of the problem of the cities, I discuss only the *urban empowerment zones*. See Gittell and others (1998); and Riposa (1996).

21. Zuckman (1992); and Rubin (1994).

22. The prior Republican iterations of the federal empowerment-zone legislation relied solely on the economic development component: offer tax incentives and reduce regulatory barriers to spur new business activity and private investment in depressed neighborhoods, which will then create new jobs and benefit the local residents. The idea was to let benefits trickle down to the poor residents of these areas; in other words, to stimulate the local economy of these depressed neighborhoods by offering tax breaks to private businesses, which would indirectly benefit the community's poor residents through the creation of new local jobs. In the mind of the Republicans, it was a win-win situation. The problem was (and still is) that there is scant evidence that these supply-side incentives actually generate *new* jobs. At best, jobs are simply redistributed throughout a region as a company that was already planning to locate in the region decides to locate in the empowerment zone to take advantage of the tax breaks. If new jobs are generated, the public expenditures per job created are high, and the benefits flow mainly to the private business owners, rather than to the employees.

23. Lemann (1994).

24. Zuckman (1992). The primary goal of the British zones was to revitalize abandoned industrial sites through the creation of new businesses and new jobs. Unlike the United States, Britain was dealing with much smaller areas, many of which had few or no residents, so there was little emphasis on improving the quality of life for the zone residents. Like the U.S. program, the British offered tax incentives to companies willing to locate in these depressed areas. A 1984 government-funded study, the Tym Report, came to three discouraging conclusions regarding British empowerment zones. First, the rate of employment growth (13 percent within the zones) was significantly slower than the 24 percent growth for comparable companies

with at the state level since the early 1980s.[25] But there was scant evidence that it worked. Assessments of its efficacy did not support the $3.5 billion that Congress approved over the 10-year life of the program.[26] Even with the inclusion of a social service component representing $1 billion of the total cost and strong community empowerment requirements, the initiative seems inadequate to reverse the myriad of problems in declining urban areas. Many scholars and even many members of Congress who voted for the initiative believed that the incentives for improving social services were insufficient to offset the costs associated with doing business in impoverished and physically distressed areas with high crime rates, high school dropout rates, a declining population, and inadequate infrastructure.[27]

Nonetheless, by the end of 1994, six urban empowerment zones had been designated throughout the country, each eligible for up to $100 million in social service block grants (SSBGs) over 10 years.[28] They were also eligible for a tax-incentive package, the main component of which was a $3,000 wage credit per employee. Designation of empowerment zones was based on specific criteria such as geographic size and poverty rate. Little program evaluation has been done to date to measure the "success" of those zones, although similar government initiatives in England suggest that the current wave of empowerment-zone activity is unlikely to turn around the most economically, physically, and socially deteriorated neighborhoods. As one observer put it, the "network of zones across the thirty-seven states has not resulted in a serious reduction in urban poverty or created enough quality jobs to alle-

---

outside the zones. The fact that some employment growth occurred within these zones could be perceived as positive, except for the subsequent salient findings. Second, only 25 percent of the jobs created within the zones since their inception could be attributed to zone designation. And third, most new economic activity—an overwhelming 86 percent—simply relocated from other areas around the zone. This is particularly troubling, since the British plan's goal was to stimulate new economic activity. On the British program, see Ladd (1994).

25. In England, the terminology was *enterprise zone*. In the 1980s, when the program was adopted at the state level, the name remained the same. *Empowerment zone* was adopted in the 1993 federal legislation.

26. This $3.5 billion includes $2.5 billion in tax incentives plus an additional $1.0 billion in Social Service Block Grant funds to be distributed over 10 years. See Lemann (1994); Riposa (1996); and Rich (1995).

27. Ladd (1994); Lemann (1994).

28. In 1997 Congress authorized the designation of an additional 20 urban and rural enterprise zones. Cities that have urban enterprise zones include Atlanta, Baltimore, Chicago, Detroit, Los Angeles, Minneapolis, New York City, and Philadelphia.

viate employment pressures on distressed communities."[29] It will take more time, program evaluation, and cost-benefit analysis to determine whether empowerment zone initiatives have been successful.

Some may argue that the federal initiative has more chance of success because the amount of money committed by the federal government is substantially larger than that committed by the states, but the federal zones are considerably larger and the needs they address therefore are greater too. Representative Charles B. Rangel (D.-New York) from Harlem, who lukewarmly supported Clinton's empowerment-zone bill, said, "I rejected the whole concept under Reagan. But people came to me and said, 'How can it hurt?' so I just said, 'What the hell.' But when it started looking like the urban policy for the nation, it was obviously inadequate."[30] Many scholars and urban historians agree: empowerment zones alone are inadequate to reverse urban decline.[31] The centrifugal forces pushing investment out of declining urban areas offset the centripetal forces represented by tax breaks to attract industry to those areas. Before empowerment-zone legislation was passed, Representative Thomas J. Downey (D.-New York) expressed the fear that "zones will masquerade as the answer."[32] And for seven years they have.

Empowerment zones alone are inadequate to reverse urban decline.

Community Development Corporations

"In the wake of ghetto uprisings since the 1960s, federal aid for community development has also become a political quick fix, a palliative for communities on the verge of revolt," opined one commentator.[33] Though only a small force on the urban scene, community develop-

29. Riposa (1996). For instance, a program evaluation by the state of Indiana in 1992 found that $20.6 million had been spent over seven years to create 2,024 new jobs: an average of $10,178 per new job. However, only 19 percent of these new jobs were held by zone residents. If the purpose of these zones is to improve the quality of life for residents of depressed areas, the cost per job given to a zone resident becomes $53,506 over seven years (Ladd 1994). According to Papke (1993). zone unemployment in Indiana had dropped 25 percent—a seemingly positive sign. But unemployment also fell by a comparable amount in nonzone areas, which suggests that something other than zone designation was responsible for the drop. Upon further inspection, she also found that the population loss was greater for the zones, and per capita income fell. According to Ladd (1994, p. 206), "On balance, the zones seem to have had little positive impact on the economic well-being of their residents." Even more discouraging, a 1987 General Accounting Office study of the zones in Maryland found absolutely no employment effect as a result of zone designation; Ladd called this study "one of the most pessimistic evaluations" to date.

30. Lemann (1994).

31. See Zuckman (1992); Ladd (1994); Lemann (1994); and Riposa (1996).

32. Zuckman (1992).

33. O'Connor (1999, p. 78).

ment is the dominant revitalization strategy for declining, low-income inner-city neighborhoods in the United States. As of 1998, after a period of rapid growth in which many new community development corporations (CDCs) appeared, an estimated 1,800 were operating in urban areas, with combined budgets of hundreds of millions of dollars.

The production and management of housing in declining inner-city neighborhoods has come to be recognized as the major success of these organizations, originally conceived as grass-roots organizations to foster community empowerment.[34] But even one community development activist has had to recognize that CDCs "fill one very important but narrow gap in the range of capacity needed to counter the economic currents undermining a community's viability."[35] That "narrow gap" is providing affordable, quality housing in areas abandoned by private builders.[36] It is widely recognized, however, that despite the billions of dollars spent on community development, the budget of the average CDC is inadequate to launch the type of sustained and comprehensive neighborhood redevelopment effort needed to resuscitate declining inner-city neighborhoods.[37] Furthermore, many argue that the focus on

34. Vidal (1992). CDCs are often involved in other activities such as commercial development, job training programs, business enterprise development, and housing advocacy, but their main focus, and what they are "best" at, is the production and management of affordable housing. See Vidal (1992); Lemann (1994); and Stoutland (1999).

35. Traynor (1992).

36. The widening gap between building costs and low-income wages, combined with the reduction in subsidies for new housing construction since the 1980s, keeps nudging affordable housing higher up on the income spectrum. It is becoming increasingly rare for the CDCs' housing activities to reach the very poorest people. This group outside the reach of local CDCs is still served by the unofficial national policy of providing low-income housing through the devitalization of our oldest housing stock. The oldest, most devalued housing in our cities is left for these people, who at times must pay upward of 50 percent of their income on rent for substandard housing. See National Low Income Housing Coalition (1998); also Stoutland (1998). In its 1998 annual report to Congress, HUD reported that 5.3 million households (1 out of every 7 renters) were in need of quality, *affordable* (30 percent of a household's monthly income) housing. Of these, 2.65 million lived in urban areas (National Low Income Housing Coalition 1998). As of 1996, CDCs were responsible for producing 30,000 to 40,000 units of affordable housing a year. This output, though impressive, does not begin to address the need (Dreier 1999). Further, because CDC activities are mainly in the inner city, they only add to the concentration of affordable housing at the center, while more affluent suburbs avoid building such housing within their boundaries.

37. See Meehan (1980); Farris (1989); Traynor (1992); Lemann (1994); Dreier (1999); and Stoutland (1999). As for CDCs' successes, "little research has attempted to systematically apply performance measures to assess their accomplishments" (Stoutland 1999). Aside from assessing the number of houses built in a year, the other activities—such as job training and housing advocacy—are much more difficult to

individual neighborhoods is much too limited and must be expanded to include the entire social and economic playing field in which metropolitan areas operate. The entire region must be the focus of a revitalization strategy.[38]

Still, community development has been both theoretically and politically attractive as a means of improving the lives of the urban poor.[39] First, it provides an opportunity for federal government and private philanthropic support for people who are trying to revitalize their neighborhoods. Second, it seems to make sense that people who live or work in a depressed neighborhood would have the best understanding of where and how money should be spent to make improvements.

Whether intentionally or not, leaving the comfortable status quo of residential segregation intact is a hallmark of in-place strategies.[40] Often, it is quietly rationalized by those outside the distressed neighborhoods with statements like "They [poor blacks] want to live near their own" or "Even when they have the opportunity to move out, they choose to stay." That convenient sentiment was expressed by a Housing and Urban Development administrator during the Johnson administration: "Many middle-class Negroes, who could move to the suburbs if they wanted to . . . decide to stay on in the central city."[41] The evidence, if not basic logic, suggests otherwise.[42]

---

assess and measure. The secondary effect of revitalizing an area in the hope of attracting private investment is even more difficult to assess.

38. Rusk (1993, 1999); Downs (1994, 1999); Jargowsky (1997); and Weir (1999).

39. Originating out of the activist spirit of the 1960s and the backlash against top-down urban renewal projects, the initial community-based development organizations were formed by community activists, seeking to take back control over their physical environment through community empowerment. The idea was that *true* urban revitalization could take place only through the involvement of the residents—the low-income and disproportionately black residents who were typically left out of the political process and denied the opportunity to shape their own future. However, "in many cities the neighborhood-based challenges to power were deflected or rewarded with symbolic recognition that left little imprint on the structure of urban power" (Weir 1999). Still, the idea took hold in Washington, as the Johnson administration began to see community development as a win-win, politically unchallenged solution to the problem of the cities.

40. Kain (1969); Downs (1994); Lemann (1994, 1991); de Oliver and Dawson-Munoz (1996); O'Connor (1999).

41. Lemann (1991).

42. For instance, David Rusk (1999) recently studied the effects of 34 of the largest and most successful CDC initiatives. In virtually all of these areas of massive CDC investment, family and individual poverty rates substantially increased and moved farther from metropolitan norms, the median household income declined and moved farther away from the metro average, and the communities grew more segregated.

Community development cannot address the regional forces that created the urban poverty and neighborhood decline in the first place.

Community development, as a primary strategy for addressing urban poverty and neighborhood decline, cannot address the regional forces that created the decline in the first place. Even when a few families and individuals manage to find good jobs and improve their standard of living, they often move to more prosperous and stable neighborhoods. In a recent study of the effects of several of the country's largest and most successful inner-city focused, antipoverty initiatives, family and individual poverty rates substantially increased and moved farther from metropolitan norms.[43] In addition, the median household income declined and moved farther away from the metro average, and the communities grew more segregated.

Although it is possible that efforts targeting poor inner-city neighborhoods have made these communities better than they might otherwise have been, it is impossible to know how they would have fared without such intense investment. Moreover, these figures do not reflect individuals who have been empowered by such programs and have left poor neighborhoods. It is also true that these programs have often represented the only available response to concentrated poverty. So far, however, it appears that central-city, antipoverty efforts alone are woefully inadequate in the face of the enormous force of metropolitan polarization.

In the end, despite the best and most admirable efforts of CDCs, poor neighborhoods typically are transitional and chronically poor.[44] No matter how well organized a poor community is, it cannot become stable and not poor as long as the people with good jobs keep moving out and the people left behind have very little income.[45]

The many who remain mired in poverty and despair can do little but ask for more money to pay for low-income housing or a few more jobs, deepening their dependence on public money to support their neighborhoods. The problem is that the neighborhoods where community development organizations work are not islands within the metropolitan political and economic landscape—they are an integral part of it. The solution? "We should be trying to bring the poor closer to the social and economic mainstream of American society, not encouraging them to develop a self-contained community apart from the mainstream."[46]

43. Rusk (1999).
44. Lemann (1994); Jargowsky (1997); Rusk (1999).
45. Lemann (1991).
46. Lemann (1991).

CDCs are expected to miraculously revitalize distressed urban neighborhoods with inadequate funding and, even more miraculously, to do it while combating the powerful forces of suburbanization that are sucking private capital and human potential out of the city core.[47] What they are being asked to do is impossible. Doing nothing would be the alternative, but it would probably make conditions worse. But, if conditions worsened, perhaps frustration would build to the point that a series of significant and equitable changes would occur. If governments at every level stopped reacting to only the symptoms of urban poverty and instead invested their energy and resources in a sustained attack on the roots of the problem—in overhauling the larger institutional frameworks in which poor communities are located—perhaps distressed neighborhoods in cities and older suburbs would stand a fighting chance.

47. In the 1970s, community development corporations relied heavily on federal funding. In the 1980s, making good on his promise to reduce domestic spending, Ronald Reagan and his administration cut spending on subsidized housing by more than 70 percent (Vidal 1992). Federal grants to central cities were also cut drastically. Many central city coffers declined between 25 and 50 percent as a result of the decrease in federal aid to central cities. See Caraley (1992); Davis (1993); Riposa (1996); and Dreier (1999).

CHAPTER 5

FISCAL EQUITY

An essential part of creating a stable, cooperative region is to gradually equalize the resources of local governments with land-use planning powers. In addition to improving equity, which will allow cities, at-risk suburbs, and many bedroom-developing suburbs to lower taxes and improve services, it will reduce the competition between places, give communities real fiscal incentives to cooperate, and make regional land-use planning easier to achieve (chapter 6). The Rubicon of local fiscal equity was crossed decades ago with the nearly universal adoption of state school equalization programs. Furthermore, state aid is already a significant source of municipal revenue in most of the regions studied here. The challenge is to take these ideas and make them gradually more extensive and efficient—a challenge of degree rather than of kind.

All state governments distribute some of their resources to local governments to help finance local public services. How much varies from state to state and across services. The states liberally support local school systems for reasons both economic and idealistic. Educating the labor force increases the country's (and states') competitiveness in the global economy. By enhancing individuals' economic mobility, education provides a means of improving income distribution. Education is also seen as a vehicle for strengthening democracy. State constitutions and the courts have long recognized the important public functions of schools. The courts have played an important role in the lengthy and still incomplete effort to equalize access for all children to at least some minimum standard of education, regardless of their parents' or their communities' economic status.

Traditionally, states have been much more willing to support local public schools than other municipal services. In 1996–97, states financed roughly half the costs of local public schools but only a fifth of the costs of municipal services (table 5-1). Also, there was much less variation among states in the extent of their support for local schools than for municipal services. The state-financed share of local school expenditures ranged from 32 percent to 66 percent for 90 percent of the states (a ratio of 2.1 to 1); the equivalent range for municipal services was 6 percent to 29 percent (a ratio of 4.8 to 1). State aid programs for schools also are much more likely to be explicitly designed to reduce inequities resulting from differences among local tax bases.

Equalizing access to municipal services has not received the same attention as education. Local governments have been left much more to their own devices in financing these services, and that is still true (table 5-1). There are several reasons for the difference. To some extent, the legal system is responsible—municipal services do not receive the same attention as schools in state constitutions and the courts. Those institutions have elevated access to education to a legal right, a status rarely achieved by any of the traditional functions of municipal governments. Similarly, many social scientists (economists in particular) view municipal services much as they do the goods and services individuals purchase privately in a market economy. Although there may be reasons to provide those services through public agencies rather than through private markets, the desirability of accommodating diverse tastes or preferences is often used to argue that such services should be financed locally to maximize consumer choice and to allow voters the greatest voice in determining how and how much of a service is provided.

About two-thirds of municipal budgets are dedicated to functions that most Americans view as a minimum acceptable menu of public services.

Nevertheless, a close look at municipal governments' functions in the U.S. economy and society makes it difficult to justify those notions. In 1996–97 roughly half of all municipal government expenditures in the United States went for core services that most people would consider essential: streets, public safety (police and fire protection), and sanitation services (sewerage and water treatment). An additional 14 percent of budgets went for income maintenance, health services, and courts (core functions financed at the county or state level in most states but at the local level in some). Thus about two-thirds of municipal budgets are dedicated to a set of functions that, although they may not attain the stature of public schools in many people's minds, are viewed as the minimum acceptable menu of public services. They are such important contributors to the quality of life in the United States that most Americans view access to a reasonable standard of service as a birthright. Nor is the remainder of the average local budget devoted to luxuries. Parks, recreation, housing, community development, and

TABLE 5-1. State Aid to Municipalities and School Districts, 1996–97

Percent

State	State aid share of municipal general expenditures	State aid share of school district general expenditures	State	State aid share of municipal general expenditures	State aid share of school district general expenditures
Alabama	6	61	Nebraska	13	32
Alaska	17	66	Nevada	28	32
Arizona	26	44	New Hampshire	12	7
Arkansas	12	60	New Jersey	30	39
California	14	56	New Mexico	27	74
Colorado	13	44	New York	27	40
Connecticut	20	38	North Carolina	15	65
Delaware	8	67	North Dakota	13	42
Florida	9	49	Ohio	13	41
Georgia	3	52	Oklahoma	4	59
Hawaii	8	90	Oregon	9	54
Idaho	16	64	Pennsylvania	20	40
Illinois	29	27	Rhode Island	10	41
Indiana	19	54	South Carolina	9	53
Iowa	12	49	South Dakota	6	30
Kansas	10	57	Tennessee	13	48
Kentucky	8	65	Texas	4	43
Louisiana	9	50	Utah	4	59
Maine	11	47	Vermont	6	28
Maryland	31	38	Virginia	20	31
Massachusetts	33	38	Washington	12	68
Michigan	24	67	West Virginia	2	63
Minnesota	20	58	Wisconsin	30	43
Mississippi	28	58	Wyoming	52	51
Missouri	6	40			
Montana	14	49	U.S. average	18	49

Source: Bureau of the Census, 1997 Census of Governments.

libraries claim 12 percent; interest on debt, 7 percent; various unallocated expenses, 7 percent; and general administration, 7 percent.[1]

There is virtue in diversity of choice—that is the central strength of a market economy and of a market-like set of local governments competing for residents. However, most of the goods and services provided by local governments are crucial building blocks for what most Americans would regard as a reasonable quality of life, and the arguments are strong for providing them through public agencies. Furthermore, the literature on demand for local government services implies that differences in the extent and quality of those services are determined largely by differences in those governments' economic resources and their costs.[2] In light of the extreme variations in tax capacities and costs revealed by the analysis in "Metropatterns," the case for reducing those disparities is clear. The question is which policies do so most efficiently and in ways that support other priorities, such as land-use planning, while minimizing intrusions on legitimate local prerogatives.

GOVERNMENT FINANCE AND FISCAL DISPARITIES

Local governments in the United States provide important public services demanded by businesses and residents and financed largely through local taxes (for example, streets, public safety, sanitation, and other basic infrastructure). At the same time, local governments have the authority to regulate land uses within their political boundaries, to determine the location and the extent of residential, commercial, industrial, parkland, and agricultural development.

Though designed for seemingly separate purposes, local tax policy and land-use regulations are closely related. The amount of revenue a local government can generate on its own depends largely on the value and types of land uses within its jurisdiction. Of the three primary sources of local tax revenues—property, sales, and income tax—the

1. U.S. Bureau of the Census (2000). The data for municipal governments are corrected to exclude spending for public schools in states where this spending shows up in municipal budgets.

2. Differences in preferences (for example, between different age groups in the population) also matter, but resources and cost differences generated by differences in the service environment are the dominant explanatory variables in most empirical analyses of this question, especially for core services like public safety. For a good example of an analysis that distinguishes the three types of variables, see Ladd and Yinger (1989).

property tax is the most common and accounts for the largest share of local tax revenues, an average of 74 percent in 1996.[3] General and selective sales taxes account for another 16 percent, and individual income taxes another 5 percent.[4] Local governments with land-use planning powers (such as municipalities or counties) therefore have direct incentives to develop a land-use plan that maximizes the value of property (if the property tax is the primary revenue source), attracts high-value retail businesses (if sales taxes are important), or tailors the housing stock to high-income residents or employers (if income taxes are important).

Incentives also can be found in local governments' expenditures. Different land uses imply different public service needs. Residential development requires water and gas lines, roads, sewerage and waste management systems, fire and police protection, schools, libraries, social services, and other public infrastructure and services. However, different types of residential development imply different degrees of need for public services. An apartment building with low-income residents is likely to entail greater social service costs than a middle-class family living in a four-bedroom single-family home. Commercial and industrial development requires a different set of local services: utilities, infrastructure, police and fire protection. Again, different types of commercial and industrial development imply different service needs—a busy commercial area with many retail businesses and an industrial park do not entail the same expenses.

Ultimately, what localities worry about is the net effect of specific types of development on revenues and expenditures. That balance (the fiscal dividend) determines whether a new development will increase or decrease current residents' financial burden. The overall incentive is therefore to allow or pursue only the kind of development that generates a positive fiscal dividend—a surplus of revenues over expenditures. Individual local governments in a fragmented local government system compete with each other for these fiscal dividends chiefly through land-use regulations to limit new activity in particular ways (fiscal zoning) and development incentives to attract particular types of activities or firms.

---

3. U.S. Bureau of the Census (2000).

4. Selective sales taxes include those on motor fuels, alcoholic beverages, tobacco, and public utilities. The balance of local tax revenues is derived from corporate income taxes, motor vehicle license taxes, and other local taxes.

Fiscal Zoning

Fiscal zoning is a deliberate attempt by a local government to reap the best fiscal dividend by limiting the types of land uses within its jurisdiction. The types of development that will do this vary from place to place, depending on local revenue sources and the way responsibilities for expenditures are divided among state, county, local, and other public entities. Research findings on this question are not in complete agreement, but some general patterns emerge.

Most notably, some general rules appear to apply when a local government seeks the most "profitable" land uses, including a hierarchy of land uses and fiscal impacts that demonstrates which land uses break even in terms of the fiscal dividend.[5] For example, municipalities generate more revenues than costs with office parks, industrial development, and small (one- or two-bedroom) apartments and condominiums. School districts break even on those types of properties as well as on retail development, two- to three-bedroom townhouses, and expensive single-family homes. The types of development that generate negative fiscal dividends include larger townhouses (three- to four-bedroom units), inexpensive single-family homes, larger apartments (three- to four-bedroom units), and mobile homes.

Two important caveats have been mentioned in this regard.[6] First, fiscal dividends have probably declined in recent decades because taxpayer revolts, which have reduced the tax benefits of development in many places, have combined with declining intergovernmental assistance to localities to force the localities to pick up a larger part of development costs. Second, recent studies have been more careful in their calculation of capital costs, the most difficult cost to estimate. One result is that fewer types of development activities actually generate a positive fiscal dividend. Another is that fiscal dividends for commercial development exceed those for residential development by less than indicated in early studies that either excluded capital costs or did not account for them well.

The overall implication is that, from the standpoint of the fiscal dividend, commercial, industrial, and high-end residential developments are the way to go. Since the ability to generate revenues depends largely on the value of property, high-value commercial, industrial, and residential properties that generate relatively little in public costs are preferred, and lower-value properties that create the need for pub-

5. Burchell (1990).
6. See Altshuler and Gomez-Ibanez (1993).

lic expenditures are avoided.[7] When determining how to allow their land to be developed, local governments have a direct incentive to favor profitable uses over others and, whenever possible, to exclude unprofitable uses such as large apartments and moderate- to low-value homes.

Local governments have tools for encouraging development of the most profitable uses. Zoning can be deployed to allow particular types of commercial or industrial development and limit others. To attract particular companies, incentives can then be proffered. Tools for regulating residential development (for example, minimum lot size or setback requirements and construction standards designed to increase the cost of building in the community) are usually less direct.

This fiscal zoning process, when played out over an entire metropolitan area, can significantly influence where people are able to live, the types and quality of public services they receive from their local government, and the presence or absence of employment opportunities near their homes. How binding those limitations are for an individual or family will for the most part be directly related to the value of the home they can afford—in other words, their income.

Competition for Tax Base

Another aspect of local governments' pursuit of positive fiscal dividends is the competition among them for desirable commercial and industrial properties. That competition, which pervades metropolitan areas throughout the United States, is likely to be both wasteful and biased. It is wasteful because, from a regional point of view, interlocal competition is largely a zero-sum game. When a business is lured to one jurisdiction in a metropolitan area by financial or other types of incentives, its arrival is unlikely to add net new activity to the regional economy. Instead, one community's gain is likely to be another's loss—a direct loss in the case of a business that relocates within the same metropolitan area and an indirect loss in the case of a new business that would have located somewhere in the metropolitan area regardless of the incentives. Communities may also find they have to spend resources to ensure that their existing businesses do not leave for other places in the metropolitan area that offer them incentives. The resources expended in such competition are largely wasted: they do not enhance the overall regional economy; they only shuffle activity from one place to another.

The fiscal zoning process can significantly influence where people are able to live, the public services they receive, and whether they can find jobs near their homes.

7. Winsor (1979); Wasylenko (1980); Cervero and Rolleston (1987).

The competition is biased because it creates the potential for a vicious, self-reinforcing cycle of decline in places that "lose" early in the game. As a locality loses activities that generate positive fiscal dividends, it must either raise taxes on its remaining tax base to maintain services at existing levels or reduce services at existing tax rates. Either choice reduces the locality's ability to compete for additions to its tax base or to keep its existing base, leading to further losses and further declines in the place's ability to compete.[8]

Similarly, as communities become segmented by housing and income type, they also become segmented by the type and amount of commercial and industrial development they can attract. Again, the commercial and industrial developments that generate the highest revenues tend to locate in the relatively few communities that have large, expensive houses. Part of the attraction lies in the low tax rates such places can maintain, but it is also related to their residents' socioeconomic status. With sufficient high-end housing available for company executives, better public services, and little social stress, those communities often offer the most attractive location for new businesses. Furthermore, higher-end retail stores also find them desirable because of the purchasing power of their middle- to upper-income residents. Just as they win the competition for revenue-generating housing, those communities win the competition for commercial properties that also generate the largest revenues.

By contrast, the newer, moderate-income communities growing at the edges of the region have little success in attracting the most desirable commercial and industrial properties. If they happen to be located along a major highway or commuter route, some of them may be able to attract retail developments that increase their tax base. Even in those cases, however, the increased costs for the roads, police and fire services, and public utilities that retail developments require tend to outstrip the revenues that they generate. Most edge communities serve primarily as bedroom communities for the rest of the region and develop at lower

---

8. Capitalization may slow down or even short-circuit this process. As a place's tax rates increase (or services decrease), demand for housing will decline, reducing local land and housing prices. The lower prices may then offset the fiscal disadvantages from the higher taxes (lower service levels) to potential buyers. However, there are good reasons to believe and empirical evidence that implies that tax or service differentials are not fully capitalized into land or housing values, so the potential for vicious cycles remains. See Younger (1982); and Fisher (1996, pp. 118–19). In any case, the changes in housing values resulting from the capitalization process represent real losses to current residents (in the losing community) and gains (in the winning community), raising genuine equity concerns.

densities than older suburban communities, generating fewer revenues and higher costs per square mile.

Finally, the older core communities that have become or are becoming home to more and more of the region's low- and moderate-income families experience significant disadvantages in attracting new business development. With higher taxes, aging infrastructure, a lack of available land, and a relatively high degree of social stress, those communities do not usually attract new investment and often lose the businesses that they have. Disinvestment by the business community can hasten community decline, as jobs evaporate and the local tax base continues to shrink. These communities thus fall farther behind other metropolitan communities as they struggle to maintain some degree of stability and competitiveness.

In sum, strong incentives for engaging in fiscal zoning and tax-base competition are built into local fiscal systems. Those processes shape metropolitan areas in important ways: they generate a highly stratified mosaic of localities in a metropolitan region, they encourage short-sighted land-use planning, and they contribute to sprawl.

Stratification of Metropolitan Areas

Fiscal zoning and tax-base competition encourage concentrations of families and individuals with the greatest need for public services in communities that are the least able to generate the revenue to provide those services. A primary reason can be seen by looking again at the hierarchy of profitable land uses and the types of people that live in different kinds of residential properties.[9] Low- or moderate-income families with children most frequently purchase cost-generating residences, relatively inexpensive housing with three or more bedrooms. Revenue-generating homes—with fewer bedrooms and costing more—are likely to be purchased by high-income families, empty-nesters, and two-income households with no children.

As municipalities in a metropolitan region compete for the limited number of "good" land uses, only a few of them succeed. Localities that attract large, expensive homes and other revenue-generating land uses see their revenues rise while their costs remain relatively stable. The resulting surplus funds allow them either to provide additional, higher-quality services or to reduce their property tax rates, making them even more attractive to people looking for housing. That increased demand allows them to continue building high-end housing, creating a continuous cycle

9. See Burchell's (1990) hierarchy.

Places that do not attract or retain high-end housing and commercial-industrial development have a hard time generating revenues and keeping taxes low.

of increasing revenue-raising capacity and lower taxes. The cluster analysis presented in the preceding chapters shows that such clear winners in the competition are rare and that the benefits accrue to a disproportionately small segment of metropolitan populations. Just 7 percent of the people in the 25 largest metropolitan areas live in communities in the two high-capacity, low-cost categories, but more than twice that percentage of office space (16 percent) is located there. Those communities commanded more than twice their region's average tax capacity, and their tax capacities have been growing faster than average, widening the gap.

Conversely, places that do not attract or keep sufficient high-end housing and commercial-industrial development have a much harder time generating revenues and keeping taxes low. In older communities at the core of the region, expenditures are often related to social stresses: poverty, crime, and aging infrastructure in need of repair. Those communities, already fully developed, have older houses that do not offer the size or amenities that more affluent homebuyers want. They thus become home to the region's lower-income families, with greater need for social services, public housing, and public safety services.

In more rapidly developing edge communities, young families with children purchase relatively affordable, newer three- and four-bedroom homes that allow them to avoid the social stresses of older core communities. School enrollments and the need for new schools expand quickly in those communities, as does the need for new roads, parks, libraries, police and fire protection, and other public services. Unable to keep up, edge communities are perpetually short of cash.

Both types of fiscally strained communities become home to families and individuals with the greatest need for additional spending and include a disproportionate share of a region's cost-generating land uses. Meanwhile, they fall farther and farther behind in their ability to generate revenues to meet their needs. Corresponding to the three at-risk categories identified in chapter 2 these communities housed 40 percent of the population in the 25 largest metropolitan areas, nearly six times the share of the high-capacity, low-cost communities. As a group, they commanded only a fraction of the tax capacity per household of the high-capacity, low-cost localities (roughly 70 percent of the regional average compared with more than 200 percent). Moreover, the gap was widening (their tax capacity grew by 6 to 12 percentage points less on average between 1993 and 1998 than that of the two high-capacity groups).

The middle ground, held by communities thought of as the prototypical suburb, is surprisingly small. They house just a quarter of the metropolitan population in the 25 largest areas, a bit more than a third of the suburban population. These communities, which have relatively low social costs but high growth rates, maintain a fragile balance between costs and revenues. They command roughly average tax capacities but are just managing to maintain that position over time.

Thus the distribution of public resources in metropolitan areas is highly skewed. A small part of metropolitan populations live in communities that are free of fiscal stress. Even if middle-ground suburbs that are just holding their own are included, just a third of the population in the 25 largest areas resides in fairly stress-free communities. Forty percent live in suburban communities with a much lower than average tax capacity that had been growing well below the average rate. The remainder (about 30 percent) of the population lives in central cities that, although they are holding their own in the competition for tax base, have a grossly disproportionate share of regional problems.

Misguided Land-Use Planning

Fiscal zoning and competition for limited "good" land uses also discourage long-term planning that might allow communities to develop in an orderly and efficient way. Because competition for certain land uses can be so intense—and the impact of losing so severe—communities often feel they have to grab all the development they can before it leaves for another community. That is especially true in newly developing communities, trying to build an adequate tax base to pay for their growing needs and to pay off debts on new infrastructure. As property tax increases threaten, tremendous pressures build to spread the costs through growth. However, they are rarely in a good position to win the competition for the most "profitable" land uses, ending up instead with single-family, moderately priced housing that generates more costs than revenues. Development of this sort at the fringe is also likely to generate long-term environmental costs—it is unlikely to be dense enough to support sewer and water treatment systems in the short term, but at the same time, it is too dense for effective use of septic systems over the longer term.

The imperative to grow in order to spread the costs of past development thus can lead instead to more new costs than new revenues, beginning a recurring cycle of budget shortfalls. In the long run, these communities would often be better off forestalling growth until metropolitan expansion generates demand for denser, more balanced use of the land—an outcome more consistent with long-term regional and environmental needs. However, they need the fiscal capacity to take the long view, capacity that current development patterns often do not provide.

Communities in the economic middle ground face strong incentives to push fiscal zoning and tax-base competition to the limit. If they do not, they become vulnerable to the downward cycle that they see in nearby at-risk communities. Since these places usually occupy the geographic middle ground of their metropolitan area, the resulting planning practices effectively push new, middle-income development even farther out into the metropolitan fringe.

Sprawling Development Patterns

The cumulative effect of fiscal zoning and tax-base competition worsens two aspects of urban sprawl: low-density development and a shift in population growth to the edges of a metropolitan region. Those characteristics are reinforced over time, fueled partly by the push of community decline in the region's older, developed areas and partly by the pull of rapidly growing communities on the metropolitan fringe. Steadily the gap widens between people who can avoid sharing the costs of public services by moving to another community and those who cannot. As businesses and homeowners migrate outward from a region's core, federal and state investment in highways, sewers, economic development, and schools follow, further diverting resources from the places that arguably need them most. There is a certain irony in the fact that taxes paid by the people left behind in the declining core often subsidize those investments.

Shifting investment in this way to previously undeveloped areas is a waste of taxpayers' limited resources, considering the significant investments in infrastructure and housing that many core areas have already made. Instead of maintaining those investments, metropolitan areas throughout the country are courting new investments—building entirely new cities to replace the ones they are throwing away.

THE PROS AND CONS OF PROMOTING REGIONAL EQUITY

Policies to reduce fiscal inequities in metropolitan areas can bring great benefits. They can narrow the disparity in local governments' capacities to provide public services; they also can reduce incentives for fiscal zoning and inefficient tax-base competition and the negative consequences of those activities. However, those gains do not always come without costs. Poorly designed policies to reduce inequality can also compromise local autonomy, derail efficient provision of local services, and create in-

Metropolitan areas across the country are building entirely new cities to replace the ones they are throwing away.

centives for inefficient patterns of migration. Finding policy designs that strike the best possible balance between trade-offs is not a trivial exercise.

Potential Benefits of Reducing Inequality

Policies that promote equity in the distribution of local taxes can reduce incentives for fiscal zoning and tax-base competition and their negative outcomes in several ways. By ensuring that all local governments can provide the infrastructure and services communities need to function, equity-enhancing policies can guarantee that all residents of a metropolitan area enjoy at least a minimum standard of service for important local public goods like public safety. By reducing the need for local governments to "steal" revenue-generating land uses from each other, such policies allow them to engage in more thoughtful and beneficial land-use planning. By reducing tax-rate disparities—leveling the playing field in the tax-base competition—these policies encourage reinvestment in the central city and other fiscally stressed communities and reduce the growth of those disparities.

Fair Provision of Basic Services. In a nation committed to equal opportunity for all citizens, all local governments must be able to provide their communities with basic infrastructure and services. However, an insufficient local tax base makes it difficult for local governments to do so at a reasonable tax rate. Equal opportunity is undercut when people living in low-tax-base communities must be taxed at burdensome levels to provide even minimum levels of public infrastructure and services while high-tax-base communities can keep local taxes low.

In every one of the 25 largest metropolitan areas in the United States, more than half the population lives in a community in one of the at-risk categories identified in chapter 2. At-risk places are not limited to central cities and core areas—they include older satellite cities, growing exurbs, and some second ring suburbs. Nearly everywhere in a metropolitan region where social needs are high or increasing, the local tax base is low and declining. By contrast, places with few social needs generally have a much greater ability to generate revenues from their local tax base, and that base has been growing at higher-than-average rates. Even to approach the goal of guaranteed access to adequate municipal services would involve a significant increase in current equity policies.

Reduction of Wasteful Competition. Intrametropolitan competition for a limited tax base harms a region. It is a waste of resources for local governments to engage in bidding wars for businesses that already have chosen to locate in the region. In such situations, public monies are used to improve the fiscal position and services of one community at the expense of another, while businesses take unfair advantage of the competition to reduce their social responsibilities. The mere threat of leaving can induce troubled communities to offer a business large public subsidies to stay.

Greater equity frees local governments from the pressure to base land-use decisions primarily on the need for additional revenues. Instead, they can focus on developing land-use plans that accommodate growth efficiently, reduce the effects of concentrated poverty, and respond to the desires of local citizens without fearing that the resources available to them will be diminished. Furthermore, reducing the incentives for competition allows local governments to focus on cooperative efforts to help build a strong, dynamic region that is attractive to employers and residents.

Reinvestment in Disadvantaged Communities. In most metropolitan areas, older communities at the core live with aging infrastructure, industrial pollution, high concentrations of poverty, and other factors that strain their limited resources. Without sufficient funds, they cannot reinvest to rebuild sewer systems and roads, rehabilitate housing, maintain parks, and clean up polluted land. The expense entailed makes it difficult for such communities to remain competitive with newer communities elsewhere in the region that offer cheaper land, new homes, and more open space.

Greater fiscal equity diminishes the difficulty in two ways. First, it reduces tax-rate disparities, which are an important factor in intra-metropolitan tax-base competition. Second, it helps to ensure that central cities and other stressed communities have the resources to maintain or enhance their competitive position by repairing crumbling infrastructure, cleaning up polluted land, and addressing other issues related to their age and social needs. Instead of being forced to leave their community because of inadequate infrastructure or crushing taxes, residents can be assured that the community will have the resources necessary to reinvest in its infrastructure and ensure its stability.

Potential Costs of Reducing Inequality

Policies designed to reduce inequality come with costs. Some may compromise local autonomy and the efficient provision of local services; they may also generate incentives for inefficient patterns of migration.

Greater equity frees local governments from the pressure to base land-use decisions primarily on the need for additional revenues.

Reduced Local Autonomy and Efficiency. The U.S. political system places a high value on local autonomy. It is often argued that policies designed to create greater equity would undermine local autonomy and the advantages derived from providing individuals with a wide range of choices. Local control is desirable for several reasons. One argument is that, because local governments are smaller and closer to voters, local service provision encourages residents to participate in the democratic process. Another is that because the actions of local governments have a direct impact on the economic well-being of voters, primarily through their effect on home values, local control creates a powerful incentive for voters to monitor those actions: the services the government produces, for example, and its efficiency in providing them. Local autonomy also rewards localities for accepting land uses with some undesirable effects—for example, commercial activity that generates congestion—by allowing them to reap the full benefit of local taxation. Finally, a system of many local governments provides consumers and voters with a variety of combinations of local services to choose from, limiting the inevitable welfare losses that result from uniform provision of services within a jurisdiction.[10]

Those are all worthy arguments. Designing policies to promote equity in a way that compromises local autonomy the least is one of the primary challenges associated with their development. However, local autonomy does not come without limitations, hence the need for higher levels of government. Some public services (such as wastewater treatment) cannot be provided efficiently at the small scale implied by a highly fragmented system of local governments. In such cases, the efficiency gained by providing that service on a larger scale—at a higher level of government—clearly outweighs the costs associated with the loss of local autonomy.

Other public services generate costs and benefits over a much larger geographic area than one, two, or several jurisdictions. Many activities currently carried out by local governments have consequences beyond local borders. Natural systems spread the costs and benefits associated with water, sewer, and sewage treatment systems; regional housing markets spread the costs and benefits of local affordable housing programs, land-use restrictions, and income redistribution policies; regional labor markets spread the costs and benefits of economic development and education programs; transportation systems spread the costs and benefits of local street and bridge maintenance and enable nonresidents to enjoy locally maintained amenities such as parks.

10. For a more complete summary of these arguments, see Fischel (1998).

When local actions have regional consequences, local and regional interests may diverge.

When local actions have regional consequences, local and regional interests may diverge. An activity that makes perfect sense on the basis of an assessment of the potential costs and benefits to a locality may be undesirable from a regional perspective because many of the costs may be felt regionally, not locally. Another may not seem worthwhile to a locality but may nevertheless be highly beneficial from a regional standpoint because many of the benefits accrue to residents of surrounding communities. In those cases, some form of regional or state participation in decisionmaking is preferable to complete local autonomy. That participation can take many forms, including assumption of full responsibility for the activity, provision of full or partial financing of the activity through intergovernmental aid, or regulation of local government activities.

Other public services provided at least in part by local governments in most states are an integral part of what most Americans would regard as an acceptable quality of life. Good examples are public safety, a healthy environment, access to the courts or legal representation, access to housing in a variety of locations (facilitating access to jobs and good schools), and various health services. To many people, even "second-tier" local services such as parks and recreation fit into that category. The implication is that all people have the right to a reasonable standard of service in those areas—a standard that a highly fragmented and fiscally stratified system with full local autonomy may not always be able to meet.

Thus the choice is not simply between having or not having local autonomy. Instead, it comes down to balancing the benefits of local autonomy against the costs, policy area by policy area, and finding equity-enhancing policies that compromise the benefits of local autonomy the least.

Negative Migration Incentives. Conventional wisdom holds that income redistribution is the job of higher levels of government. Local governments pursue income redistribution at their peril because, in most metropolitan areas, it is easy for the losers in a locality that redistributes income to escape to a nearby locality that does not. Policies designed to reduce fiscal inequities in metropolitan areas must recognize that limitation. The clear implication is that the geographic scope of equity-enhancing policies must, at a minimum, include entire metropolitan areas—entire housing and labor markets. Programs that do not include the entire area run the risk of being undermined by migration. A program that affects only the inner portions of a metropolitan region, for instance, may inadvertently encourage sprawl by pushing higher-income residents to outer areas beyond the scope of the program.

Areas that do implement properly scaled programs to promote fiscal equity reduce the incentives for residents to move in pursuit of "personal" fiscal dividends or to flee small changes in the fiscal position of their neighborhood or community. Many people value the result—greater neighborhood and community stability.

POLICIES TO PROMOTE FISCAL EQUITY

State governments have long recognized the need to promote fiscal equity among local governments. They have followed three primary strategies to reduce interlocal fiscal disparities: "institutional" aid to jurisdictions with especially high needs (often central cities); state revenue-sharing programs that distribute state revenues to local governments; and metropolitan tax base–sharing programs that share tax resources within a single region.[11]

Institutional Aid

States can help specific localities balance their capacity to raise revenues and their service needs or costs in ways that do not involve giving them direct financial aid. They can ease the burden on low-capacity or high-need places either by relieving them of financial responsibility for a service that is a local responsibility in their state (reducing their expenditures relative to those of other localities in the state) or by allowing them to levy taxes that other localities in the state are not permitted to levy (increasing their capacity). The capacity-increasing type of aid is most commonly provided to central cities or other large localities where the need for such measures is most evident.

The use of expenditure-reducing aid is hard to document, except when it is given to city/counties. On the surface, this type of institutional aid is negative: city/counties have responsibilities for more services than their counterparts, not fewer. However, city/counties also have access to more resources than their counterparts. They do not share their tax base with an overlying county, enabling them to tax at higher rates without competitive disadvantage. They also usually receive more state aid than their counterparts in the rest of the state—aid the state would give the municipality plus aid it would give the county.

11. Ladd and Yinger (1989) were the first to emphasize the importance of "institutional" aid.

101

If the extra county aid they receive more than compensates them for their extra expenditure burdens, their overall fiscal status could be improved.

The city/counties in our sample do not seem to be helped fiscally by their special status, especially with regard to aid flows. The six city/counties in the sample (Baltimore, Denver, New York, Philadelphia, San Francisco, and St. Louis) did have 1998 tax capacities greater on average than those of the other cities in the sample: 112 percent of their regional average compared with 98 percent (table 2-2).[12] That is not because they do not share their tax base with a county; the tax-capacity calculation controls for that factor. Three of the cities (New York, Philadelphia, and St. Louis) do have access to taxes not generally available to their regional counterparts (an issue discussed in more detail later). However, because two of the three (Philadelphia and New York) still have capacities below their regional average, access to taxes does not explain the higher-than-average capacity for the six as a group. It is more likely that their city/county status confers no great benefit with regard to tax capacity. Removing the one high outlier (St. Louis) from the calculation reduces the average capacity for the group to roughly 93 percent of regional averages.

More revealing is the extent to which these city/counties receive additional aid to compensate for their additional responsibilities. Their fiscal position in relation to that of their regional counterparts worsens when aid is considered. When aid is added to tax capacity, the six city/counties average just 105 percent of their regional average total revenue capacity. Since the data for these places were adjusted to control for the extra aid they receive for county functions (appendix A), that means that these city/counties are undercompensated either for their municipal functions or for their county functions, compared with other cities and counties in their states. The available data do not suggest which, but it is clear that their city/county status hurts them in that regard. In contrast, tax capacity in the other 24 cities averages 100 percent of the regional averages and this *improves* to 114 percent when aid is added to the comparison.

In a regional context, a much more meaningful approach to easing demands on local budgets would be to relieve all localities of all or some of the responsibility for activities involving costs and benefits beyond

---

12. Washington, D.C., is also technically a city/county. However, it was not included in this analysis because it does not receive state aid, as the other city/county places do, and its inclusion would distort the analysis.

their borders. A variety of activities for which local governments are responsible in many states are candidates for institutional reform of that sort, including wastewater treatment, many transportation-related activities, a variety of income-redistribution programs, and assistance for housing that does not generate positive fiscal dividends in a specific locality but is needed within a region. All such activities can entail a wide divergence of local and regional interests, implying the need for regional action. Current practices and recommendations for policy reform in those areas are discussed in later chapters.

The second form of institutional aid—special taxing power—is easier to document. Several cities in the sample receive this form of aid. Washington, D.C., Minneapolis, St. Paul, and New York have special access to the sales tax.[13] Washington, D.C., Detroit, Kansas City (Missouri), New York, and St. Louis assess local income taxes that other cities in their region generally cannot assess, and Philadelphia is the only city in its region with the power to tax the income of nonresidents who work in the city.[14] These cities receive a real benefit in terms of their ability to raise revenues. Their tax capacities are 121 percent of their regional average, compared with an average of just 95 percent for other central cities. However, like city/counties, they do not benefit as much from state aid as the other central cities: their index increases by only 2 percent (to 124 percent), compared with an increase of 12 percent (to 107 percent) for the other cities. In effect, some of the increase in capacity from institutional aid is offset by financial aid forgone. As noted in chapter 2, this form of aid presents an additional drawback: special taxes mark these cities as higher tax places than their suburban counterparts. This distinction puts them at a disadvantage in the competition for economic activity within their metropolitan area.

Overall, the central cities in the sample do not appear to benefit greatly, if at all, from institutional aid. Indeed, any advantages gained appear to be more than offset by disadvantages in other areas. More fundamental reforms are called for in the way local services are organized—reforms that explicitly recognize the regional costs and benefits of local activities.

13. In the Washington, D.C., and New York metropolitan areas, a small number of other municipalities also assess a sales tax. Minneapolis and St. Paul are the only cities in the Twin Cities metropolitan area with this power.

14. In the Detroit and New York metropolitan areas, a small number of other municipalities assess income taxes. Kansas City and St. Louis are the only cities in their metropolitan areas with this power.

State Aid Programs

Many states attempt to reduce fiscal inequity among jurisdictions through revenue-sharing programs that distribute a portion of the revenues from one or more state taxes to local governments through a variety of formulas. Massachusetts, Michigan, and Wisconsin are conspicuous examples of states with large revenue-sharing programs. Whether fiscal inequities are reduced in this way depends largely on the formula used to distribute revenues to local governments. Most programs began with a simple per-capita (return-to-origin) approach to distributing funds. As those programs evolved, however, it became clear that such approaches did little to reduce the fiscal inequities among localities.

Most distribution formulas now place greater emphasis on the communities' needs, typically determined by characteristics such as tax base, revenues, spending, or some combination of the three. For instance, in Wisconsin, revenues are distributed on the basis of five criteria, including population, the value of the local tax base, and compensation for the presence of a power company property not taxable locally.[15] In Michigan, the legislature recently revised its revenue-sharing program so that a portion of the revenues collected from the state sales tax is distributed to local governments according to three separate formulas—one accounting for population and the type of jurisdiction, and two based on taxable value per capita.[16] Detroit, which is excluded from those formulas, receives a fixed payment, protecting it from potential decreases due to future population declines.

Tables 5-2 and 2-2 provide information on the extent to which current state aid programs reflect revenue-raising capacity and needs. From table 5-2 it is clear that most aid programs do equalize revenue-raising capacity to some extent. The equity measure shown in the table (the Gini coefficient) improves in all but two metropolitan areas when aid is added to local tax capacity. However, the effects of aid vary considerably, ranging from a 63 percent change for the better in the inequality measure to an 11 percent change for the worse. In addition, a great deal of inequality remains after accounting for aid flows. On average, revenue capacity (tax capacity plus aid) in the ninety-fifth percentile jurisdiction exceeded that in the fifth percentile jurisdiction by nearly 7 to 1 in the 25 metropolitan areas in the sample, down from roughly 11 to 1 before aid.

15. Wisconsin Department of Revenue (2001).
16. Citizens Research Council of Michigan (2000).

Table 2-2 provides a rough measure of the extent to which aid programs reflect needs. The disproportionate shares of aid to individual central cities reflect their greater needs. The fiscal status of 22 of the 30 cities improved compared with that of their metropolitan neighbors when they received aid, implying some correlation between state aid programs and needs. The pattern of improvements implies that New Jersey, Wisconsin, Minnesota, Maryland, Massachusetts, and Michigan do the most for their largest cities and suggests that those states target needs fairly well. However, the changes in the relative positions of all the cities (difference between the index for tax capacity and the index for total capacity) are more closely correlated with tax capacity than with any of the need measures included in the table, implying that capacity rather than needs has the greater influence on aid flows overall. Analysis of the data for the full sample, including suburban areas, generates the same result.[17]

Tax-Base Sharing

Tax-base sharing, an alternative way to reduce tax base inequities, has several advantages over the patchwork quilt of aid programs common to most states. First, tax-base sharing provides resources to multiple taxing jurisdictions at the same time. Unlike separate programs that distribute state revenues to counties, cities, townships, and special districts, tax-base sharing simply redistributes the common base from which each local jurisdiction derives its revenues. Second, it helps to equalize the resources available to local governments without removing local control over tax rates. Third, by requiring local governments to relinquish some of their fiscal dividend from new commercial-industrial development, tax-base sharing weakens their incentive to waste taxpayer dollars by stealing it away from other communities. Similarly, including residential property in tax-base sharing dilutes local governments' incentives

17. For central cities, the correlation coefficients between the change in relative fiscal position (the total capacity index minus the tax-capacity index) and the indexes for tax capacity, free-lunch percentage, population density, age of housing stock, and population growth are –0.66, 0.20, 0.55, 0.07, and 0.21, respectively. Only the coefficients for tax capacity and density are statistically significant at the 95 percent confidence level. The results are similar for the full sample (including suburban areas). The equivalent correlation coefficients are –0.19, 0.06, 0.03, 0.05, and –0.004. (All but the population growth coefficient are significant at 95 percent.) Similarly, in a multiple regression of the change in relative fiscal position on indexes for the four cost variables, only the coefficients on tax capacity and housing age are statistically significant, and the standardized coefficient for the tax-capacity index is more than four times that for housing age. Allowing for nonlinear relationships with population growth and density does not substantively change the results.

to use fiscal zoning or its substitutes to restrict residential development to "profitable" types of housing, making cooperative, efficient land-use planning easier. Minnesota's experience with tax-base sharing is evidence of those effects. In the Twin Cities region in the early 1970s, reformers attempting to pass legislation for metropolitan land-use planning used tax-base sharing as a quid pro quo to gain political support in the low-fiscal capacity, developing suburbs.[18] These suburbs initially cried foul when told that an urban service line would be drawn through the middle of their towns and that land outside that boundary would be zoned at agricultural densities. They argued that they desperately needed the land to develop their tax base so that they could keep their tax rates down and still relieve overcrowding in their schools. Compromise and acceptance was reached when they were shown the potential benefits of a tax-base-sharing system: that is, that they would share in the full region's new tax base and would gain fiscal capacity per capita faster than they would by developing lower-value residential property. In the end, low-tax-base communities in the region accepted land-use planning in exchange for tax-base sharing.

Flexibility is a fourth advantage of tax-base sharing. This tool can be designed to offset intraregional variations in the need for or cost of public services as well as variations in revenue-raising capacity.[19] It can also be implemented at the regional level to avoid the problems associated with designing aid formulas to simultaneously accommodate the vastly different needs and costs of urban and rural areas. Furthermore, if properly structured, it avoids migration issues.

With tax-base sharing, a portion of each locality's tax base is contributed to a regional pool and redistributed according to some criteria other than the locality's original contribution to the pool.[20] A community's contribution can be set as a percentage of growth in tax base or as a percentage of current tax base. The tax-base pool can be limited to particular types of tax base (for example, commercial-industrial property), or it can include all types (sales tax, income tax, and property tax). Distributions from the pool can be determined by tax capacity, service cost or need indicators, land-use decisions, or other criteria. The essen-

18. Albert (1979).

19. This can be achieved without altering the disincentives for tax-base competition since only the distribution formula need be changed to achieve this result.

20. The program can be structured in a way that both allows localities to tax their distribution from the pool at local tax rates and taxes the pooled portion of the regional tax base at a uniform rate. The former maintains local control over tax rates while the latter narrows interlocal tax-rate disparities.

tial features of tax-base sharing are that it distributes tax base or revenues by criteria other than the origin or collection point (unlike piggyback taxes, for instance); it provides resources for the full range of local services (unlike special district assessments); and it provides additional resources for the provision of local services (unlike county or state taxes).

Tax-base sharing across a metropolitan area has been attempted in only one place in the United States: the Minneapolis–St. Paul (Twin Cities) region of Minnesota. Created by the Minnesota Fiscal Disparities Act of 1971 as an alternative to annexation and consolidation of local governments, the Twin Cities' tax-base-sharing program was an attempt to respond to a number of concerns, including increasing property tax rates, tax-base and tax-rate disparities, and interjurisdictional competition for development.

Under the Twin Cities program, each taxing jurisdiction in a seven-county area must contribute to a regional pool 40 percent of the growth in the value of its commercial-industrial tax capacity since 1971. Municipalities are assigned a portion of that pool, based on population and the ratio of the total market value of property per capita in the jurisdiction and the average market value of property per capita in the region. The formula assigns a share of the pool that is greater than their share of population to municipalities with lower-than-average market value per capita; high-market-value localities receive a lower portion than their population share.

The program's overall design balances regional goals with local autonomy. It is designed to narrow interlocal business tax-rate disparities by taxing part of commercial-industry property at a uniform regional rate, but it also allows each locality to set the rate at which the locality taxes its distribution from the pool.[21]

In 2000 the Twin Cities program shared about 28 percent of the region's commercial-industrial tax base, an amount that would have generated roughly $300 million in revenue at the regional average tax rate on commercial-industrial property. That amount represented about 12 percent of total tax base.[22] The program reduced local tax-base disparities by roughly 20 percent (as measured by the Gini coefficient) and reduced the ratio of the ninety-fifth to fifth percentile tax base by about 25 percent. For cities with a population of at least 9,000, the ratio of the

---

21. For more complete descriptions of the program design, see Baker and Hinze (1995) and Luce (1998).

22. Hinze and Baker (2000).

Tax-base sharing is a much more cost-effective means of reducing tax-base inequity than existing aid programs.

largest tax base per capita to the smallest dropped from 15:1 to 5:1 as a result of the program.[23]

As just noted, a tax-base-sharing program can be created in any number of ways, depending on the political support for such a program and its public policy goals. Table 5-2 shows the impact a program similar to the Twin Cities program would have on tax-capacity inequities in the 25 largest metropolitan areas in the sample. (Minneapolis–St. Paul is excluded because tax capacities there already reflect the effects of the Fiscal Disparities Act.) The simulations generate a regional tax-base pool with contributions equal to 10 percent of each municipality's tax capacity. Distributions from the pool are determined by population and the ratio of local tax capacity per household to the regional average tax capacity per household.[24]

The results of the simulations show that tax-base sharing is a much more cost-effective means of reducing tax-base inequity than existing aid programs. On average, tax-base sharing reduces inequities by a greater amount than current state aid programs with a pool of money that is less than one-third the amount of current aid.[25] Tax-base sharing reduces disparities by 2 percentage points for each percentage point of shared revenues, while current aid programs reduce disparities by just half of a percentage point for each percentage point of aid. Tax-base sharing reduces disparities more than current aid does in 10 of the 24 metropolitan areas and less than current aid does in 11; in three areas the reductions are equal. However, even in the 11 areas where current aid is more equalizing, disparities are reduced just 0.7 percentage point per percentage point of aid compared with 2.0 percentage points per percentage point of shared tax base. Although current aid is not designed solely to equalize the tax base, that is still an impressive difference in "bang for the buck."

AN AGENDA FOR REFORM

Policies designed to reduce inequality can be controversial and divisive. On the surface, they create winners and losers. The potential losers often argue that, in addition to their direct losses, equity-enhancing activities generate economic losses in the form of a less efficient regional economy and public sector. However, as seen in the tax-capacity and cluster

23. Schroeder (2000).
24. See appendix A for a description of the formula.
25. This is a 20 percent reduction in the Gini coefficients on average from pools equal to 10 percent of tax capacity compared with a 17 percent average reduction in the Gini coefficients from aid averaging 32 percent of tax capacity.

TABLE 5-2. Revenue Capacity Equity before and after Aid from State Governments and Tax-Base Sharing

Metropolitan area	Tax-capacity Gini coefficient	Gini coefficient after tax-base sharing	Percent change	Gini coefficient after aid	Percent change	Shared pool as a percentage of tax capacity	Aid as a percentage of tax capacity
Atlanta	0.17	0.13	−21	0.17	3	10	5
Boston	0.25	0.20	−20	0.19	−22	10	28
Chicago	0.27	0.22	−20	0.17	−36	10	48
Cincinnati	0.36	0.29	−20	0.35	−2	10	13
Cleveland	0.24	0.20	−19	0.22	−9	10	14
Dallas	0.19	0.15	−21	n.a.	n.a.	10	n.a.
Denver	0.21	0.17	−19	0.20	−7	10	14
Detroit	0.21	0.17	−21	0.24	11	10	41
Houston	0.15	0.12	−22	n.a.	n.a.	10	n.a.
Kansas City	0.25	0.20	−21	0.22	−11	10	14
Los Angeles	0.22	0.18	−19	0.15	−33	10	53
Miami	0.21	0.17	−18	0.17	−18	10	30
Milwaukee	0.27	0.22	−18	0.10	−63	10	51
Minneapolis–St. Paul	0.17	n.a.	n.a.	0.17	−3	n.a.	77
New York	0.23	0.18	−22	0.18	−22	10	26
Philadelphia	0.33	0.28	−16	0.26	21	10	26
Phoenix	0.15	0.12	−21	0.09	−41	10	61
Pittsburgh	0.26	0.21	−19	0.25	−4	10	35
Portland	0.15	0.12	−18	0.13	−12	10	12
San Diego	0.11	0.08	−20	0.08	−20	10	49
San Francisco	0.17	0.14	−20	0.13	−27	10	41
Seattle	0.21	0.17	−21	0.20	−7	10	16
St. Louis	0.37	0.29	−20	0.24	−36	10	39
Tampa	0.13	0.11	−19	0.12	−14	10	47
Washington, D.C.	0.22	0.18	−21	0.17	−24	10	18
24 Metro area average	**0.22**	**0.178**	**−20**	**0.182**	**−18**	**10**	**32**

Sources: Various state and local government agencies.
n.a. = Not applicable.

analyses in chapter 2, resources are so skewed in most metropolitan areas that winners are likely to far outnumber losers, even for relatively modest proposals to share the benefits of metropolitan growth. Nor need one appeal to unenlightened self-interest for support of such programs. Properly designed institutional reform, aid, and tax-base-sharing programs offer real efficiency gains in addition to the equity benefits.

The arguments for institutional reform are primarily efficiency arguments. Public services should be designed and financed on a scale commensurate with the scope of their costs and benefits. If they are not, then local and regional interests diverge. Strict local control can result in waste—wasteful tax-base competition, excessive depletion of water and other resources, overconsumption of land, and segregation and concentration of impoverished populations in specific areas, all of which increase the social and public costs of income inequality. A growing body of research implies that suburban growth is tied to the economic health of central cities.[26] Strict local control of land-use planning also increases the physical separation between rich and poor, to the detriment of everyone.[27]

Similarly, aid and tax-base-sharing programs can be designed to enhance the efficiency of both the local and regional economies and the public sector as well as to improve equity. Attenuating the link between growth in particular types of local land uses and the tax base available to produce local services reduces wasteful competition. Providing financial incentives for particular types of development that provide regional benefits but do not generate local fiscal dividends can improve the functioning of regional housing and labor markets.

Reforms in these policy areas need not be radical. All states provide at least some financial support to local governments. A reform agenda can begin with incremental improvements in the way current aid is allocated. Tax-base-sharing programs can be designed to capture a portion of tax-base growth, as occurred in the Twin Cities, rather than part of existing tax bases, allowing regions to reap the efficiency benefits immediately while the redistributive impacts grow more slowly.

Nor does institutional reform necessarily imply designing a regional government from whole cloth. New or existing cooperative arrangements in areas in which the argument for regional control is strongest (water management and transportation, for instance) can be the building blocks for future reform.

26. See Altshuler and others (1999, pp. 34–36).
27. Fischel (1999).

6

LAND-USE REFORM

The central objective of a regional reform agenda is to achieve "smart growth," meaning the close coordination of local land-use planning. Smart growth is an efficient and environmentally friendly pattern of development. It provides people with additional travel, housing, and employment choices and focuses future growth away from rural areas and closer to existing and planned job centers and public facilities.[1] The desire for smart growth and "regionalism" usually reflects dissatisfaction with some aspect of local land-use decisions and the way they are made—from sprawling residential and commercial growth, to automobile-dependent development patterns, lack of affordable housing, or inequitable public investments in building new communities at the edge while allowing existing communities to decline. Because land-use decisions have such a wide-ranging impact on real and perceived quality of life, this area of reform is often the most visible and talked-about part of a regional reform agenda.

With this awareness has come support for local comprehensive and cooperative land-use planning by local governments. In the 1998 elections, for instance, 240 state and local ballot initiatives dealt with land use and growth. Voters approved more than 70 percent of these initiatives.[2] In 1999, 107 of the 139 measures on the ballot passed—nearly 77 percent. In the 2000 elections, growth-related ballot initiatives numbered more than 550, and 72 percent passed. These ballot initiatives, covering a wide range of issues from comprehensive coordinated planning to the establishment of state land trusts to preserve

---

1. Paraphrased from San Diego Association of Governments, "Smart Growth Principles and Designations" (www.sandag.cog.ca.us/region2020/definitions.pdf).
2. Myers (2000).

111

Individual communities can do little to deal with the underlying regional forces contributing to sprawling development patterns.

land and moratoriums on new growth, enabled local governments to use various smart-growth tools. Overall, 44 percent of these initiatives proposed to preserve open space, 26 percent involved infrastructure issues, and 16 percent involved growth management. Of the 94 growth-management ballots, 89 (95 percent) involved local unilateral growth management. Thus while there is great energy for change, much of this burgeoning smart-growth sentiment has been directed toward local action that is unlikely to respond effectively to either the problems stimulating the initiative in the community itself or the larger series of growth-related problems that affect the region as a whole.

The bond between local land-use planning and fiscal health described in chapter 5 creates clear incentives for local governments to pursue local planning objectives that contribute to regional problems such as sprawl. Local growth moratoriums are one good example of this. Because they reflect a purely local response, efforts by individual communities to prevent any further development within their boundaries often end up contributing to sprawl instead of reducing it.

Petaluma, California, provides a case in point. In 1972 that city decided to slow growth by limiting the number of building permits issued annually, and this caused a dramatic increase in housing demand in farther-out Santa Rosa.[3] According to U.S. Census figures, the population of the Santa Rosa area nearly doubled between 1970 and 1980. Actions like this cause regions to become geographically larger than they would be under a plan to accommodate orderly growth. In the end, Santa Rosa had to build new roads and sewers, and residents of Petaluma were forced to deal with the increased traffic through their community.

Individual communities can do little to deal with the underlying regional forces contributing to sprawling development patterns. For instance, communities that impose development moratoriums or other restrictions are often trying to preserve desired features such as open spaces, panoramic views, and quiet and uncongested streets. Many of the places that support growth moratoriums are bedroom-developing communities and the affluent job centers identified in chapter 2 and represent a relatively small percentage of the overall population in a region. Still, the affluence and many amenities found in these places make them a magnet for further development.

While local development moratoriums, slowdowns, or other local restrictions may seem like a good strategy for reducing the negative impacts of increased development, ultimately they only throw develop-

3. Downs (1994).

ment further out to surrounding communities eager to attract additional development to add to their tax base and help them keep up with the costs of their residential growth. In many cases, these surrounding communities are the at-risk, developing, and bedroom-developing communities trying to keep up with their growing costs. Thus such well-intentioned actions by individual communities to halt growth can make the problems associated with sprawl worse instead of better.

EXISTING STATE AND REGIONAL EFFORTS TO MANAGE GROWTH

A number of states and regions have tried to tackle the difficulties associated with purely local planning through a variety of approaches: most notably, statewide planning, legislation empowering or encouraging localities to use various smart-growth tools, and comprehensive planning by regional authorities.

Statewide Comprehensive Planning

At present, 16 states have some sort of land-use planning system in place; 10 of these states actually require comprehensive local planning, while the other 6 encourage it.[4] Many states have attempted to counteract the influences of sprawling development patterns by requiring or encouraging local governments to develop a local land-use plan. While not always explicit, these efforts can also help to reduce problems related to growing social separation. In some cases, these local land-use plans must be coordinated with a comprehensive state land-use plan or with the land-use plans of nearby local governments. They vary in degree of state oversight and local control, and in the consequences for not planning (box 6-1). In many cases, the consequence for not planning is the loss of state capital investments or ineligibility for planning grants.

Each of these states has some sort of system in place that either requires (in 10 of the states) or encourages (in 6 of the states) local jurisdictions to plan comprehensively for growth. Under the most stringent systems, jurisdictions that do not plan face legal sanctions (Hawaii), financial sanctions (Florida), a real estate excise tax (Washington), or loss

4. Minnesota Planning (2000). This document includes a table of 15 states that have statutes requiring local jurisdictions to plan for growth. Pennsylvania passed local land-use planning legislation in June 2000.

BOX 6-1. Model State Comprehensive Planning Programs

Oregon. Concerned about the impact of rapid, unplanned growth on its natural resources and economy, Oregon passed its Land Use Act in 1973. This landmark legislation provides a statewide planning framework, requiring each of the state's 240 cities and 36 counties to adopt a long-range, comprehensive plan for development consistent with the state's 19 planning goals. Among these are strong citizen involvement in the planning process; protection of agricultural, forest, and scenic areas; provision of opportunities for economic development; provision of safe, convenient, and economic transportation; and the establishment of urban growth boundaries (UGBs) around every municipality and the Portland metropolitan area.

Florida. In the early 1970s Florida passed a planning act, but the resulting system has been less successful than Oregon's. It requires all cities to plan and to have infrastructure in place before development occurs. Localities that do not plan face strict financial sanctions, at least on paper. After being amended and refined numerous times, the legislation was finally implemented in 1985. Lack of consistent support from the governor's office and from other elected officials has also hampered the effectiveness the system.

Washington. With its Growth Management Act of 1990, Washington introduced urban growth boundaries—the only state since Oregon to include such strategy in its planning legislation. Washington's program was stronger and more comprehensive than any other state planning system implemented since Oregon's in 1973.

Rhode Island. Rhode Island passed its initial land-use legislation in 1978 and after some refinement passed a stronger Comprehensive Planning and Land Use Regulation Act in 1988. This act requires cities and towns to develop land-use plans that are regularly reviewed by a state agency. The act also has concurrency requirements to ensure adequate infrastructure before starting new development.

Other state programs. In the late 1980s states across the nation renewed their interest in directing localities to plan for growth, beginning with Vermont and Maine in 1988 and Georgia in 1989.

Maine's Comprehensive Planning and Land Use Management Act, which called for a required program, could not be implemented until 1992 for lack of funding. The legislation was then changed to a voluntary program. Georgia's Planning Act, originally an optional program, is now required of all counties and municipalities. In Vermont, localities that choose to plan must meet the state's planning requirements, one of which is to develop plans consistent with state goals.

Connecticut's Conservation and Policies Plan Public Act of 1991 requires cities with a planning commission to plan for growth. In 1992 Maryland passed its Economic Growth, Resource Protection and Planning Act, and New Jersey passed its Communities of Place, Development and Redevelopment Plan, a voluntary program.

Delaware's comprehensive planning program is based on a series of acts passed in the 1990s, including the 1995 Shaping Delaware's Future Act and the 1996 Land Use Planning Act. In 1996 New Hampshire passed legislation calling for cities and towns to plan for growth, but it is one of the few states that does not require plans to conform to state planning goals and guidelines. In 1998 Tennessee passed legislation requiring localities to develop plans that include urban growth boundaries around developing municipalities—the third state to require UGBs.

Smart Growth Wisconsin (1999) came about through the state's budget process. Like most of the other voluntary programs, it provides a planning framework for localities and offers incentives in the form of planning grants. In 2000 Pennsylvania passed Growing Smarter, legislation that will empower cities to establish planning commissions and plan for future growth.

In 1997 Minnesota passed a voluntary pilot program, the Community-Based Planning Act, establishing 11 planning goals and offering limited funds to participating jurisdictions. Although the program is scheduled to sunset in 2001, an effort is under way to make the 11 goals required guidelines for localities that develop comprehensive plans.

of their authority to issue building permits and approve land subdivisions (Oregon) or to make other land-use decisions (Vermont). Some have proved successful and enduring; others are still too new to evaluate. In nearly every case, the plans must be consistent with state goals and completed according to specific guidelines and methods. For the most part, the local plans must be reviewed and approved by a state or other agency.

Smart-Growth Toolbox Legislation

While the drive for statewide comprehensive land-use planning remains a priority in many states,[5] another popular strategy has been to authorize and encourage the use of various smart-growth tools—often through legislation based on model statutes developed by the American Planning Association.[6] The popularity of this strategy is likely due to that fact that it relies on voluntary and incentive-based tools. Today, nearly every state in the union allows for or promotes the use of at least one kind of tool for the smart management of growth.[7]

The overall goal of smart-growth planning is to be prepared for inevitable growth and to be able to enhance the economic development opportunities that come with it. At the same time, smart-growth planning attempts to ensure that new communities are attractive, affordable, and livable; that natural resources will be protected; and that all communities will benefit from the anticipated growth. The idea is not to stop all growth. Indeed, smart-growth planning accepts that growth is inevitable and even desirable—if done correctly and intelligently.[8]

Smart-growth planning accepts that growth is inevitable and even desirable —if it is correctly and intelligently done.

---

5. In the 2000 elections, initiatives were on the ballot in Arizona and Colorado that would have required localities to develop growth-management plans (but both failed). Legislation passed in New Hampshire improved upon the state's 1996 planning legislation.

6. In October 1994, the American Planning Association launched its Growing Smart[SM] initiative. Growing Smart[SM] is a major effort to help states manage change and modernize their planning statutes, many of them 75 years old (American Planning Association [APA] 1998). As part of this effort in 1998, the APA updated its *Growing Smart[SM] Legislative Guidebook: Model Statutes for Planning and the Management of Change*, originally developed and promulgated in 1996. The model statutes have become the basis for extensive new planning legislation nationwide, setting off a widespread smart-growth movement.

7. Sprawl Watch Clearinghouse, www.sprawlwatch.org (November 15, 2000).

8. This definition of smart growth is based on the following sources: Smart Growth America, "Greetings from Smart Growth America," www.smartgrowthamerica.org (November 13, 2000); Urban Land Institute, www.uli.org/pub/pages/a_issues/a_sml4_nepr.htm (November 10); Smart Growth Network, www.smartgrowth.org/information/aboutsg.html (November 13, 2000); O'Neill (1999, p. 3); Katz and Liu (2000, p. 31).

Some of the most common strategies for accomplishing smart growth are to manage the location and timing of growth and development, to protect and preserve land, and to design livable and sustainable communities.

Growth Management. Common growth-management techniques nationwide include the urban growth boundary (UGB), which prevents or limits development outside a designated area;[9] the urban service area, which limits provision of public services (for example, sewerage and water) to a designated area (an urban service area);[10] designated areas where growth will be focused;[11] and concurrency, which requires adequate public infrastructure to be in place before (or at the same time as) development occurs.[12]

9. An *urban growth boundary* is a line that separates urban land from nonurban land. It is a line delineated by a government entity through an assessment of projected growth and the land needed to accommodate that growth for a given period (often 20 years calculated at present growth rates but expandable to accommodate changes in growth projections as they occur). One of the best examples of the use of UGBs is found in Oregon, where, in accordance with the 1973 Oregon Land Use Act, every city and town in the state and the Portland metropolitan region has delineated boundaries, outside of which development is not allowed. Other states that have passed legislation requiring or encouraging all (or nearly all) jurisdictions to create UGBs include Washington (1990) and Tennessee (1998). A number of local governments have acted independently to create UGBs, including Boulder, Colorado; Lexington, Kentucky; Lancaster County, Pennsylvania; Santa Barbara, California; Modesto, California; and 17communities in the San Francisco Bay Area, including San Jose (Sprawl Watch Clearinghouse).

10. An *urban service area* (USA) is an area delineated by a government entity, outside of which urban services (such as sewerage and water) will not be provided. Low-cost infrastructure, with debt service underwritten by a large pool of ratepayers, often makes this system attractive to local officials and the public. A USA is less rigid than a UGB in that it does not *prohibit* development outside the boundary; it only says that the government will not provide services beyond the designated area. Thus if a developer or a city outside the USA provides the necessary services, development can still occur. Examples of urban service areas include the Minneapolis–St. Paul area's metropolitan urban services area (MUSA), established in the 1980s, and, in Florida, Sarasota County's urban service area, established in 1975.

11. An example of this is Maryland's 1997 Smart Growth Areas Act. Instead of drawing a line around the area preferred for development, the Maryland legislation allows counties to designate their own "priority funding areas." These areas are targeted for high-density development and will receive priority over all other areas for funding from the state for infrastructure, economic development, housing, and other projects.

12. An "adequate public facilities requirement" or "concurrency" requires infrastructure to be in place or under construction when new development begins. It encompasses everything from roads, sewerage, and water services to schools and police and fire services. Besides helping to manage the location and timing of development, concurrency requirements protect the region from environmental harm often

These can be effective tools. Misused or used in isolation without complementary policies in the nondeveloping portions of regions, however, they can contribute to low-density dispersed development instead of preventing it. For instance, if an urban service boundary limiting the provision of sewerage is implemented without concurrent regulation of land use beyond the boundary, lower land costs just beyond the boundary may push developers who can bypass the urban service boundary to build housing on private septic systems. This leapfrog development creates the need for larger lots, with enough space for these septic systems, and can greatly expand the size of the new development, destroying farmland and open spaces that might otherwise have been preserved.

Although these lots may be large by urban standards, they are often too small to effectively absorb sewer effluent and can contribute to the pollution of groundwater, rivers, and lakes. If wells are a local source of water, septic systems can pose a serious threat to public health. In the face of uncontrolled growth and the threat of pollution from ineffective septic systems, public sewerage must eventually be installed in any event. The remediation that this requires (digging up roads, lawns, and basements to connect to the new sewer systems) will cost the community and homeowners many times what it would have cost to do it right in the first instance. This leapfrog development creates the fiscal and environmental challenges characteristic of at-risk, low-density communities.

Agricultural Land and Open Space Preservation. As a region grows, pressure inevitably builds to develop prime agricultural lands and coveted open space. According to the American Farmland Trust, about a million acres of land a year are lost to development. Smart-growth planning attempts to protect agricultural lands and open space from development, preserving such areas for future generations. To this end, many states and regions, create agricultural district programs, purchase agriculture conservation easements or development rights through state land trust funds, and allow the transfer of development rights from a rural to an urban location. These land-preservation tools, though well

About a million acres of land are lost to development each year.

---

related to poorly planned septic development. They also save cities money. Montgomery County, Maryland, has had an adequate facilities ordinance in place since 1973. Florida's 1985 Growth Management Act provides one of the strongest concurrency requirements of all statewide planning acts. Other states with some form of concurrency requirement include Washington, Oregon, Rhode Island, New Jersey, and Vermont.

intentioned, are extremely costly and cannot on their own truly change the nature of U.S. development patterns.

Despite intense investment in land trusts by government agencies and foundations, every year sprawl development eats up more land on the edge of metropolitan regions than all these land trusts have saved in 20 years.[13] According to a survey by the Land Trust Alliance, about 4.7 million acres of land have been protected by private land conservation efforts since they began tracking these numbers in 1982.[14] It is difficult to determine how much of this figure relates to metropolitan development and how much to the preservation of largely rural tracts. These numbers, though large, do not come close to compensating for the 20 million acres of agricultural and fragile lands lost to development over the same time period. In the absence of a regional land-use plan that encourages orderly growth, development prevented in one area by preservationists simply relocates to another area that has less political power and organization and probably less fiscal capacity to handle the growth.

New Urbanist Design. A central strategy of smart-growth planning is to create communities that will remain livable well into the future. Sustainable communities are compact, moderate- to high-density developments, planned in a way that minimizes reliance on the automobile (thereby helping to limit air pollution) and on local resources, both natural and man-made. Livable communities are attractive places, where people know their neighbors and can get around easily. People in various income brackets can afford to live there, and they are desirable places to live, work, and play.

Such places may be created through various strategies, often integrated to address multiple issues such as transportation, housing, open space, and employment. These methods include a multimodal transportation system, integrated land-use and transportation planning, new urbanism design standards, high-density housing and employment development along transit corridors, and affordable housing opportunities in all communities.

The Federal Government's Role in Smart Growth

Beginning in the early 1990s, former U.S. Housing and Urban Development Secretary Henry Cisneros advocated that the federal govern-

13. Richmond (1997).
14. Land Trust Alliance (2000).

ment strengthen metropolitan coordination of affordable housing, land use, environmental protection, and transportation. In 1994 President Bill Clinton issued an executive order beginning this process.[15] In September 1998 Vice President Al Gore announced a federal agenda "to help encourage smarter growth and more livable communities all across America."[16] And in 2000 the Congress took an important step toward acting on this new agenda when Republican Senator Lincoln Chafee (R-Rhode Island) introduced legislation to enact the Community Character Act. As reintroduced in the new Congress (S.975), the legislation would make available grants of up to $1 million to individual states to help states revise their land-use plans to incorporate smart growth.

Regional Comprehensive Planning

Two regions—Portland, Oregon (Portland Metro), and Minneapolis–St. Paul (Twin Cities Metropolitan Council)—have vested significant and comprehensive planning powers in a single regional entity. These regional governments are particularly effective because they have the authority to design and implement regional policies regionwide. Both have been granted authority by citizens and their respective state governments to take on crucial service provision and growth-management functions. Portland Metro regulates development patterns through its administration of the state-mandated regional urban growth boundary. Metro uses a tight boundary policy limiting expansion of the urbanized area to implement its transportation, housing, and environmental protection plans. In the Twin Cities, the Metropolitan Council administers a similar policy tool, regulating the expansion of its Metropolitan Urban Service Area through its authority to plan for and permit extensions to the regional sewer system.

These formal powers, complemented by council members' accountability to the governor in Minnesota and directly to the voters in Portland, give these regional governments political leverage that other metropolitan planning organizations (MPOs) and regional councils lack. The 17 governor-appointed members of the Twin Cities Metropolitan Council and the 7 directly elected members of the Portland Metro Council are unaffiliated with local governments and state agencies, whose representatives make up the policy boards of most MPOs. This detachment from the parochial interests of local governments'

15. Clinton (1994).
16. Al Gore, *Brookings Policy Series*, September 2, 1998.

fragmented units gives Metro and the Met Council unique freedom to focus exclusively on regional needs and concerns.[17]

In a number of other places, county governments—either as required by state law or on their own—have engaged in planning activities or worked to coordinate local planning efforts. Long before Maryland instituted its 1992 Economic Growth, Resource Protection and Planning Act, for instance, Montgomery County was conducting comprehensive planning on its own. This affluent suburb of Washington, D.C., has had a planning program in place since the 1920s and is nationally considered a pioneer of comprehensive planning. Its first countywide master plan, adopted in 1957, included several innovative growth-management techniques that are becoming increasingly popular smart-growth tools. They include a concurrency requirement, transit-oriented development, transfer of development rights, preservation of farmland and open space, and a moderately priced dwelling unit ordinance.

AN AGENDA FOR REFORM

Effective regional land-use reform hinges on three elements: coordinated infrastructure planning, a regional housing plan, and regional review and coordination of local planning.

Coordinated Infrastructure Planning

The location and extent of basic infrastructure investments is one of the most important determinants of local and regional land-use patterns. Roads, highways, sewerage and water, and electric utilities (often called growth shapers) all play a major role in opening up land to development that, without them, would be less profitable to developers and landowners. The location and magnitude of these investments also determine whether investment patterns strike a balance between making efficient use of existing infrastructure and expanding infrastructure at the edges of the region, drawing people and resources out.

For most regions, basic infrastructure is provided at the local level by individual units of governments or special districts set up to provide this infrastructure to a small number of cities, with little thought to regional networks. Similarly, cities or counties often plan local roadways

17. Although the Twin Cities' appointed council has periodically been captured by developers close to Minnesota governors, it nevertheless represents a huge improvement over uncoordinated local government decisions.

without trying to fit them into the regional system that would make public transportation a viable option for getting from one area of the region to another. Piecemeal provision of the basic infrastructure that guides regional investment and development patterns is a major contributor to inefficient, sprawling development, congested roadways, and environmental strains.

Regional provision and planning of any type of infrastructure helps guide development in more efficient and equitable ways. Coordinating this planning with other basic infrastructure investments amplifies benefits by ensuring that these investments do not work in opposing directions. The Metropolitan Council of the Twin Cities, for instance, was created in the 1970s to provide a regional sewerage system, maintain a network of regional parks, and plan and operate public transportation throughout the region.

Regionalizing infrastructure provision and planning can help reduce per capita costs throughout the region by creating an orderly pattern of development. Transportation investments are an especially important part of regional infrastructure that should be coordinated with other investments. Giving a regional agency authority over transportation investments, instead of vesting it solely in the state Department of Transportation, is one way to help achieve this goal.

Some of the more common tools used to coordinate infrastructure planning are urban growth boundaries, urban service areas, concurrency requirements, and provision by a regional authority. However, as noted, these policies cannot work unless combined with regulation of undeveloped areas to avoid leapfrog development and overuse of technologies (like septic systems) with hidden long-run costs. For instance, the Twin Cities Metropolitan Council combines its urban service area with minimum size limitations for lots in the areas outside the boundary. The objective is to limit new development beyond the boundary to lot sizes that are environmentally sound (for septic systems) and that are large enough to allow infill development at a later date when the boundary is expanded. Ineffective regulation of housing densities beyond the urban services boundary could lead to the development of large tracts of land in two-acre lots with septic systems, for instance, a pattern both environmentally unsound and poorly suited for future infill development.

Regionalizing infrastructure planning and provision helps guide development in more efficient and equitable ways.

Regional Housing Plan

The objective of a regional housing plan is to provide balance in housing choices within every community of the region. To do this, metropolitan areas need to increase the construction of entry-level housing in developing suburban areas and at the same time increase upper-income housing opportunities in the region's core.

Affordable housing allows individuals to live close to new suburban jobs, divorced mothers to remain in their children's school district, and old people to remain in their communities and close to friends as their life situation changes. At least one large experiment demonstrates that when poor individuals are freed from poor neighborhoods and provided with such opportunities, their lives can change dramatically. Under a 1976 court order in the case of *Hills* v. *Gautreaux,* thousands of single-parent black families living in Chicago public housing have been provided with housing opportunities in predominantly middle-class suburbs.[18] Under the consent decree in a fair housing lawsuit originally brought in 1966, more than 5,000 low-income households have been given housing opportunities in the Chicago area. By random assignment, more than half of these households moved to affluent suburbs, while the other participants moved to neighborhoods that were poor. The pool of *Gautreaux* families thus provides a strong sample to study the effects of suburban housing opportunities on very poor residents.

In-depth studies of the *Gautreaux* families established, first, that the low-income women who moved to the suburbs "clearly experienced improved employment and earnings, even though the program provided no job training or placement services."[19] Very rapidly after the moves, the suburbanites were about 15 percent more likely to be employed.[20] The children of the suburban movers dropped out of high school less frequently than the city movers (5 percent vs. 20 percent), maintained similar grades despite higher standards in suburban schools, were significantly more likely to be on a college track (40.3 percent vs. 23.5 percent), and went to college at a rate of 54 percent, compared with 21 percent for those who stayed in the city.[21] In terms of employment, 75 percent of the suburban youth had jobs compared with 41 percent in the city. Moreover, the suburban youth had a significant advantage in wages and were more likely to have a high-quality job with benefits.

18. *Hills* v. *Gautreaux*, 425 US 284 (1976).
19. Rosenbaum and Popkin (1991). For details of this research, see also Rosenbaum, Kulieke, and Rubinowitz (1988); Rosenbaum and Kaufman (1991); Rosenbaum and Popkin (1991); and Rosenbaum and others (1991).
20. Rosenbaum and Popkin (1991).
21. Rosenbaum and Kaufman (1991, p. 4).

Also, 90 percent of the suburban youth were either working or in school compared with 74 percent of the city youth.[22]

Most regional housing efforts have focused heavily on constructing affordable housing in the core of regions. For housing opportunities to truly be expanded, however, middle- and upper-class households also have to be brought back into the city through neighborhood revitalization or gentrification. Attracting middle-class households into a struggling community helps provide a needed tax base, and these families, through their presence, support and demand an appropriate level of public and private services.

At the same time, it is important to recognize that revitalization and gentrification require low-income (and often minority) families to relocate elsewhere.[23] Without adequate housing opportunities in other parts of the region, these families have little opportunity to escape the social and economic stress of their neighborhoods and can end up in a worse neighborhood than the one they have left. This phenomenon has led minority and affordable housing advocates to associate gentrification with economic and racial segregation and fight bitterly against efforts to attract middle- and upper-class families into struggling neighborhoods.[24]

Promoting the supply of affordable housing in suburban areas requires three complementary policies: reduced barriers to affordable housing, fair-share requirements to ensure that all municipalities contribute to a pool of affordable housing, and financial assistance for very low-income housing. Regional housing markets are also highly segregated by race, and any remedies in this dimension must necessarily also

Promoting affordable housing in suburban areas requires three complementary policies: barrier reduction, fair-share requirements, and financial assistance.

22. Rosenbaum and Kaufman (1991, pp. 5–7). The acceptance of these poor black families in affluent, predominantly white suburbs was not painless or immediate. At the outset, about 52 percent of the suburban movers reported incidents of racial harassment, compared with 23 percent in the city. However, these incidents rapidly decreased over time. Interestingly, both the suburban and city movers reported similar amounts of neighbor support and assistance and essentially no difference in the degree of contact with neighbors. The suburban movers were actually slightly more likely to have friends in their new neighborhoods than the city movers. The suburban movers had more than two times the number of white friends than the city movers and slightly fewer black friends. Furthermore, over time, the degree of integration continued for suburban movers, and resegregation did not occur.

23. See powell (forthcoming), who cites Maureen Kennedy and Paul Leonard, "Dealing with Neighborhood Change: A Primer on Gentrification and Policy Choices," paper prepared for the Brookings Institution Center on Urban and Metropolitan Policy and Policy Link (http://www.brook.edu/urban/gentrification/gentrificationexsum.htm).

24. powell (forthcoming).

be regional. Therefore an important fourth component of a regional housing plan is a policy to maintain stable integration in situations where communities are becoming naturally diverse and to eliminate racial discrimination in other suburban housing markets.

Barrier Reduction. A regional strategy to reduce zoning, financial, and other barriers to the development of affordable housing is the logical first step toward the goal of mixed-income housing in every community within a region. Removing discriminatory, nonmarket-oriented barriers is an essential first step of developing a regional strategy: it costs little, can make a big difference in the availability of affordable housing, and is philosophically difficult for opponents to attack. It is a deregulatory step that the building community can support, actively or passively. The housing industry has long argued that regulatory barriers such as large lot sizes, prohibitions on multifamily housing, and assorted fees hurt the natural marketplace for affordable housing. A barrier-reduction strategy is also a way to build an early relationship with an important private sector actor in land development.

Fair-Share Affordable Housing. Fair-share housing requirements ensure that all places contribute to the regionwide supply of affordable housing. Without them, a few communities are likely to continue to provide a disproportionate share of housing for moderate and lower-income households—a practice that ultimately harms the entire region. Fair-share housing programs allocate to each city a part of the region's affordable housing, on the basis of the jurisdiction's population, previous efforts to create affordable housing, and job availability. An effective fair-share housing program seeks a sustainable balance of lower-cost and more expensive housing in all areas of the region, whether they are greenfield suburban sites or gentrifying neighborhoods. The Massachusetts fair-share housing program ("Chapter 40B"), for example, reduces barriers to affordable housing in all cities and allows a Zoning Board of Appeals to override local zoning codes when less than 10 percent of a community's housing stock is listed on the state's 40B subsidized housing inventory. In the past 30 years, more than 25,000 units of housing have been built as a result of this legislation.[25]

Regional Housing Fund. Even with fair-share housing programs and barrier reductions, the market is still unlikely to provide housing for

25. Citizens' Housing and Planning Association (1999).

very low-income families. A regional housing fund can help ensure that adequate low-income housing is constructed and that existing housing is property maintained. Such funds could also be used for rental assistance for market-rate housing.

Measures to Support Stable Integration

Black and Hispanic middle-class populations seeking opportunity in the suburbs are comparable to those already living there in most measurable ways. However, as noted earlier, they are often steered to certain suburbs already on the path of decline. To help regions achieve and maintain racially integrated communities, states must also take active measures to detect and fight discrimination. States may provide or contract with a housing-testing agency to constantly monitor the housing market for vestiges of discrimination and to enforce severe penalties for sellers or landlords who discriminate on the basis of race and for real estate agents who steer black or Hispanic buyers or sellers.

Given the reality of economic and racial segregation, it is particularly important to stabilize communities in the midst of racial transition. Thus achieving racially integrated neighborhoods that are viable and stable over time should be a goal of metropolitan comprehensive planning. Strong tools will be needed to do this.

Several cities have taken steps to maintain their communities' stability and diversity as they begin to change. These include some of the nation's older suburbs, such as Shaker Heights, Cleveland Heights, Ohio; Oak Park, Illinois; and Southfield, Michigan. Often called managed integration, these programs encourage communities not only to acknowledge and value their diversity, but also to track social and racial changes as they occur in their housing markets and to aggressively market local housing to middle-class and white families upon reaching a certain ratio of poor and minority households to the middle class or white. This helps maintain social and racial balance and prevents resegregation and disinvestment.[26] As stability is attained, normal marketing resumes to families of any race. Though controversial, targeted

Racially integrated neighborhoods that are viable and stable over time should be a goal of metropolitan comprehensive planning. It will require strong tools.

26. Keating (1994) talks about the success and failure of various suburban communities in managing to remain economically stable at the onset of racial change. He compares communities such as East Cleveland, which underwent a rapid dramatic downward movement when it resegregated from white to black, to the adjacent community in Shaker Heights, which practiced a managed integration system and remained stable. Similarly, in the Chicago region, places such as Oak Park have maintained integration and stability while surrounding communities, such as Maywood, have undergone rapid resegregation and disinvestments.

marketing to families of a specific race has been upheld by federal courts as a prointegrative strategy.[27]

A variety of financial instruments are logical complements to managed integration programs. These may include low-rate housing loans for blacks seeking to move into white areas and for whites seeking to move into black areas or a regional or state fund to guarantee housing prices in transitional neighborhoods.

Regional Review and Coordination of Local Comprehensive Planning

Much land-use planning and infrastructure are best provided at the local level. Therefore comprehensive, regional land-use reform requires a coordinated framework in which local governments develop comprehensive land-use plans that are consistent with state or regional planning goals. Ideally, these goals are clearly laid out and applicable to all communities within the region, and any local plans and policies inconsistent with these goals may be challenged in court or in special forums created for such adjudication. This is consistent with Oregon's Land Use Plan, for instance, which outlines 19 goals that local plans must address. Similarly, Florida's Growth Management Act covers 25 "goal areas"; Maryland's 1992 legislation outlines 7 "visions"; Rhode Island's plan includes 11 general goals; and Wisconsin's new planning legislation includes 9 such elements. Most other statewide comprehensive planning programs also include a set of goals to be addressed, including Minnesota's community-based planning pilot program, which outlines 11 planning goals that participating communities must consider.

All local plans should be coordinated among participating communities within a region. The plans should be reviewed for consistency with state- or regionally defined goals and guidelines. There should be strong penalties for noncompliance, such as financial sanctions or the loss of authority to make land-use decisions and to grant building permits. As already mentioned, these are all components of current planning requirements in many states.

In addition, states could revise their planning statutes to include important smart-growth planning tools such as those included in the American Planning Association model. Metropolitan regions and their communities should be encouraged to use these tools to achieve the goals of the land-use planning framework. For example, a fund for cleaning up and redeveloping polluted brownfields can be used to

27. Keating (1994, p. 221).

126

achieve the goal of urban revitalization, a moderately priced dwelling unit ordinance can promote mixed-income housing in all communities, and a purchase of agricultural conservation easement (PACE) program can protect farmland and open space. This comprehensive regional planning system would be most effective if, in each region, the plan were integrated with a regional fiscal equity system such as tax-base sharing and operated under an elected metropolitan planning organization (see chapter 2).

Of all the statewide land-use plans currently in place, Oregon's has the longest track record and has been the most successful in creating stability, equity, and sustainability. The debate about land-use planning throughout the country is extremely positive and the various solutions that are being proposed provide new and important models for the way growth management can work. However, the Oregon model—also used in general terms by Florida, Rhode Island, Maine, Washington, and Maryland   remains the most effective effort to date.[28]

An important aspect of the Oregon model is that a state or regional entity has the authority to review local plans for consistency with state or regional guidelines and to suggest revision of any inconsistencies. This entity also has the power to withhold approval from regional plans, which prevents the municipality from receiving beneficial services such as regional roads, sewerage, or other aid from state and federal governments. The same entity could also coordinate local transportation, utility regulation, environmental protection, and activities of other governmental units that have a regional significance. This would ensure that all state agencies' actions within the region are consistent with regional plans, local plans, and other agency decisions.

28. Porter (1997, p. 251).

CHAPTER 7

METROPOLITAN GOVERNANCE REFORM

U.S. regions need a forum to discuss and resolve the growing inter-related problems of central cities, at-risk and bedroom-developing communities, and affluent job centers. They cannot address these by themselves or in competition with each other. Many recognized this even before World War II and took some steps toward regional cooperation through annexation and consolidation, which can still be seen to some degree. What complicates matters today, however, is a strong local identity and a difficult legal terrain.

Every large U.S. region has a metropolitan government, the metropolitan planning organization mandated by federal law and created by an act of state law. These structures range from full-service regional governments to weak entities in the thrall of state highway departments. For 50 years, with a brief interruption in the 1980s, Congress has been expanding the reach, authority, and visibility of these metropolitan governments. By the millennium, these governments were allocating hundreds of millions, often billions, of federal and state transportation dollars and in many ways, if only by default, were planning the physical if not social future of their regions. As this chapter shows, it is time for these important organizations to become more accountable to the cities and citizens of their regions and ultimately become stronger forums for resolving difficult metropolitan issues.

Persistent urban poverty, increasing traffic congestion, and the relentless pressure to develop open space and farmland have made the public uneasy about urban growth. Many are demanding action from their representatives in local, state, and national government.[1] Because

---

1. According to a recent national survey, 26 percent of urban and suburban residents cite urban sprawl as their community's worst problem—more than any

of the fragmented nature of governance in America's metropolitan regions, however, local representatives are ill-equipped to meet regional challenges. Planners and politicians are torn between mitigating the localized effects of regional problems and addressing the common concerns and long-range interests of their larger metropolitan areas. This governance dilemma is particularly acute in America's largest urban regions, where the physical boundaries of elected and accountable units of government do not match the regional scale of equity problems and major service delivery and infrastructure needs.

This fragmentation of metropolitan areas into many local governments is not only a barrier to effective growth management, but also a leading cause of social separation, sprawl, and fiscal disparities within those areas.[2] In regions without a shared tax base or dominant central city, competing jurisdictions often duplicate infrastructure and services that could be provided more cost effectively in older suburbs and central cities. Duplication of services and infrastructure in turn contributes to fiscal, social, and environmental stresses in the at-risk communities at the core of metropolitan regions as well as in those at the edge. Zoning incentives to attract high-value residential and commercial development result in exclusive neighborhoods, segregated by race and income. Meanwhile, the new office and commercial centers in suburban edge cities siphon customers and resources from established business districts and allow the commuter zone to expand, further inducing sprawl.

Growing awareness of these inefficiencies and the inequities fostered by governmental structures has led to a resurgence of support for some form of regional governance. Evidence of the continued interdependence between cities and their surrounding suburbs and of the heightened importance of regional efficiency and productivity in the competitive global economy provides additional economic incentives for cities to abandon parochial laws and attitudes in favor of collaboration and, ultimately, structural reform of government systems.

FRAGMENTATION OF METROPOLITAN GOVERNANCE

The population explosion in suburban communities over the past several decades has led some commentators to suggest that "the" suburbs

---

other traditional local concern including crime, education, and the economy (survey conducted in February 2000 by the Princeton Survey Research Associates for the Pew Center for Civic Journalism: www.pewcenter.org/doingcj/research/r_ST2000nat1.html).

2. Rusk (1993, 1999).

have become politically, socially, and economically independent from the central cities—unaffected by the concentrated poverty, aging infrastructure, and high crime that plagues many of the nation's largest cities. Despite the perceived independence of "the" suburbs, there is mounting evidence and a growing awareness among regional leaders that the fortunes of central cities and their surrounding suburbs are closely intertwined. Empirical research shows that suburban home value appreciation, income growth, and population growth all depend on income growth in central cities.[3] Even the price of office space in suburban edge cities varies with the price of office space in central cities.[4] Moreover, cities that include a larger share of the population of their entire metropolitan area are more prosperous.

Despite the growing evidence of their interdependence, many regions become even more fragmented with growth and expansion into new communities. Instead of fostering cooperative planning that benefits the entire region, this fragmentation has made it more difficult for metropolitan areas to address regional problems such as concentrated poverty, social and fiscal disparities, traffic congestion, and urban sprawl. With hundreds of local governments, each making its own land-use and investment decisions, there is little sense of how all of the pieces fit together into a comprehensive whole.

Measures of Fragmentation

A common measure of regional fragmentation is the number of local governments per 100,000 residents. Table 7-1 summarizes the number of local governments with land-use planning powers for the 25 largest U.S. metropolitan regions. The most fragmented regions are found in older metropolitan areas of the Midwest and the Northeast. Pittsburgh tops the list, with nearly 18 local governments for every 100,000 residents. Western and southeastern metro areas are less fragmented, with metros in California, Arizona, and Florida all having fewer than 2 local governments per 100,000 residents.

The total number of government units per metropolitan area and per 100,000 residents is a good general indicator of political fragmentation in urban regions, but these measures do not reflect variations in the size and influence of central cities, which are important elements of regional reform. One good measure of geopolitical fragmentation captures the influence of central cities in the political geography of

There is mounting evidence and growing awareness that the fortunes of central cities and their surrounding suburbs are closely intertwined.

3. Voith (1995).
4. Savitch (1993).

TABLE 7-1. Political Fragmentation in the 25 Largest Metropolitan Areas

Metropolitan area	Counties	Municipalities and townships	Total local governments	Local governments per 100,000 residents
Pittsburgh	6	412	418	17.7
Minneapolis–St. Paul	13	331	344	12.3
St. Louis	12	300	312	12.2
Cincinnati	13	222	235	12.2
Kansas City	11	171	182	10.6
Cleveland	8	259	267	9.2
Philadelphia	14	428	442	7.4
Milwaukee	5	108	113	6.9
Chicago	13	554	567	6.6
Detroit	10	325	335	6.2
Boston	14	282	296	5.1
Dallas	12	184	196	4.2
Portland	8	79	87	4.1
New York	27	729	756	3.8
Atlanta	20	107	127	3.5
Denver	7	67	74	3.2
Houston	8	115	123	2.8
Seattle	6	88	94	2.8
Tampa	4	35	39	1.8
San Francisco	10	104	114	1.7
Miami	2	55	57	1.6
Phoenix	2	32	34	1.2
Los Angeles	5	177	182	1.2
San Diego	1	18	19	0.7
Washington, D.C.	33	125	158	2.2

Source: U.S. Census Bureau.

their metropolitan areas.[5] It is the total number of local governments per 10,000 people divided by the share of the total metropolitan population living in the central city. Regions where the central city is declining in population in relation to other metropolitan communities have a high geopolitical fragmentation index. Metropolitan areas in

5. Ziegler and Brunn (1980).

Northeastern and North central states have the highest geopolitical fragmentation indexes, a sign that people who can afford housing elsewhere are abandoning the central city for surrounding suburban communities. Southern and Western metropolitan areas, with larger central cities and higher proportions of people living in these cities, have relatively low levels of geopolitical fragmentation.

Table 7-2, using data from the 1997 Census of Governments, shows much the same pattern. Pittsburgh has the most severe geopolitical fragmentation, with more than 400 local governments and less than 15 percent of the population living in the central city. St. Louis, Cincinnati, Minneapolis–St. Paul, and Cleveland also have high indexes. Southeastern and Western metropolitan areas such as Portland, Seattle, Denver, and Houston have much lower indexes, mainly because they have relatively few local governments.

TOWARD MORE EFFECTIVE REGIONAL GOVERNANCE

Recognizing fragmentation's negative effects, a number of regions have acted to bring a greater regional focus to local governance. These efforts center on three main strategies: annexation, consolidation, and special-purpose regional bodies such as the metropolitan planning organization. Each of these strategies has had some success in dealing with the regional pitfalls of fragmentation. But experience has also shown that these strategies are limited in their ability to reduce social separation, sprawl, and fiscal inequities over the long term.

Annexation

Annexation refers to the power granted to cities in some states to expand their boundaries to capture undeveloped land, unincorporated areas, or existing communities. Traditionally, cities have used annexation to expand their local tax base, while providing needed sewerage, water, public safety, and other city services to surrounding areas. Annexation as such can reduce the negative effects of fragmentation by reducing the number of local governments within a region and ensuring greater uniformity in the public services and infrastructure provided for city residents.

Liberal annexation policies before 1900 allowed central cities to regionalize their governments, but by the turn of the century there was growing political opposition to the process. With increased migration and immigration to cities, class and ethnicity began to sharply divide

TABLE 7-2. **Geopolitical Fragmentation in the 25 Largest Metropolitan Areas**

Metropolitan area	Total local governments	Population living in central city (%)	Geopolitical fragmentation index
Pittsburgh	418	14.8	12.0
St. Louis	312	13.8	8.8
Cincinnati	235	18.0	6.7
Minneapolis–St. Paul	344	22.4	5.5
Cleveland	267	17.1	5.4
Boston	296	9.6	5.3
Detroit	335	18.4	3.3
Kansas City	182	34.6	3.1
Atlanta	127	11.4	3.1
Philadelphia	442	24.7	3.0
Chicago	567	31.7	2.1
Milwaukee	113	36.1	1.9
Dallas	196	23.1	1.8
Portland	87	23.2	1.8
Seattle	94	15.9	1.8
Miami	57	10.5	1.5
San Francisco	114	11.1	1.5
Denver	74	21.9	1.5
Tampa	39	13.0	1.4
Washington, D.C.	158	17.1	1.3
New York	756	37.3	1.0
Houston	123	41.1	0.7
Los Angeles	182	23.0	0.5
Phoenix	34	42.1	0.3
San Diego	19	43.7	0.2

Source: U.S. Census Bureau.

American society. Meanwhile, urban areas were expanding so rapidly that inflexible governments could not adjust and keep pace. Recognizing the growing differences between themselves and central city residents, the suburban middle class began to push for the creation of their own towns and cities. With growing support for autonomous local government, political pressure mounted for changes in state laws to facilitate incorporation and limit cities' powers to annex new territories.

In the ensuing rush to incorporate, the major cities of the Northeast and North central regions were "hemmed in" by new suburban towns and cities. With the accompanying limitations on their powers to annex, central cities found they were no longer able to regionalize their government structures. Thus began the era of fragmented regional governance.

Houston, Texas, provides an example of the aggressive use of annexation powers. With a consistent expansion policy, Houston annexed many of the new suburban communities that developed on its fringes throughout the twentieth century. Between 1960 and 1990, the city increased its total land area by 65 percent, adding 212 square miles, and has annexed more territory since. Although Houston lost 26 percent of its share of the metropolitan area population over the same period, it has retained influence in the region. It still has 49 percent of the metropolitan population, a larger share than in any other central city in this study.

Despite the increasing share of the metropolitan population living outside its jurisdiction, aggressive annexation has allowed the city of Houston to secure and maintain a strong position within the larger functional region. It has been able to address issues of regional competitiveness by securing representation and leadership roles in regional bodies from the Metropolitan Transit Authority to the Port of Houston Authority. In another show of strength, the city mobilized prominent business leaders and regional resources for the construction of the Intercontinental Airport (IAH) in the 1960s.

Although Texas annexation statutes remain liberal, significant expansion of Houston's boundaries may no longer be politically feasible. Several recent annexations have been challenged in court, including the 1997 annexation of Kingman, an affluent Houston suburb. This annexation met with resistance from Kingman's 55,000 mostly white residents as well as from Houston's African American community, concerned about the potential dilution of its voting power within city limits. This latter factor has proved a significant hurdle for the regional reform movement—particularly in metropolitan areas where minorities make up a large part of the central city population.

Consolidation

Multijurisdictional consolidation is another method that has been used to regionalize government in several American metropolitan areas. Consolidation means joining multiple jurisdictions into one larger jurisdiction. In most cases, consolidation occurs when a city joins with its county and all of its cities. Like annexation, consolidation is contingent on individual state laws. By combining several independent municipalities into one local government, consolidation can help to eliminate wasteful competition between individual cities, promote coordinated land-use and transportation planning, avoid duplication of public services, and efficiently provide capital-intensive infrastructure and services.

Whereas annexation consists of incremental expansion of central city boundaries and influence, consolidation immediately unites cities with surrounding areas, many of which have separate local governments of their own. But these independent cities are often fiercely protective of their autonomy, and minority and other residents of central cities oppose consolidation, fearing dilution of their voting power. Such opposition has limited the number of consolidations in the United States.[6]

The most striking recent example of consolidation comes from Indianapolis. The 1970 merger between the city of Indianapolis and surrounding Marion County, Indiana, stands as a unique 30-year experiment with local government structural reform. Through this consolidation, Indianapolis has received several important benefits, beginning with higher per capita income.[7] It also has a stronger tax base from additional commercial and office space, and greater borrowing power.[8] In addition, consolidation has concentrated land-use planning and zoning powers, allowing for more coordinated and orderly development.

Despite the conspicuous gains since the 1970 restructuring of local governance in central Indiana, the potential for equitable and efficient regional reform has not been fully realized. The political compromises used to gain approval of the reforms offer evidence of the pitfalls and limitations of consolidation as a means of regionalizing government. As in Houston, the architects of the structural reform isolated the expansion of central city political boundaries from the heated and polarized issue of school district boundaries by excluding all school districts from the new Unigov jurisdiction. Also left unconsolidated were local police and fire departments, court systems, hospitals, poverty alleviation pro-

6. Of the 22 city/county consolidations approved since 1921, only 3 involved central cities with populations larger than 250,000 (Indianapolis, Indiana; Nashville, Tennessee; and Jacksonville, Florida). See Altshuler and others (1999).

7. The 1990 per capita income of the Unigov city was $14,478 compared with $13,485 for residents of the old city. Rusk (1994, p. 2).

8. David Rusk suggests that with a less stable, lower-income population, the old city of Indianapolis would today have a relatively low A1 general obligation bond rating, while the current Unigov city benefits from an AAA rating (Rusk 1994).

grams, and local property tax bases—all still administered by township governments and special districts. Without comprehensive consolidation in these areas, the Unigov reform has done little to directly address intraregional equity concerns.

Still, steps such as those taken by Houston and Indianapolis provide an institutional framework that enables necessary regional reforms and paves the way for further structural changes, including the creation of an elected metropolitan governing body or substantial policy changes. Overall, evidence from Indianapolis, Houston, and other "elastic" cities in the United States suggests that annexation and consolidation cannot fully address many of the regional challenges facing metropolitan areas, but they are steps in the right direction.

A measure of central city elasticity, quantifying the degree to which central cities have been able to expand and capture new growth in the region, was developed by David Rusk, former mayor of Albuquerque, New Mexico.[9] An individual metropolitan area's elasticity for the period 1950–90 is a relative score, based on the central city's population density in 1950 (a measure of the central cities' potential to capture new growth within existing boundaries through increased density) and the percentage increase in the area inside central city boundaries due to annexation of new territory, or consolidation with other jurisdictions (most often counties).[10]

Table 7-3 shows Rusk's findings for the 25 largest metropolitan regions in the United States. The metros with higher elasticity (a greater ability to expand their boundaries and capture new growth) were primarily in Western areas with relatively few local governments and little political fragmentation. Older Midwestern and Northeastern metros, where annexation powers are usually weaker and central cities are hemmed in by suburbs outside their borders, had much lower elasticity in Rusk's measures.

Evidence from Houston, Indianapolis, and other "elastic" cities suggests that annexation and consolidation are steps in the right direction.

Metropolitan Planning Organizations

Responsible for planning and programming transportation investments, metropolitan planning organizations are the most widespread form of regional governance in the United States today. MPOs were created by the U.S. Congress in the early 1970s to address the growing

9. Rusk (1993).

10. For the purposes of interregional comparison, a city's relative rank (among sample cities) for initial population density is multiplied by its relative rank for boundary expansion, producing a composite score for relative elasticity (Rusk 1993, p. 53).

TABLE 7-3. **Relative Elasticity of Selected Central Cities, 1950–90**

Hyper	High	Medium	Low	Zero
Houston	Dallas	Tampa	Atlanta	Cincinnati
San Diego	Phoenix	Kansas City	Seattle	Miami
		Denver		Milwaukee
		Portland		Chicago
				Minneapolis
				Baltimore
				Philadelphia
				San Francisco
				Cleveland
				Pittsburgh
				Washington, D.C.
				Detroit
				St. Louis
				Boston
				New York

Source: Rusk (1993).

transportation challenges in metropolitan regions. Most of these organizations took the form of a council or association of locally elected officials and representatives of state and regional agencies.

MPOs slowly gained prominence in regional affairs during the 1990s—in large part because of the quasi-governmental authority vested in them by the Intermodal Surface Transportation Efficiency Act (ISTEA-1991) and the Transportation Efficiency Act for the Twenty-First Century (TEA-21, 1998). Under ISTEA and TEA-21, MPOs' primary responsibilities were expanded to identify long-range needs and to program state and federal investments to ensure that regional transportation systems are efficient, integrated, and multimodal. Given broad powers to guide regional growth through long-range transportation planning and the allocation of federal transportation funds to individual jurisdictions, the MPOs in America's 25 largest metropolitan areas are, in a very real sense, special-purpose regional governing bodies.[11]

11. In two notable cases, Portland and the Twin Cities, designated MPOs function as multiple-purpose or comprehensive regional governments.

However, despite their ability to approve billion-dollar highway and transportation plans, MPOs are not directly accountable to voters and do not always make their transportation investments with social separation, sprawl, and fiscal inequities in mind. Furthermore, although transportation infrastructure investments have an enormous impact on land-use and development patterns, MPOs do not have the authority to coordinate these investments in a comprehensive, region-focused manner. Without broader authority and a mandate to address these assorted issues comprehensively, MPOs, as currently structured, are limited in what they can accomplish on regional concerns.

Several regional councils and associations designated as MPOs have, either by state mandate or through their own initiative, taken on a myriad of other functions, attempting to fill the void in regional governance created by political fragmentation. Some of the most common duties taken on by MPO staff include air quality conformity planning, local and regional economic development initiatives, land-use plan review and coordination, rideshare services (carpool programming), and regional demographic and economic forecasting.[12] Like other MPOs, Portland's Metro and the Twin Cities' Metropolitan Council prepare long-range transportation plans and perform other transportation-planning functions. In contrast to other MPOs, however, the regional governments in Portland and the Twin Cities have been able to advance both efficiency and equity reforms at a regional scale because of their land-use plan review and coordination powers.

MPOs in other regions have also succeeded in pushing for coordination of regional investments. In the Seattle area, the Puget Sound Regional Council (PSRC) maintains the region's growth-management plan in addition to its transportation investments. In keeping with the council's mission, the PSRC has taken pains to involve the public in choosing between land-use and growth alternatives instead of simply declaring specific transportation investments.[13]

12. As required under the Amendments to the Clean Air Act (1990), transportation plans for each region must provide for infrastructure and resulting emissions patterns that will allow "attainment" of federal standards for maximum levels of certain air pollutants

13. The PSRC has gained prominence and visibility in the Seattle region because of its outreach to the business community, civic leaders, and citizens at large throughout the 10-year development of its VISION 2020 growth-management plan. This exemplary public involvement process, and the council's efforts to meet regional needs from demographic and economic forecasting to economic development planning, have solidified its role within the Greater Seattle region.

The PSRC and counterpart organizations in San Diego (SANDAG), Los Angeles (Southern California Association of Governments, SCAG), and Denver (DRCOG) are models of the ideal MPO envisioned in the ISTEA and TEA-21 legislation. All of these MPOs conduct limited, voluntary land-use and growth-management planning in addition to their transportation planning duties. They also have authority under state mandate to review the land-use and transportation plans of local jurisdictions to ensure they are coordinated and comply with state goals and laws regarding growth management, smart growth, and air quality. More important, these councils and associations of governments are much more inclusive and democratic than other MPOs. All have provisions for weighted voting or representation. SCAG has the most proportionally representative board structure, with a council composed of one county supervisor from each county and one representative from each of 64 distinct districts (each of equal size, with approximately 200,000 residents).[14]

Also crucial for implementing incremental reform, the planning region of each of these prominent MPOs encompasses most of the population and territory in their respective metropolitan areas. In the six-county Greater Los Angeles Region, the SCAG planning area covers 38,000 square miles and contains more than 95 percent of the metropolitan area's population.[15] (SCAG's territory is more than four times more extensive than the next largest MPO planning area, Maricopa AOG, 9,226 square miles.) Their democratic structures, effective planning, and growing regional significance put these MPOs in an excellent position to take on greater responsibility for regional governance through structural reform.

FEDERAL SUPPORT FOR REGIONAL PLANNING

Federal support of regional planning goes back a long way. As part of the New Deal, the Public Works Administration moved to institutionalize metropolitan regional planning by making federal infrastructure aid contingent upon cooperative planning by local governments. This

14. See the Southern California Association of Governments at http://www.scag.ca.gov.

15. See 2000 Profiles of Metropolitan Planning Organizations (Washington, D.C.: AMPO, May 2000).

arrangement set a precedent for federal involvement in regional affairs and the requirement for local government cooperation and planning.[16]

In the postwar period, there has been a strong movement to increase regional coordination at the federal level through a series of acts from the Departments of Housing and Urban Development and Transportation. Progress has been consistent, despite a brief interruption during the 1980s. Even while Newt Gingrich was Speaker of the House, Congress consistently expanded its emphasis on regional governance.

In the postwar period, there has been a strong movement to increase regional coordination at the federal level.

The Early Years: 1950–73. Throughout the second half of the twentieth century, the urban-regional planning organizations and the planning process itself were defined and redefined by each major federal act dealing with urban and transportation policy. Federal support for metropolitan planning increased in the postwar years, reaching a peak in the 1970s, when the powers and composition of MPOs were formally addressed in the Federal-Aid Highway Act of 1973. A series of legislative acts, focusing on housing and transportation, marked the years leading up to formation of MPOs in the 1970s and provided the framework for metropolitan planning and incentives for cooperation among local governments in regional infrastructure investments.

Housing Act of 1954. Section 701 of the Housing Act of 1954 marked the first attempt to authorize federal funding for local and regional planning. Available to state agencies, cities, and other municipalities with more than 50,000 residents, the 701 planning grants gave many cities and counties an incentive to create planning departments and initiate formal planning processes. In several regions, local governments formed joint metropolitan or regional planning commissions, which used the federal funds to plan major regional infrastructure investments.

Housing Act of 1961. This act further defined Section 701 of the Housing Act of 1954 with an amendment permitting the use of grant

16. Established in 1933, the Tennessee Valley Authority (TVA) was among the first multipurpose regional authorities created by a federal mandate. President Franklin Roosevelt asked Congress to create a "corporation clothed with the power of government, but possessed of the flexibility and initiative of a private enterprise" that would be responsible for balancing the needs and integrating solutions for power production, navigation, erosion control, flood control, reforestation, and malaria prevention in the Tennessee Valley (www.tva.gov/abouttva/history.htm).

funding to "facilitate comprehensive planning for urban development, including coordinated transportation systems, on a continuing basis."

Federal-Aid Highway Act of 1962. This landmark bill was the first to make federal capital assistance funds contingent upon "continuing," "comprehensive," and "cooperative" (CCC) planning by local and state governments. It also further defined the planning process initiated in many cities after the Housing Act of 1954.[17] Comprehensive planning required that plans specifically address economic factors affecting development, population, land use, zoning codes and regulations, financial resources, and social and community impacts of new infrastructure and development. To perform continued planning, the Highway Act of 1962 required that each region have an institution or organization dedicated primarily to regional or areawide transportation planning. Cooperative planning was defined to include joint planning by the individual local governments within a given region, in addition to the coordination of state and local government planning efforts. These provisions essentially defined the entire urbanized area of a city, rather than the jurisdiction of any local government unit, as the scale for the required CCC planning process.

The 1962 bill also provided federal funds to support regions in their planning efforts, requiring that 1.5 percent of federal transportation funding be restricted to use in research and planning. This provided a guaranteed source of funding for planning, further institutionalizing the regional planning process and the emerging metropolitan planning organizations.

Housing and Urban Development Act of 1965. The 1965 act, which created the Department of Housing and Urban Development (HUD) from the former Department of Housing and Home Finance (HHF), had a major impact on metropolitan governance and planning processes. Amendments to Section 701 of the Housing Act of 1954 stipulated that planning grants could be made only to regional organizations governed by "public officials representative of the political jurisdictions within a metropolitan area."[18] The act's requirement that planning agency boards consist of "public officials" led many regions to create new councils of governments (COGs) with representatives from individual juris-

17. For further discussion of the Federal Aid Highway Act of 1962, see Weiner (1992).
18. Weiner (1992, p. 65).

142

dictions, but not directly elected metropolitan governments. In many metropolitan areas, appointed commissions and agencies responsible for regional planning and coordination functions were converted into COGs by bringing locally elected officials to the table. These new regional entities have been defined as "voluntary associations of elected public officials from most or all of the governments of a metropolitan area, formed to develop a consensus regarding metropolitan needs and actions to be taken in solving their problems."[19]

The Supervisor's Inter-County Committee (SICC)—the first recognized COG in the nation—was created in the greater Detroit region in 1954, establishing a model structure of regional governance that was soon emulated in every major metropolitan area.[20] With elected officials from towns, cities, counties, and special districts represented, new COGs were more democratic and accountable than the appointed commissions and voluntary associations that had preceded them. While the COG movement was spreading throughout the country, President Dwight D. Eisenhower's new Advisory Commission on Intergovernmental Relations examined the potential coordination of federal programs and new government structures.

Demonstration Cities and Metropolitan Development Act of 1966. A new national focus on integrated approaches to solving America's metropolitan problems of poverty, inequality, and inefficient growth resulted in the passage of the Demonstration Cities and Metropolitan Development Act of 1966. Provisions of this act required that all applications for federal government aid—including, but not limited to, transportation projects—be reviewed for their consistency with regional plans by areawide coordinating agencies, a move that further strengthened the authority of the emerging COGs.[21]

19. Beckman (1964).

20. In 1968 the SICC was modified by the inclusion of representatives from all the cities and special districts in the Greater Detroit Metropolitan Area. It was renamed the South East Michigan Council of Governments (SEMCOG), an intergovernmental body that exists today as Detroit's designated MPO. Councils of Governments in many other major cities evolved in similar fashion through the years (and the notably different presidential administrations)—tweaking board structures and government representation but ultimately preserving their mission of regional consensus on the way to becoming federally designated MPOs. See Wickstrom (1977).

21. The Demonstration Cities Act also opened the door to the creation of two-tier metropolitan governments by extending the definition of "areawide planning agencies" in the HUD Act of 1965 to include "any areawide agency which is designated to perform metropolitan or regional planning for the area within which the assistance is to be used and which is, to the greatest practicable extent, composed of or

While the COGs were gaining power, a tug of war over highway funds was under way in Congress. Concern over pollution and the loss of natural resources prompted Congress to pass the National Environmental Policy Act (NEPA, 1969), and the Clean Air Act (1970). Both acts required close consideration of alternative transportation methods (transit, nonmotorized, and demand management) in the national policy debate.[22]

Federal-Aid Highway Act of 1973. With growing support for multimodal transportation investments, transit advocates began struggling for a share of the federal highway funding pie. In 1972 a massive highway-funding bill was proposed but did not pass until a compromise was struck a year later. Under the Federal-Aid Highway Act of 1973, Highway Trust Fund money previously earmarked exclusively for road construction and maintenance was authorized for urban mass transit investments.[23]

This landmark bill also gave birth to the federally designated MPO. To enhance regional coordination and ensure that state Departments of Transportation (DOTs) did not evade its multimodal objectives, the 1973 Highway Act authorized federal funding for new MPOs in every metropolitan area with more than 50,000 residents. MPOs had to create both long-range transportation improvement plans (TIPs) and shorter-range transportation systems management elements (TSMEs), to improve operations of existing facilities. Also, a five-year TIP was to provide a plan for "immediate feasible implementation." This legislation also required each MPO to be certified by the federal government in order to receive program or project funds.

By 1975 the Federal Highway and Federal Transit Administrations solidified the rules governing the MPOs, which would be bodies of locally elected officials. Meeting this requirement, the COGs of most major metropolitan areas gained federal designation as their regions' official MPOs. In addition to long-range planning, the MPOs' primary responsibility was to create "fiscally constrained" three- to five-year

---

responsible to the elected officials of a unit of areawide government or of the units of general local government within whose jurisdiction such agency is authorized to engage in such planning." (Demonstration Cities and Metropolitan Development Act of 1966, Public Law 89-754, Title II: Planned Metropolitan Development, Section 204: Coordination of Aids in Metropolitan Areas).

22. Solof (1997).

23. Federal-Aid Highway Act of 1973, Public Law 93-87. For further analysis of the Highway Act of 1973, see Weiner (1992, p. 107).

transportation improvement programs. This short-term planning requirement forced local government officials to set priorities in their wish list of projects and expanded the planning process to cover financing and implementation. Going one step farther than earlier national transportation policy, which required CCC planning for receipt of federal funds, MPOs were given authority to approve or deny state and local applications for transportation aid, on the basis of their consistency with both TIPs and long-range plans.

MPOs Turn toward Their Regions: 1980–90

Several years after settling into their planning and allocative roles, the mission and functions of the nation's MPOs were threatened by a new challenge from the federal government. The increased review, regulation, and coordination of transportation planning had been accompanied throughout the 1970s by increased federal involvement in other sectors, from housing to education, and created a widespread perception that local governments were unnecessarily burdened. These regulations and certifications were the "red tape" the public associated with a growing bureaucracy.

To combat the growing influence of the federal government, President Ronald Reagan instructed all federal agencies to "postpone implementation of all new regulations." Afterward, the Reagan administration set about simplifying the regulatory process across all sectors, including transportation planning. Federal support for regionalism and the MPO model of governance were all but eliminated in the early 1980s by Reagan's efforts to pare down the federal government and delegate allocative authority to the states. Between 1979 and 1984, all but one of the federal programs requiring and funding regional planning were either sharply downsized or eliminated all together.[24]

The reduction in direct federal support for MPO planning operations, and the transfer of many transportation programming functions to the state level, blunted the MPOs' tools for coordinating regional transportation investments.[25] Throughout the country, MPOs were forced to look to local sources for work and funding and to seek authority from their state governments.[26] In response to their new isolation, regional councils, including designated MPOs, became

24. McDowell (1984).

25. The share of regional council (including MPOs) operating funds coming from federal sources was reduced from 76 percent in 1978 to 45 percent in 1988. See National Association of Regional Councils (1989).

26. Solof (1997).

increasingly entrepreneurial in their operations, putting more emphasis on providing services for their member governments and developing their relationships with the private sector. By offering credit pooling, training, regional demographic data collection, and standard technical assistance to local governments, regional councils and MPOs improved the efficiency of individual jurisdictions, increased their own revenues from local sources, and solidified their position in emerging regional governance networks.

ISTEA and TEA-21 Legislation: 1991–Present

Having shuffled their priorities and strengthened their ties to regional business and governance networks during the federal funding dry spell of the 1980s, MPOs in major metropolitan areas were better attuned to the needs and objectives of their constituent communities and governments. With the revival of federal support for regionalism and recognition of their value to regional governance and economic development, MPOs and other regional councils were ready for deeper involvement in metropolitan affairs by 1990. The passage of ISTEA in 1991 allowed MPOs to regain control over the allocation of federal transportation funds, and once again they refocused their efforts on regional coordination and planning.

The resurgence of metropolitan planning occurred initially as a response to growing concern for environmental quality and the resultant tightening of air quality standards. The Clean Air Act Amendments of 1990 required states to develop attainment plans (state implementation plans, SIPs) for all urban areas failing to meet national ambient air quality standards (NAAQS). All plans, including the TIP and long-range plans prepared by MPOs, must be consistent with projected vehicle miles traveled and emissions budgets in SIPs, which heavily affect total vehicle miles traveled and consequent emissions levels in nonattainment areas. States with MPOs that fail to coordinate transportation and air quality plans are subject to federal sanctions, including the withholding of approval for federal aid highway projects.

These requirements for the conformity of transportation and air quality plans in the Clean Air Act Amendments of 1990 are a product of widespread recognition that the integrated problems of metropolitan areas demand integrated solutions. An integrated, multimodal strategy for improving the efficiency of the nation's transportation systems was formalized one year after the Clean Air Act Amendments in 1991, when Congress passed ISTEA.

Acknowledging that transportation investments could be balanced only with land use, air quality, economic development, and social equity objectives at the regional level, the authors of ISTEA provided strong measures to ensure that federally designated and certified MPOs were vested with the power and obligation to meet these stated goals.[27] ISTEA immediately revived MPOs' planning capacity, doubling federal funding for planning operations. More important, the landmark bill included provisions to further democratize MPOs and increase their flexibility in using federal funds.

With their provisions for flexible funding, ISTEA and TEA-21 allowed MPOs discretion to use Federal Highway Trust Fund money and general funds appropriated to various highway construction and maintenance programs for other projects, including recreational trails, pedestrian and bicycle facilities, congestion mitigation, air quality programs, and mass transit. As an indication of the influence these provisions had over transportation investment decisions, between 1992 and 1999, 12.5 percent of available federal highway funds were transferred to transit programs nationwide.[28] Almost half of all flexed funds during the study period were transferred in New York (38.4 percent) and California (33.7 percent), the states with the largest transit systems and authorities. As these are also the two largest states by population, some observers have suggested that ISTEA was considerably less than a nationwide transportation revolution.[29] Excluding California and New York, only 8 percent of available funds were transferred, but several MPOs and their partner state DOTs have been more assertive in meeting ISTEA's multimodal goals. The District of Columbia (Metro Washington Council of Governments) distinguished itself by transferring more than 48 percent of available funds between 1992 and 1999. Among the regions that transferred more than 15 percent of their available highway funds to transit projects were Portland (Portland Metro), Seattle (Puget Sound Regional Council), Philadelphia (Delaware Valley Regional Council), Boston (Boston MPO), Minneapolis–St. Paul (Metropolitan Council of the Twin Cities), and Pittsburgh (Southwest Pennsylvania Regional Planning Commission).

27. Solof (1997).

28. Puentes (2000). Puentes calculated the percentage of available funds in the Surface Transportation Program (STP) and the Congestion Mitigation and Air Quality Program that were transferred to Federal Transit Administration projects.

29. Puentes (2000).

STRATEGIES FOR MOVING TOWARD GREATER REGIONAL GOVERNANCE

The challenges facing metropolitan America require a representative, accountable regional governing body with the authority to guide regional development.

The energy behind the efforts discussed in this chapter and growing endorsement across the country for similar efforts point to popular support for a coordinated, regional approach to local and regional land-use issues. The fragmented nature of land-use planning in the United States, however, has meant that there are few, if any, coordinated strategies for regionwide efforts to deal with the challenges facing metropolitan areas. Government and business leaders, environmental and historical preservation organizations, affordable housing and poverty advocates, and many other organizations working to address the effects of concentrated poverty, segregation, and sprawl are all beginning to recognize that this fragmentation and the lack of power to oversee regional land use and public investment hinders their ability to succeed over the long term.

Responding to the many challenges facing metropolitan America will require a strong, representative, and accountable regional governing body with the authority to guide regional development patterns. Where they do not have this authority already, existing regional governments (MPOs) should gradually assume the power to promulgate an efficient and orderly regional land-use plan. This plan should be coherent with an MPO's transportation investment and other regional goals forwarded by the people or their representatives. This plan could be advisory. If advisory authority does not help rationalize development, it could, by vote of the people or their representatives, become a mandatory plan. In cases where local zoning and land-use plans do not conform to the regional plan, the governing body could establish the authority to deny land-use permits or funding for infrastructure until they are brought into compliance.

As power to address regional issues is transferred, however, any regional governing body must be held directly accountable for its actions to ensure that all residents of the region are represented. Over time, a fairly apportioned, accountable, directly elected regional body could help to ensure that it represents the best interests of every part of the entire region as it coordinates strategies to address regional challenges.

Most critics of regional governance argue that it would violate the principle of local autonomy and unnecessarily add another layer of government. However, effective, efficient regional governance strikes a balance that allows local control over issues best addressed by smaller local governments (such as public safety, licensing, street maintenance, garbage collection, and purely local land-use or zoning issues), while promoting cooperation among local governments on larger issues affecting the entire region (such as highway and sewer investments, affordable housing, transit, land-use planning, air and water quality, and economic development). The need for regional governance reflects the reality of modern metropolitan challenges—challenges that are too large for any one local government to address alone and that are often exacerbated by excessive fragmentation.

In fact, multijurisdictional governance has been occurring in every metropolitan area of the country for more than 30 years—through the metropolitan planning organizations created to allocate federal resources and to plan for the construction and maintenance of regional transportation systems. Although these MPOs have significant authority over transportation investments, they typically serve only in an advisory role on other, interconnected regional land-use and economic development decisions. Since these MPOs already serve as regional transportation planning bodies and as a forum for efforts on other regional issues, they are a natural candidate for the type of regional governing body discussed here. Broadening their authority and accountability to address regional investments and development patterns comprehensively is perhaps the most feasible strategy for creating an appropriate structure for addressing regional challenges effectively and equitably.

A strong, accountable regional governing body is an essential part of a comprehensive regional reform plan. The following strategies will help to ensure the long-term viability of any regional governing body, whether an MPO with expanded authority or some other regional body.

—Strategy 1: Apportion voting membership by population. MPOs spending millions, often billions, of transportation planning dollars should be equally apportioned so that all parts of the region have equal voting power. Decisions on how and where to spend taxpayer dollars for regional investments should be made in a fair and equitable manner, giving equal representation to all types of communities and residents in a region. The way voting membership is apportioned and power is shared on the board can lead to very different types of spending decisions.

—Strategy 2: Hold direct elections for voting members. Direct elections of members of regional governing bodies would make regional decisionmaking more open and participatory. The major infrastructure and development issues of the region would become a matter of public decisionmaking. Even without expanding the scope of MPO powers, direct election of MPO boards would create a legitimate forum to discuss regional issues. Any increase in MPOs' powers would make direct election even more important.

—Strategy 3: Broaden and deepen public awareness of the way transportation investments contribute to or alleviate social separation and sprawl. Regional bodies should be required to evaluate their transportation decisions to see whether they worsen or alleviate social separation and sprawling development patterns in the region. This evaluation could lead to alternative investment plans.

—Strategy 4: Broaden the scope of land-use planning. MPOs or another regional body should develop an advisory land-use plan for the region that embodies a vision for coordinating all major forms of developmental infrastructure efficiently. These advisory land-use plans might ask cities to voluntarily submit comprehensive plans for review or offer them incentives to do so. These comprehensive plans can cover any number of issues, including sustainable development, affordable housing, and public transit. Depending on how well these advisory plans coordinate regional investments and planning, mandatory requirements may not be necessary.

PART

3

METRO
POLITICS

METRO POLITICS

"M etropatterns" detailed the great diversity of America's suburbs and central cities and the spreading pattern of social and fiscal disparity and competition for resources that is sapping the energies of metropolitan communities throughout the nation. "Metropolicy" outlined a reform agenda based on gradually altering *existing* concepts of government cooperation to heal festering wounds, curb growing waste, and provide a framework for tight regional cooperation. "Metropolitics" lays out a bipartisan political strategy to achieve these reforms.

"Metropolitics" argues that *all regional communities* benefit from regional reform. To translate this reality into policy and politics, "Metropolitics," as a first step, draws political maps of the suburbs and their metropolitan regions. From these pictures, large U.S. regions, and their suburbs, emerge as districts that the two parties vie over. The most volatile ones—the swing districts, which either party can win in the contest for legislative and congressional control—are located largely in the at-risk and bedroom-developing suburbs. These are the types of suburbs that can benefit most from the tax equity, land-use planning, and metropolitan governance inherent in metropolitan reform.

Central cities and the very affluent suburbs also stand to gain from regional reform. The central cities—with their tremendous social needs—have an obvious stake. For the citizens of affluent job centers, at the hub of fast-growing congestion and dwindling open space, regional cooperation offers the only practical way of containing the harsh consequences of rapid growth and preserving their pleasant way of life.

Finally, "Metropolitics" argues that an effectively communicated regional agenda could be a powerful tool for realigning American politics in a way that would foster social mobility and basic equity; more efficient, less complex, and more representative government; and a clean and livable metropolitan environment.

8

METROPOLITICS AND THE
CASE FOR REGIONALISM

In the 1998 elections, the suburbs were "up for grabs" by the two main parties. The Republicans were in charge of the Congress, most governorships, and 17 state legislatures. Of the other state legislatures, 1 was nonpartisan, 13 were divided between the two main parties, and the Democrats held 19. State lower houses in the country's 25 largest regions were 56 percent Democratic and 42 percent Republican (table 8-1).

The most solidly Republican strongholds in the 25 largest metropolitan areas were Tampa (86 percent of state House seats), Phoenix (71 percent), Dallas (70 percent), and Cincinnati (65 percent). The most Democratic places in the nation were San Francisco (85 percent of seats), Boston (77 percent), Pittsburgh (77 percent), and St. Louis (67 percent). Two of the places with the most extensive regional policies in place were Republican-majority regions: Minneapolis–St. Paul (54 percent) and Portland, Oregon (57 percent). Some of the nation's most affluent regions, such as San Francisco (85 percent), Boston (77 percent), Washington, D.C. (58 percent), and Seattle (52 percent), were predominantly Democratic, while some of the lower-income regions, such as Phoenix (71 percent), Dallas (70 percent), and Tampa (86 percent) were Republican.

The prevailing stereotype is one of Republican politicians dominating the suburbs. However, in terms of state House seats, this was not true in 1998. In metropolitan districts located entirely or partly in suburban areas, less than half (48 percent) were represented by Republican state House members. In terms of fully suburban districts, Republican members of the state House represented only 50 percent of the districts.

Northeast regions like Boston and New York were among the most Democratic areas in the nation. With this exception, geography did not

TABLE 8-1. Party Affiliation of State House
Representative Districts in the
25 Largest Metropolitan Areas, 1998

Metropolitan area	Number	Democratic (%)	Republican (%)
Atlanta	88	43	57
Boston	182	77	23
Chicago	93	60	40
Cincinnati	26	35	65
Cleveland	27	59	41
Dallas	37	30	70
Denver	42	50	50
Detroit	62	60	40
Houston	34	56	44
Kansas City	66	48	52
Los Angeles	41	59	41
Miami	33	65	35
Milwaukee	35	54	46
Minneapolis–St. Paul	89	46	54
New York	256	60	40
Philadelphia	114	43	57
Phoenix	21	29	71
Pittsburgh	43	77	23
Portland	42	43	57
St. Louis	72	67	33
San Diego	8	38	62
San Francisco	19	85	15
Seattle	62	52	48
Tampa	22	14	86
Washington, D.C.	164	58	42
Total	**1,678**	**56**	**44**

Source: State election records.

seem to affect partisan balance in any region. In the Midwest, St. Louis was a Democrat stronghold (67 percent) while Cincinnati (with 35 percent Democrats) was strongly Republican. In the southeast, the Miami region was overwhelmingly Democratic (65 percent) while Tampa (with 14 percent Democrats) was the country's most Republican region. In Houston, Democrats formed a majority (56 percent) while in Dallas they consisted of less than a third (30 percent). The large California regions were divided between Democratic places like San Francisco (85 percent) and Republican places like San Diego (with 38 percent Democrats). For examples of the geographic distribution of seats by party, see maps 8-1 through 8-6, which illustrate Democratic safe seats, Republican safe seats, and swing seats for the study's six representative metropolitan areas.

In 1998 only 50 percent of fully suburban districts were represented by Republicans in their state House.

In terms of geographic party strategy, the Democratic party appears to base its operations in the central cities of major regions. Building from there, Democrats first campaign in older declining suburbs. If successful, they contest rapidly developing modest-income bedroom communities.

The Republicans find their most solid base in the affluent job centers. They generally hold a slight advantage in the bedroom-developing suburbs and a slight disadvantage in the at-risk suburbs. As the next section makes clear, the two parties would do well to focus their energies on the swing districts.

METROPOLITAN SWING DISTRICTS

A swing voter is an individual who is weakly attached to a political party and has a tendency to switch back and forth between parties from one election to the next. Swing voters fall into various categories. In the 2000 election, according to the popular press, both presidential candidates appeared to concentrate their efforts on a demographic group between 40 and 55 years of age, with household incomes between $30,000 and $65,000 a year, and living in blue-collar suburbs.[1] This group was also heavily courted in the election of 1992.[2] Other swing voters cultivated in the past include suburban women, "soccer moms," who are likely to have a deeper interest in education spending and the environment than their male counterparts. Older voters are also frequently cultivated, as seen in the last election from the constant debate about a

1. Berke (2000).
2. Greenberg (1996).

157

prescription drug benefit for seniors. The list of theoretically volatile voters is so endless that, at least within the Democratic party, there is some disagreement about who they are. One faction, led by Stan Greenberg, the pollster in President Bill Clinton's 1992 election, believes that swing voters are middle-income families, struggling to make ends meet in places like Macomb County, Michigan. Another, led by Mark Penn, President Clinton's pollster in his 1996 election, thinks the important swing voters are more affluent, educated, and "wired" than the Greenberg group does. In the end, capturing as many groups of swing voters as possible—whoever they may be—is an important part of a winning electoral strategy.

A swing district is an electoral district with a high proportion of voters who vote for candidates from either party. Every legislative and congressional party caucus makes its own calculation concerning the location of these districts in order to strategize the campaign for the next election. Most develop a district index based on cumulating the district-specific results of hard-fought national and statewide elections for major offices, statewide elections for minor offices such as state treasurer or secretary of state (where fewer voters are likely to know the candidates and voting is usually based on party preferences), and, if relevant, the electoral track record of the incumbent serving the district.

This type of index is hard to generalize across the entire nation, so a simple, widely accepted academic swing index developed by political scientists studying voting behavior was used in this study. The Flanigan/Zingle index uses a weighted history of all elections cast in the 1990s to determine a district's "safety index." The less safe the district, the more likely it is to be a volatile or swing district.[3]

The country's 25 largest regions have about 43 percent of the U.S. population but only about 30 percent of the volatile political districts. Thus the large metro regions appear to be somewhat underrepresented in terms of political volatility. Table 8-2 shows the distribution of swing districts across the community types. Thirty-six percent of swing districts are predominately at-risk suburbs; 43 percent are predominately bedroom-developing suburbs; and just 10 percent are affluent job centers. The political battleground in these metropolitan areas falls squarely in at-risk and bedroom-developing suburbs.

Put another way, of the suburban jurisdictions that are entirely or partly within swing districts, 40 percent are at-risk suburbs (containing

3. Flanigan and Zingle (1974).

158

TABLE 8-2. **Distribution of Swing Districts across Suburban Community Types**[a]

Metropolitan area	Number of swing districts	Distribution (%)			
		High-density at-risk	Low-density at-risk	Bedroom-developing	Affluent job center
Atlanta	12	8	42	50	0
Boston	68	12	6	60	19
Chicago	18	0	0	83	17
Cincinnati	4	50	0	50	0
Cleveland	6	0	0	83	0
Dallas	5	0	80	20	0
Denver	20	25	50	5	10
Detroit	16	31	0	69	0
Houston	5	0	40	40	0
Kansas City	15	13	33	53	0
Los Angeles	11	9	55	36	0
Miami	2	0	50	0	50
Milwaukee	2	0	0	0	50
Minneapolis–St. Paul	21	38	10	48	0
New York	32	16	3	53	16
Philadelphia	17	24	24	41	6
Phoenix	4	50	25	0	0
Pittsburgh	14	21	7	57	14
Portland	22	5	59	18	5
San Diego	1	0	0	0	0
San Francisco	5	0	100	0	0
Seattle	12	50	17	0	33
St. Louis	14	0	29	50	7
Tampa	8	0	100	0	0
Washington, D.C.	35	0	9	29	9
Total	**369**	**14**	**22**	**43**	**10**

Source: State election records and U.S. Bureau of the Census.

a. Swing districts are assigned to the category that represents the majority (by area) of the district. Thirty-nine swing districts are in jurisdictions not assigned a classification.

In terms of electoral strategy, understanding the distinction between swing voters and swing districts is critical.

60 percent of the population in suburban swing jurisdictions); 50 percent are bedroom-developing municipalities (containing 34 percent of the population); and just less than 1 percent are high-capacity, low-cost places (representing 6 percent of the population). Thus an important part of the battleground of U.S. politics is in the low fiscal capacity suburbs, struggling either with the pressures of growth or the stresses of decline.

In terms of electoral strategy, understanding the distinction between swing voters and swing districts is critical. Coalitions of base and swing voters may be able to build a popular vote majority for statewide or national office. But, in terms of a legislative strategy, there may be fewer opportunities. In a state where metropolitan areas form a significant part of the population, Republicans and Democrats must control at-risk or bedroom-developing suburbs, or both, as, without them, they cannot maintain legislative majorities. Many of the closely contested races in the battle to control the U.S. House of Representatives have also taken place in at-risk and bedroom-developing suburbs.

The swing district maps of the Atlanta metropolitan region show a Democratic advantage in the city, in the at-risk communities in Fulton, Clayton, and DeKalb Counties (particularly those undergoing rapid racial change), and in outlying at-risk and bedroom-developing areas to the west. The Republicans dominate the affluent job centers in Newt Gingrich's former congressional district and most of the bedroom-developing suburbs. In 1998 the battleground in Atlanta was at-risk low-density and bedroom-developing districts.

In Chicago, the Democrats held the advantage in the city, most of the close-in at-risk suburbs, and bedroom-developing areas to the south and west. The Republicans controlled the affluent job centers and most bedroom-developing areas elsewhere in the metropolitan region. The swing districts were in close-in at-risk and bedroom-developing districts to the south and west. In the 1990s, control of the Illinois House shifted back and forth between parties twice with the deciding races in the at-risk suburbs. In Denver, Democrats had the advantage in most of the central city, at-risk suburbs to the north, and bedroom-developing areas to the northwest, while the Republican vote was strong in the bedroom-developing suburbs to the southeast. The swing districts were in at-risk suburban areas to the north and west.

In the Twin Cities, the Democrats controlled the central cities and most of the at-risk suburbs, whereas the Republicans controlled the affluent job centers and a large share of bedroom-developing areas. As in

MAP 8-1. ATLANTA REGION
Legislative Swing Districts

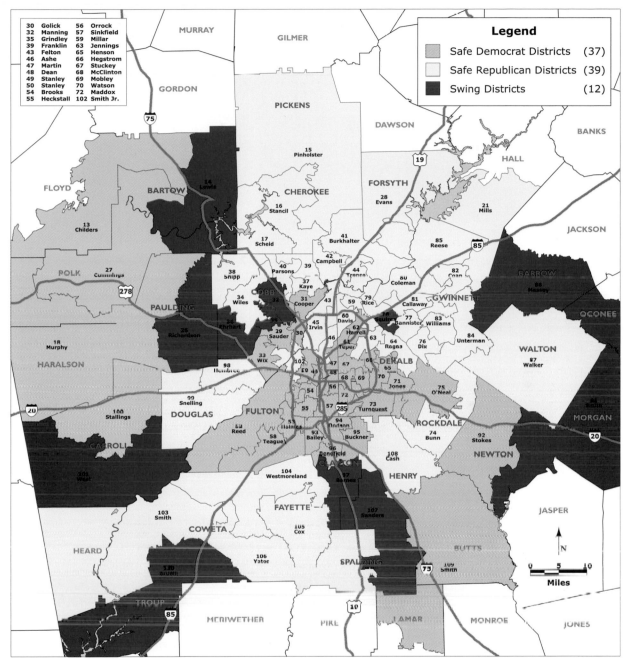

30	Golick	56	Orrock
32	Manning	57	Sinkfield
35	Grindley	59	Millar
39	Franklin	63	Jennings
43	Felton	65	Henson
46	Ashe	66	Hegstrom
47	Martin	67	Stuckey
48	Dean	68	McClinton
49	Stanley	69	Mobley
50	Stanley	70	Watson
54	Brooks	72	Maddox
55	Heckstall	102	Smith Jr.

Legend

Safe Democrat Districts	(37)
Safe Republican Districts	(39)
Swing Districts	(12)

Data Source: Georgia Secretary of State.

MAP 8-2. CHICAGO REGION
Legislative Swing Districts

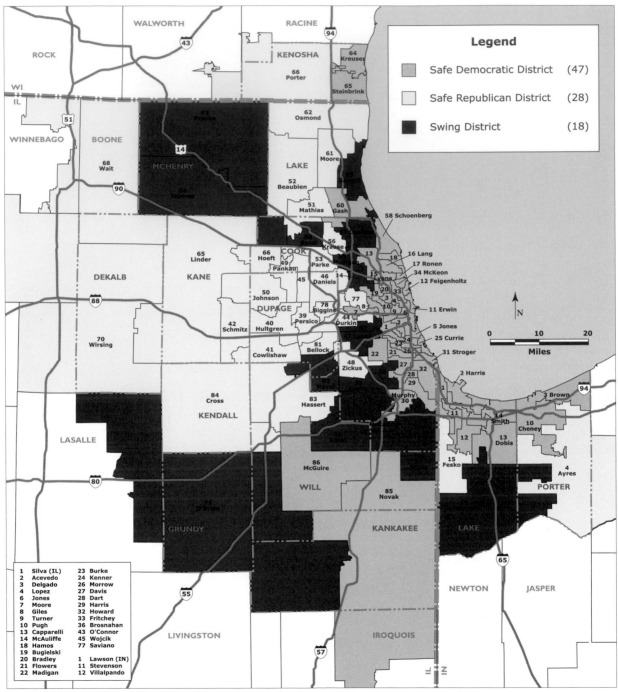

Legend

▨	Safe Democratic District	(47)
▧	Safe Republican District	(28)
▧	Swing District	(18)

1	Silva (IL)	23	Burke
2	Acevedo	24	Kenner
3	Delgado	26	Morrow
4	Lopez	27	Davis
6	Jones	28	Dart
7	Moore	29	Harris
8	Giles	32	Howard
9	Turner	33	Fritchey
10	Pugh	36	Brosnahan
13	Capparelli	43	O'Connor
14	McAuliffe	45	Wojcik
18	Hamos	77	Saviano
19	Bugielski		
20	Bradley	1	Lawson (IN)
21	Flowers	11	Stevenson
22	Madigan	12	Villalpando

Data Source: State of Illinois Official Vote; Wisconsin Secretary of State; Indiana Secretary of State.

MAP 8-3. DENVER REGION
Legislative Swing Districts

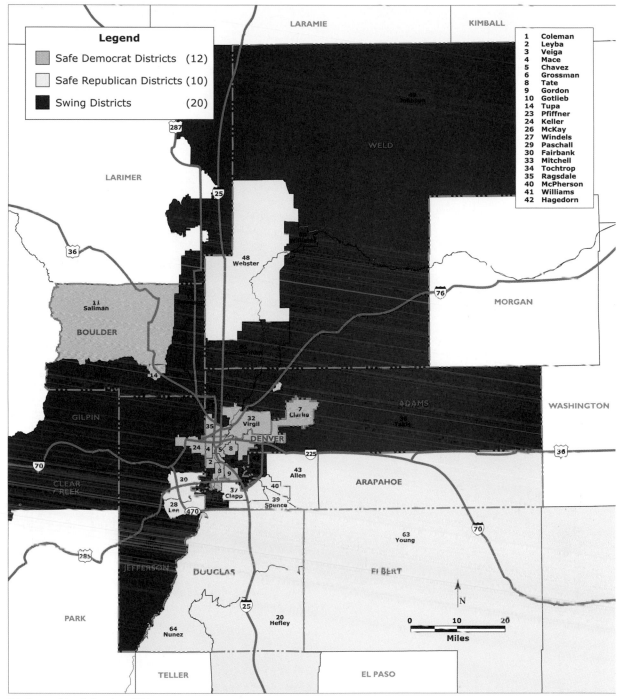

Legend

- Safe Democrat Districts (12)
- Safe Republican Districts (10)
- Swing Districts (20)

1	Coleman
2	Leyba
3	Veiga
4	Mace
5	Chavez
6	Grossman
8	Tate
9	Gordon
10	Gotlieb
14	Tupa
23	Pfiffner
24	Keller
26	McKay
27	Windels
29	Paschall
30	Fairbank
33	Mitchell
34	Tochtrop
35	Ragsdale
40	McPherson
41	Williams
42	Hagedorn

Data Source: Colorado Secretary of State.

MAP 8-4. MINNEAPOLIS–ST. PAUL REGION
Legislative Swing Districts

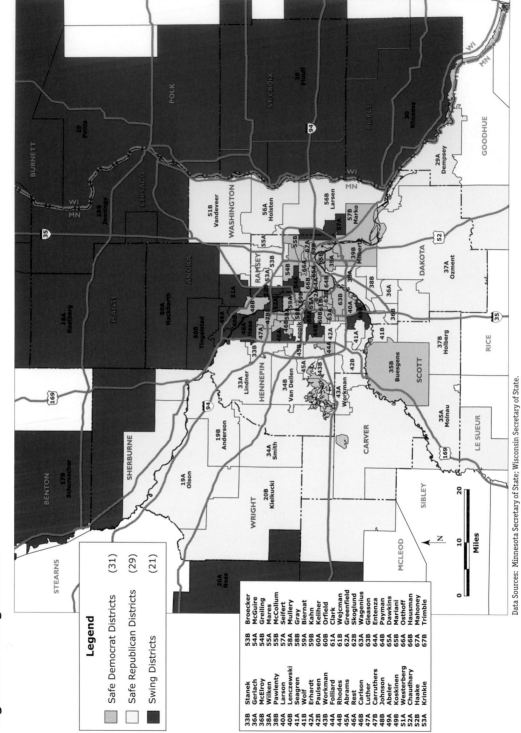

Legend

	Safe Democrat Districts	(31)
	Safe Republican Districts	(29)
	Swing Districts	(21)

33B	Stanek	53B	Broecker
36A	Gerlach	54A	McGuire
36B	McElroy	54B	Greiling
38A	Wilken	55A	Mares
38B	Pawlenty	55B	McCollum
40A	Larson	57A	Seifert
40B	Lenczewski	58A	Mullery
41A	Seagren	58B	Gray
41B	Wolf	59A	Biernat
42A	Erhardt	59B	Kahn
42B	Paulsen	60A	Keliher
43B	Workman	60B	Orfield
44A	Folliard	61A	Clark
44B	Rhodes	61B	Wejcman
45A	Abrams	62A	Greenfield
46A	Rest	62B	Skoglund
46B	Carlson	63A	Wagenius
47A	Luther	63B	Gleason
47B	Carruthers	64A	Entenza
48B	Johnson	64B	Payman
49A	Abeler	65A	Dawkins
49B	Koskinen	65B	Mariani
51A	Westerberg	66A	Osthoff
52A	Chaudhary	66B	Hausman
52B	Haake	67A	Mahoney
53A	Krinkie	67B	Trimble

Data Sources: Minnesota Secretary of State; Wisconsin Secretary of State.

MAP 8-5. NEW YORK REGION
Legislative Swing Districts

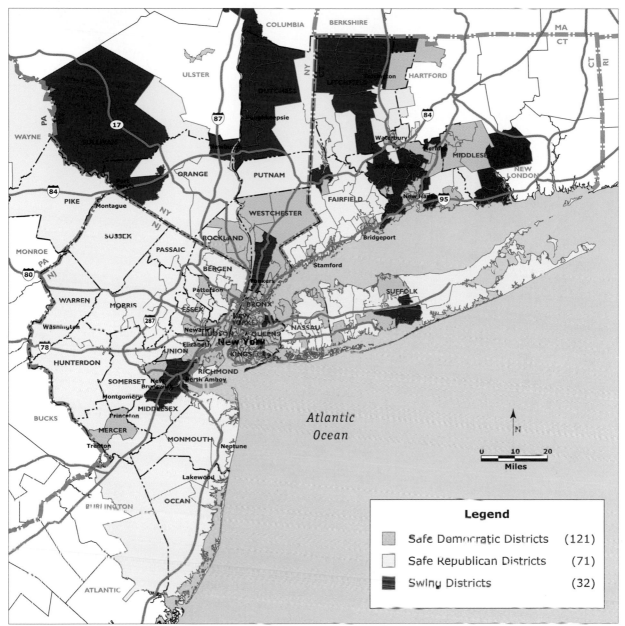

Legend

	Safe Democratic Districts	(121)
	Safe Republican Districts	(71)
	Swing Districts	(32)

Data Sources: Connecticut Secretary of State, New Jersey Secretary of State, New York State Board of Elections, Pennsylvania Secretary of State.

MAP 8-6. SAN FRANCISCO REGION
Legislative Swing Districts

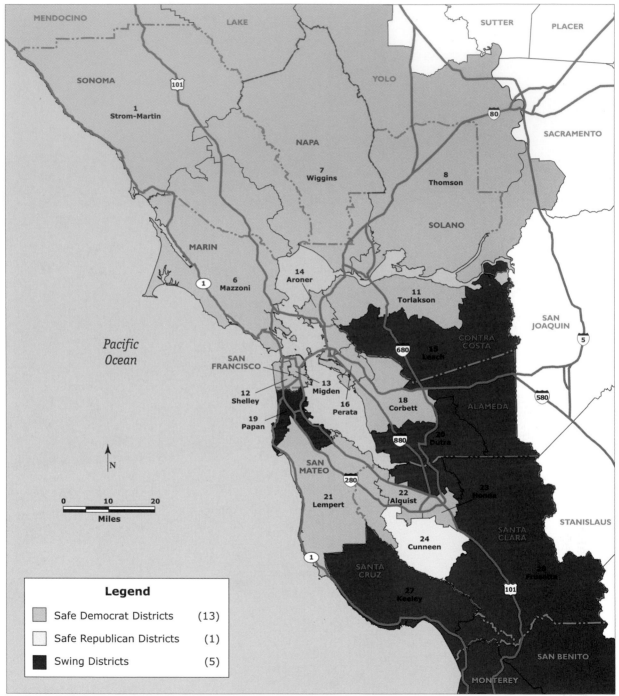

MENDOCINO LAKE SUTTER PLACER

SONOMA

101

YOLO

SACRAMENTO

80

1
Strom-Martin

NAPA

7
Wiggins

8
Thomson

SOLANO

MARIN

6
Mazzoni

14
Aroner

11
Torlakson

SAN
JOAQUIN

Pacific
Ocean

680

15
Leach

CONTRA
COSTA

5

SAN
FRANCISCO

12
Shelley

13
Migden

16
Perata

18
Corbett

ALAMEDA

580

19
Papan

880

20
Dutra

N

SAN
MATEO

280

22
Alguist

23
Honda

STANISLAUS

0   10   20

21
Lempert

24
Cunneen

SANTA
CLARA

Miles

1

26
Firebaugh

101

SANTA
CRUZ

27
Keeley

Legend

	Safe Democrat Districts	(13)
	Safe Republican Districts	(1)
	Swing Districts	(5)

SAN BENITO

MONTEREY

Data Source: California Secretary of State.

MAP 8-7. MINNEAPOLIS–ST. PAUL REGION
Gubernatorial Race, 1998: Winner by Minnesota House District

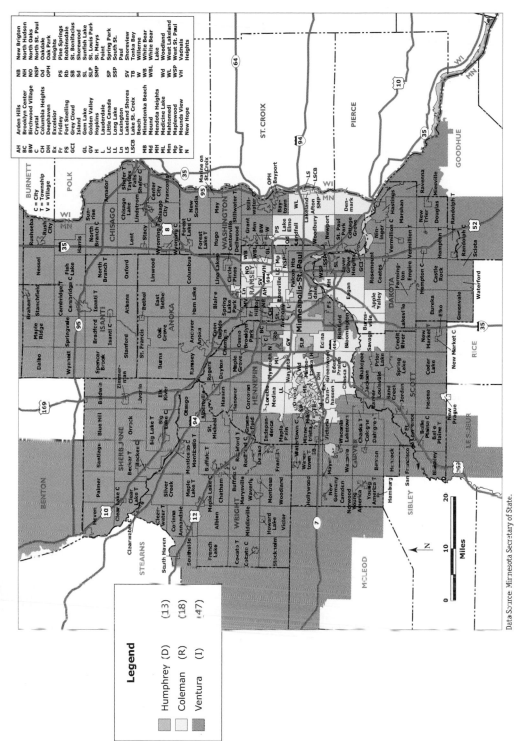

Legend

Humphrey (D) (13)

Coleman (R) (18)

Ventura (I) (47)

Data Source: Minnesota Secretary of State.

Illinois, control of the Minnesota House in the last two elections has been based on electoral outcomes in northern at-risk and developing suburban districts. In the course of a decade, these Minnesota communities voted for one of the nation's most liberal senators (Paul Wellstone in 1992 and 1998), one of the nation's most conservative senators (Rod Grams in 1994), and Democratic Senator Mark Dayton in 2000, and, in a three-way gubernatorial race in 1998, they flocked to the iconoclastic, blue-collar-oriented Reform Party candidate, Jesse Ventura. Ventura, who did not carry a single truly rural Minnesota county and who had a poor showing in the affluent job centers, beat both major party candidates combined in the bedroom-developing suburbs! Map 8-7 shows the distribution of Ventura votes in the Twin Cities, exemplifying the importance of swing districts in electing a candidate.

In the New York region, Democrats were dominant in New York City (except for outlying parts of Queens) and the old, larger cities of New Jersey and Connecticut. They had the advantage in about half the interior at-risk suburbs of New Jersey, a very few interior at-risk suburbs on Long Island, and many of the bedroom-developing suburbs of Connecticut. The Republicans controlled most of the affluent job centers, a large share of the bedroom-developing suburbs in New York and New Jersey, and had an advantage in many of the at-risk communities of New Jersey and Long Island (places where former Senator Alfonse D'Amato began his political career). The election battleground was located in some of the outlying districts in the borough of Queens (in the city), the Yonkers area of the inner at-risk suburbs to the north, and the bedroom-developing areas of New Jersey, New York, and Connecticut. Finally, the Bay Area, the most Democratic metropolitan area in the nation, had only one safe Republican district—an area in the heart of the Silicon Valley that includes Palo Alto, Cupertino, Santa Clara, Los Altos, and many of the communities commonly associated with America's high-tech boom. The business community in this area is one of the business communities most firmly united around the issues of "smart growth."

In the end, Republican, Democratic, and independent officials have to heed the pressing needs of at-risk and rapidly developing bedroom communities. If these places become aware of their pivotal role in American politics as well as the detrimental consequences for their communities of social and fiscal separation, intense intrametropolitan competition for tax base, and sprawling development, then the party that addresses these issues will wield great political power. Educating these communities about their power and future within the heretofore monolithic conception of "the" suburbs, and convincing them only regional approaches can solve their problems, is one of the central challenges of regionalism. In this, regional reformers and local, state, and national politicians have their job cut out for them.

MAKING THE CASE FOR REGIONALISM

Economists and others have made the important point that regional cooperation helps every community, but the parochial costs and benefits of regional reforms vary by community type within metropolitan areas. Therefore making the case for regionalism requires an understanding of the nature of the different community types and the ways they may benefit from the various reforms.

The Central Cities

Little has changed in the American central cities' prospects despite a decade of reform-minded, cost-cutting, entrepreneurial mayors and urban leaders, growing philanthropic commitment to cities, and unparalleled economic growth. Elementary schools in all but one of the selected cities grew poorer and more segregated in the mid-1990s, and core neighborhoods became increasingly isolated racially.[4] In terms of tax capacity, although several cities gained business and development in certain areas, more often than not it was offset by decline and loss in other areas. Cities as a whole, with large and proliferating challenges, lost fiscal ground against their surrounding metropolitan areas. With the current cooling of the economy, further challenges lurk on the horizon, since many city residents, those among the last hired, will probably be the first fired. Central cities clearly need the support of regional institutions that will distribute the fruits of growth more equitably.

The At-Risk Developed Suburbs

The first two groups of at-risk suburbs—the at-risk segregated and at-risk older suburbs—together represent about 15 percent of the population of large regions. Like the central cities, they are both fully developed. Together with the central cities, they represent 44 percent of the population in the 25 largest metropolitan areas. The case to present to the de-

---

4. U.S. Bureau of the Census, 2000. See also chapter 2, pages 23–25.

veloped at-risk suburbs is simple. Regional equity gives them lower taxes and better services. Regional land-use planning stabilizes housing markets in the older, declining areas by requiring affordable housing to be more dispersed, reduces their subsidies to new sprawling development, and redirects regional growth back into their communities.

What the high-density at-risk suburbs are experiencing has already befallen central cities, and their greater fragility impairs their ability to respond. The schools in these suburbs are growing poorer and, in many cases, racially isolated. As schools are often a predictor of the future, their current deficiencies illuminate the fiscal and social challenges these at-risk communities are beginning to face. Many of their streets, sewer systems, parks, and schools need restoration beyond the capacity of the local government. Outdated business buildings and shopping malls, long ignored by the private sector, may need to be remodeled or demolished. Land has to be assembled for redevelopment. Industrially polluted brownfield sites are common and expensive to restore.

To make matters worse, the fiscal capacity of the at-risk suburbs as a group is only about 70 percent of their regional average, with the slowest growth in fiscal capacity of all the suburban classifications. Their residents are less affluent and their housing less valuable than those in the other groups of suburbs. Their residential real estate values are not competitive with other parts of suburbia and may be declining in the slow-growth regions of the Midwest. Finally, these at-risk communities are home not only to a struggling middle class and increasingly poor population but also to elderly residents, all of whom may be in need of cars and good public transportation to get to work, go shopping, or visit a physician.

The evidence shows that the at-risk suburbs are more fragile and vulnerable to the forces of social separation and sprawl than the central cities they surround. While some central cities like San Francisco, Seattle, Portland, Minneapolis, Boston, and Washington, D.C., are building around their assets of regional centrality—parks, cultural activities, amenities, and elite neighborhoods—at-risk places are bedroom communities of comparatively inexpensive construction, hard-to-restore housing, and few urban amenities. In the nation's largest regions, unlike the central cities, there is no measurable evidence of resurgence in the at-risk places.

Fiscal Equity. In the at-risk suburbs, taxes are comparatively high for the mix of services provided. In states and regions without substantial state-supported school equity, these taxes can be the highest in metropolitan America. To the older suburbs, regional tax equity means what everyone promises in American politics, but almost no one can deliver: lower taxes and better services. Simulations of property-tax sharing throughout the country show the older suburbs as the largest net gainers of resources of any of the subregions. New equity resources would help at-risk suburbs both reduce tax rates and provide the essential services necessary to compete and retool in the metropolitan economy. Such resources could help older suburbs shore up old infrastructure they cannot now maintain, undertake projects such as sewer separation or other long-deferred public facility upgrades, clean up brownfield sites, reconfigure abandoned malls or industrial facilities, and invest in housing in declining neighborhoods. Underfunded schools could get a boost and, depending on the comprehensiveness of the equity, such measures could be taken even as the local tax rates were being reduced.

To the older suburbs, regional tax equity means what everyone promises but almost no one can deliver: lower taxes and better services.

Land-Use Planning and Transportation. For at-risk communities, properly implemented regional land-use planning is a powerful stabilizing tool that serves to make edge communities share the responsibilities of affordable housing, redirect some regional growth to older suburbs, provide new transit resources for all suburban areas, and force priority setting for the use of regional infrastructure resources for redevelopment in preference to new development of greenfield sites.

Affordable Housing. At-risk suburban communities are often in downward residential transition or threatened on their borders by rapid change. For them, it is critical to understand that a strong, well-implemented regional housing plan is the only way to avoid this transition. Although many have tried, in the end at-risk communities simply cannot afford to knock down enough old houses and apartment buildings to keep out the poor. Even if they could, the poor would turn up in the next vulnerable suburb. A good regional housing plan requires newer suburbs to gradually take up some of the responsibility for affordable housing. It takes pressure off the older suburbs and prevents the concentration of poverty and decline in these places. In the end, a regional plan will let them supply less affordable housing than they would have done by default and maintain more middle-class residents, too.

In this light, well-conceived, well-explained housing initiatives could become a powerful political positive rather than a negative. Once older declining suburbs understand that they already have their fair share of affordable housing (often many times their fair share), they could use a good regional housing plan as a powerful defensive strategy to maintain their communities' stability. This was the way public support worked in the Twin Cities during the debates on the Comprehensive Choice Housing bill in the 1993–95 legislative sessions.[5] The older suburbs strongly supported an affordable housing plan in their own self-defensive interest. In metropolitan Boston, blue-collar urbanites grew angry with blue-blooded suburban liberals, pushing for intra-Boston, instead of metropolitan, busing. In response, the "Southies" pushed through the legislature a sweeping suburban fair-housing act that began to open up Boston suburbs to apartment buildings and other forms of affordable housing.[6]

By the same token, neglecting the defensive aspect of affordable housing for at-risk suburbs can have lethal consequences for reform advocates. In the early 1990s, Henry Cisneros, secretary of the U.S. Department of Housing and Urban Development (HUD), launched a program called "Moving to Opportunity," based on Chicago's Gautreaux project, with the goal of deconcentrating poverty and providing housing opportunities in job rich suburbs. One of the pilot regions was metropolitan Baltimore. Almost as soon as the initiative was announced, the declining blue-collar, at-risk suburban communities of Essex and Dundalk were in frantic public revolt against the idea. Politician after politician lined up to blast the program. Essex and Dundalk, communities in steep residential decline, were not slated to receive new affordable housing units, and HUD made it clear to them that they would not. However, as declining suburbs, they had been on the receiving end of subsidized housing for years, units that probably contributed to their instability. They simply did not trust HUD or the concept of affordable housing programs. In the end, liberal Senator Barbara Mikulski, a powerful member of the HUD budget committee in the Senate, forced an end to the initiative in Baltimore. Perhaps had HUD been more successful in showing Essex and Dundalk that they would not receive additional subsidized housing units and that a strong regional housing effort would make them less, not more, poor, the outcome might have been different.

5. See Orfield (1997, pp. 114–20).
6. Orfield and Luce (2001).

An additional component of a regional housing plan that might win the support of the at-risk suburbs would involve elements of the managed integration approaches of Oak Park, Illinois, or Shaker Heights, Ohio. By creating mechanisms that strongly regulated sales in at-risk communities, created insurance pools for first-time homeowners, and helped maintain middle-class demand, such an effort could help at-risk communities deal with the issues of transition and stability. However, such plans take resources and planning that these communities do not have the experience, staff, or funds to implement. Providing such tools as resources and guidance from experienced planners who help to monitor community change would enable these communities to protect their stability.

Next, infrastructure concurrency requirements for development prevent older suburbs from subsidizing the cost of poorly planned new development and its remediation. Many status-quo systems of highway and sewer financing require older suburban residents, through their taxes, to subsidize communities elsewhere in the region that are siphoning off their most desirable citizens and businesses. Regional planning can help by either ending these subsidies or making them explicit and requiring newly built communities to contribute resources to help with the needs of older communities. Often, sprawl development needs expensive sewer and road remediation. Ultimately, remediation will be financed, if at all, by state or regional grants, and the older suburbs that lost out in the beginning will be forced to help pay for the poorly planned communities that lured away their residents and businesses. Regional land-use planning would convey to the developing competitors of the older suburbs that they could not compete until adequate infrastructure is in place. This would make the competition fairer and would relieve older suburban voters of expensive remediation costs in other parts of the region.

Well-implemented regional urban growth boundaries help redirect growth toward older available suburban sites. Urban growth boundaries, whether created by state law or natural environmental boundaries such as mountains, lakes, or swamps, have had a tendency to be correlated with lower social and fiscal disparities and stronger patterns of fiscal and social health in older communities.

Finally, one of the precepts of smart growth is to take advantage of infrastructure funds to fix old developed at-risk communities before building new communities in greenfield sites. This is a central principle of Maryland's celebrated series of smart-growth laws. This sort of boundary requirement could help rebuild many of the crumbling roads in older suburban America and perhaps be expanded to other forms of infrastructure. Another common smart-growth principle involves opening up funding systems dedicated to highways for metropolitan transit initiatives. This could be a strong benefit to the growing carless working and elderly population in at-risk suburbs.

Regional Governance. Making sure regional governance includes the older suburbs proportionate to their population is likely to return more federal and state funds under the control of the MPO back to the older suburbs and to improve the balance in funding between transit and highways and between remediation of old highways and new capacity built into greenfields.

To the extent that the regional governance system encompasses more than just transportation decisions, involving land planning and affordable housing as well, older communities need seats at the table to make sure newer communities provide affordable housing and follow sound plans in their development. In light of this, it is important to realize that most regional land-use planning regulation affects the developing edge of the region and, if the at-risk suburbs are fully developed, it is unlikely to constrain their activities.

Without regional solutions, the future of these at-risk places is bleak. In a competitive regional economy, they have little to offer middle- and upper-class households and lack businesses that would make them desirable residential or work places. Their only message to the populace is: "Please come to our community. Our schools are fast becoming impoverished, we will tax you to death or skimp on your services." With their low fiscal capacity and lack of amenities, they have little hope of improving their competitive position. If they cut taxes, they cannot generate the revenues needed to deal with their old infrastructure or poverty problems in their schools. If they raise taxes to deal with these challenges, they cannot attract businesses or homeowners. While efficient management and cost-cutting strategies are important and should be encouraged, the regional forces contributing to their decline often overwhelm these efforts. Clearly, the at-risk suburbs will have a very difficult time surviving without significant regional reforms. In the end, these places have no haven in America outside regional cooperation—and the sooner they realize that, the better off they will be.

At-Risk and Bedroom-Developing Communities

There are two types of developing suburbs: the "developing" category of at-risk communities and the bedroom-developing suburb. Each type represents about a quarter of the population of large regions and together they represent about two-thirds of swing districts. Of these districts, about 27 percent are in the at-risk and a whopping 43 percent in the bedroom-developing communities. Both types of communities face significant growth-related challenges. The at-risk developing communities are often exurbs with significant pockets of rural poverty and only about two-thirds of the average regional fiscal capacity per household. As they grow, they lose fiscal capacity per household. The bedroom-developing suburbs have low poverty and average fiscal capacity, but with only a quarter of regional population they are receiving 60 percent of regional population growth and have by far the highest ratio of school children per household.

Beyond the obvious concerns about the health of the entire region, the at-risk-developing and bedroom-developing suburbs have three compelling reasons to support regional cooperation. First, it will reduce their taxes and increase their services, most notably in terms of schools. Second, it will help them get the infrastructure they need for safe and orderly development. Third, it will provide a better alternative to local unilateral growth moratoriums or slow-growth action to respond to the increasingly negative reaction within these communities to the development status quo.

Without significant commercial capacity and with only a small number of local jobs, most of these communities depend chiefly on residential property taxes for their tax base. As a result, many have low per-pupil spending and stressed or inadequate school, transportation, and sewerage infrastructure. Because few jobs are available locally, their residents have unusually long commutes to work. In light of these inconveniences, a negative groundswell is developing in these communities against the status-quo pattern of growth.

Equity. While the bedroom-developing communities are places of comparatively low poverty and diversity, their children-to-household ratio is high, sometimes two to three times higher than in the developed core. Schools are the most expensive local public services in America and hence a high ratio of children means extremely high school costs per household. In every region of the country, at-risk and rapidly developing, moderate-capacity places are the lowest spending districts per pupil. In areas without significant school equity, these places combine high property taxes and low school spending. In addition, at-risk developing suburbs, burdened with high rates of student poverty, compete for middle-class households.

Through school equity and almost any form of tax sharing, these communities can be among the largest recipients of aid per student, and as with the older suburbs, regional fiscal equity often gives these places both money for schools and lower tax rates. This is a hard combination to beat in American politics. Once a system of significant school aids is established, both Democratic and Republican legislative leadership will compete to see which party can give the most money to developing suburban school districts.

Infrastructure. Because of the lack of a local tax base, the governments of at-risk and bedroom-developing communities often hunt much more aggressively for additional development than the affluent job centers. In this hunt, they tend to neglect long-range planning for schools, roads, and sewerage, leaving such issues to a happier future. Instead, they finance their daily costs through revenues from building permits, property taxes, and public debt—much like many of their residents who make ends meet through credit card debt. As many commentators have noted, these communities are gambling that they can throw up rooftops fast enough to create the demand for a shopping mall and accompanying office space that will bail them out. In light of the statistics cited in this volume, this strategy more closely resembles buying a lottery ticket than planning responsibly for maturity and old age. In the end, the cost of neglected infrastructure and schools catches up with them. Then these communities find that, like paying off high-interest credit card balances, digging themselves out of debt costs much more than facing the challenges would have to begin with.

Many at-risk and bedroom-developing communities have allowed significant population growth along small country roads that cannot handle the traffic that accompanies new development. Rebuilding the roads and moving strip malls and houses back from the right of way to widen the roads costs many times more than doing it right in the first place.

Similarly, the septic systems built in low fiscal capacity communities instead of more expensive sewerage invariably fail, polluting the groundwater and endangering public health. This is a huge problem in the Midwest and the Northeast, as illustrated by the Macomb County example. Yet it often escapes the radar of public concern. Again, as in the case of roads, remediation is often many times more expensive than

Governments of developing suburbs finance daily costs through building permits, property taxes, and public debt—just as their residents make ends meet with credit card debt.

doing it right would have been in the first instance. This is because septic systems need large lots, and serving low-density areas raises per-capita costs.[7] Eventually installing sewerage involves building expensive interceptors and trunk lines through developed areas—digging up roads and other public infrastructure, homeowner's lawns, bypassing lakes and stands of trees—all very costly.

Regionalism provides assistance for infrastructure problems in developing communities in two ways. First, through equity, it can give them money to build their own infrastructure. This money can also relieve recurrent cash-flow crises and allow communities to step back from the aggressive hunt for development at any price. Second, by sharing treatment facility costs and long-range road and interceptor planning, pooling regional resources, and creating regional funds and bonding authorities, regionalism can help get infrastructure to these communities in a cost-effective way. Thus, in addition to tax equity, regionally planned and financed infrastructure can relieve bedroom-developing communities of an enormous and unavoidable obligation.

Sprawl. At the millennium, sprawl is a major concern among the American electorate, rivaling education, taxes, crime, and health care.[8] Loss of open space, intensive development, increasing traffic congestion, long commutes, lack of parks and other amenities—all of these things are important quality-of-life issues to suburban voters, especially residents of bedroom-developing suburbs.

Moreover, residents of these communities seem to be increasingly distrustful of their locally elected officials' ability to handle growth appropriately. Consequently, the number and frequency of local ballot initiatives have exploded in the bedroom-developing suburbs. Most of the initiatives that can be connected to cities also came from growth-stressed bedroom-developing suburbs.[9] And most of this smart-growth sentiment was directed toward a pattern of local action that is unlikely to solve either the problem stimulating these community initiatives or the larger growth-related problems affecting entire metropolitan regions.

7. Burchell (1990).

8. In early 2000, a survey conducted for the Pew Center for Civic Journalism identified sprawl. (Princeton Survey Research Associates, February 2000: www.pewcenter.org/doingcj/research/r_ST2000nat1/html.

9. Meyers (2000); Puentes (2000).

A single community can have little effect on the growth of a region. Acting alone, a community is not only unlikely to solve its own growth-related problems but is likely to impose higher costs on the region when it tries. Take the case of Petaluma, California, with its growth moratorium that swamped neighboring Santa Rosa with growth (chapter 6).

In the end, regional or statewide planning to protect open space and create a regional growth boundary has been more effective than unilateral action for bedroom-developing communities to achieve their goal of remaining close to a natural or farmlike setting. Regionally funded transit commuting alternatives are one of the most promising ways to respond to growing congestion. A cooperative regional approach, encouraging affordable housing close to affluent job centers and helping to spread job growth to more regional development nodes, is also likely to provide more help than local Not-in-My-Back-Yard (NIMBY) approaches. In the past, cash-strapped bedroom-developing suburbs have had difficulty affording parks and open space. A regional park fund and comprehensive planning requirement that encourage all fiscally competing communities to set aside park land could better serve all communities. The status-quo reaction against sprawl has made the problem worse.

Affluent Job Centers

In many parts of the nation, affluent job centers are in a revolt against the status quo of regional development. Regionalism will give the affluent job centers a far more effective growth-management regime than local moratoriums, keeping them closer to the urban edge and less likely to be surrounded by sprawling development. Regionalism will also give the regional business leaders and managers who disproportionately live in these communities a more economically prosperous region.

The affluent job centers form a very small proportion of metropolitan regions, with only about 7 percent of regional residents and few swing districts. They have very little poverty and more than twice the regional average fiscal capacity. Despite their quick growth, through careful fiscal zoning they have even managed to keep the number of children at the regional average.

Despite all this, even the affluent job centers are harmed by the lack of regional cooperation. Because they are intense centers of job growth, these communities are often troubled by higher rates of congestion than other suburban areas, particularly in the country's fast-growth regions. Open space is harder to preserve in these communities, because land becomes very valuable. In the most extreme cases, suburban "edge cities" can become as densely urban and congested as city business districts.[10]

Although most ballot initiatives seem to come from the bedroom-developing suburbs, antigrowth ballot initiatives also originate disproportionately in the affluent job centers. Some of the most celebrated and extreme fights against status-quo development patterns have occurred in this small group of suburbs. Here, too, regionalism presents the only possible response to these concerns, the only real way to maintain a suburban rural edge, the only plausible plan for dealing with traffic congestion. It is the only way to have an effect on a neighboring community's poor decisions.

A final consideration becomes important here. Residents of these areas are often the region's economic chieftains, deeply concerned about the regional economy's health and growth. It is increasingly clear that regions with healthy central cities have stronger economic growth and work forces, and the more equitable and regionally focused regions appear to be leading the nation's economic growth. To the extent that these economic leaders—residents in affluent job centers—care about the economy's overall health and well-being of the economy, such communities might be stimulated to support regional cooperation. Clearly, all communities are winners when it comes to regionalism.

CONCLUSION

In the twenty-first century, American politics is almost entirely metropolitan politics. Today's metropolitan politics is based on an inaccurate model of poor cities and rich suburbs. It does not acknowledge that almost half of the U.S. population lives in places that have finished developing and have increasing urban problems. Nor does it come to terms with the fiscal pressure of growth and the public's growing discontent with sprawl and loss of open space. A new metropolitics must understand the diversity of U.S. suburbs and build a broad bipartisan movement for greater regional cooperation. If metropolitics does not succeed, our metropolitan regions will continue to become more unequal, and more energy will be spent growing against ourselves.

10. Garreau (1991).

AN AGENDA FOR REGIONALISM

Four major new steps will advance the cause of regional reform:

—Place regional reform on the agendas of both major parties.

—Build an association of suburbs with a clear interest in reform.

—Strengthen the environmental movement's efforts to reform state land-use laws.

—Renew the civil rights movement in a new campaign against housing discrimination.

STEP 1: PLACE REGIONAL REFORM ON PARTY AGENDAS

Fiscal equity (fixing the tax system), land-use reform (using our resources wisely and efficiently), and accountable regional governance (obtaining fair representation in regional decisions) must be placed on the agendas of both the Republican and Democratic political parties. Initially, most of the nation's significant regional reforms were championed by and identified with Republican political leaders. In tax reform, there has been no clearer backer of fiscal equity than Governor John Engler of Michigan, who in 1994 worked with the legislature to increase the state's share of school funding from 20 to 80 percent, one of the most dramatic improvements of equity in the nation. A few years later, Engler signed into law a state revenue-sharing reform basing distributions to cities more on local fiscal capacity than past spending. Although elements of this bill harmed the city of Detroit, in the long run using fiscal capacity as a factor for aid distribution is a powerful step toward rationalizing Michigan's aid system and ultimately integrating its aid programs with comprehensive land-use reform. In 1997, Governor James Edgar of Illinois, also a Republican, followed Engler's lead by spearheading a movement to dramatically increase school equity funding in Illinois. He was less successful than Engler, but not for lack of courage or outspoken leadership. In 2000 Governor Robert Taft of Ohio proposed a more equitable system of state funding in Ohio but has yet to have legislative leadership match his own. Finally, Minnesota's tax-sharing system's chief proponent was a Republican state House member, Charlie Weaver Sr., and the bill was passed by a Republican-dominated legislature.

The nation's most significant state system of land-use planning, the Oregon Land Use Act, was championed by a Republican, Governor Tom McCall, who has become a great conservationist icon of that state. Recently, Pennsylvania's Tom Ridge signed a new statewide land-use planning bill, former New Jersey Governor Christine Todd Whitman pushed for millions of state dollars for land trusts, Utah's Mike Leavitt has been a leader in state land-use planning efforts, and Minnesota's former governor Arne Carlson has supported the creation of state legislation to deal with the problem of sprawl in the Twin Cities metropolitan area and statewide.

In terms of fair housing, no national leader has been clearer about the detrimental consequences of local Not-in-My-Backyard zoning than Jack Kemp, former secretary of the U.S. Department of Housing and Urban Development and Republican vice-presidential candidate. Kemp declared that NIMBY zoning was one of the worst drags on the U.S. housing market and hence the entire U.S. economy.[1] Newly appointed HUD Secretary Mel Martinez considers economic segregation one of his biggest challenges as HUD secretary.[2]

In terms of structural reform, both of the nation's most extensive systems of regional governance were created in Republican-dominated regions and were championed by Republican governors: Tom McCall of Oregon and Harold Levander of Minnesota. In addition, in 1994 Arne Carlson of Minnesota signed a metropolitan reform act that consolidated all regional sewerage, transportation, transit, and review of land-use planning under the Met Council, which made it the nation's strongest and largest regional government. Similarly, one of the most significant city-county consolidations north of the Mason-Dixon line, that of Indianapolis–Marion County—the Indianapolis Unigov—was

1. Kemp (1991).
2. Interview with Martinez, on "Morning Edition," National Public Radio, April 20, 2001.

championed by a Republican, U.S. Senator Richard Lugar, when he was mayor of Indianapolis. Two of his Republican successors have both become national leaders in the regional movement: William Hudnut, first as a congressman, later as a high-ranking official with the Urban Land Institute; and Steven Goldsmith, a close adviser to President George W. Bush. In the end, regionalism squares with some bedrock Republican values: efficiency, simplicity, and opportunity.

Democratic politicians are also quite open to the issues of regionalism, once they understand them. Democrats tend to represent cities, at-risk suburbs, and bedroom-developing suburbs. Most, if not all, metropolitan Democratic districts have low property wealth (as do more than half the Republican districts). Therefore the basic principles of equity, environmental leadership, and government cooperation should not be difficult ones for Democrats to accept.

STEP 2: BUILD AN ASSOCIATION OF AT-RISK SUBURBAN COMMUNITIES

The regionalist movement would benefit from the formation of an association of at-risk suburban governments that would educate the public about the consequences of social separation and sprawling development and advocate for reform before regional, state, and federal governments. The most distressed older governments should form the local organization's core. From there, the group should expand to include developing suburbs that can support the principles of metropolitan tax equity, land-use planning, and a representative and comprehensive system of regional governance. The local organization would employ professional staff and would have the ability to do research to inform its participation in regional, state, and federal-level tax, land-use, and governance discussions.

The beginnings of such a model exist in the First Suburbs Consortium in Ohio, the North Metro Mayors Association in the Twin Cities, the South Suburban Mayors and Managers Association in Chicago, and the Gateway Cities in Los Angeles. These are essential organizations: they represent the local units of government in the most fragile places in America. Because they represent significant population and political strength, they could be powerful. Ultimately, each region of the country should have such an organization. These local regional associations should, in turn, form statewide organizations when multiple metropolitan areas are present (as in Ohio), and a national organization with a presence in Washington, D.C.

Regionalism squares with Republican values: efficiency, simplicity, opportunity; while its principles of equity, environmental leadership, and government cooperation should not be hard for Democrats to accept.

If such a structure could be organized, it would enable these groups to share information about best practices locally and about legislative progress in each state and at the federal level. It would also allow older suburbs to overcome some of the fragmentation that has so long divided them and silenced their voices. This would give the at-risk suburbs, like the central cities, a presence before regional, state, and federal governments. The process of organizing such an association has begun as a joint project of the Metropolitan Area Research Corporation (MARC) and the Brookings Center on Urban and Metropolitan Policy.[3]

STEP 3: STRENGTHEN THE ENVIRONMENTAL MOVEMENT'S EFFORTS TO REFORM STATE LAND-USE LAWS

Sprawl is an upsetting issue for more and more voters, especially residents of the fast-growth regions in the United States. Responding to those concerns, governmental and philanthropic commitment is growing. However, too much of this energy has been dissipated in sidetrack strategies unlikely to alter detrimental trends. More often than not, citizen opposition to the metropolitan growth machine results only in a localized growth moratorium, which aggravates metropolitan sprawl. A purely local moratorium simply pushes development into other communities—often tax-hungry exurbs lacking the capacity to plan properly. Local moratoriums feed regional sprawl, congestion, and decentralization and do nothing at all for the declining core regions.

A second, though not harmful, sidetrack strategy is the land trust movement. Tremendous amounts of energy and enormous governmental and philanthropic resources are being devoted to an effort to solve sprawl by buying land and preserving it from development. In effect, this movement is occupying the field of most states in terms of reform. In places like New Jersey and Maryland, the government is devoting vast sums to purchase land. Large U.S. foundations have given single grants in the tens of millions for this purpose. Although any land protected from development is an undisputed gain in open space preserved, such efforts are unlikely to have any real effect on metropolitan sprawl. For example, every year the Oregon land-use law saves more land from development than all the U.S. land trusts do in a decade.[4] Land purchased just shifts potential development to another regional

> *A purely local growth moratorium simply pushes development into other communities —often tax-hungry exurbs lacking the capacity to plan properly.*

3. See www.brook.edu/urban.
4. Richmond (1997).

176

venue. In any case, there is not enough money in philanthropy, in government, or in the wealthy U.S. economy to buy even a fraction of the land that needs protection and planning.

To really protect our environment, we have to change the rules of the game—through land-use laws. In the states where this has happened or is beginning to happen, public interest groups are already fighting for changes in state law. This process, though often controversial and always difficult and long, is the real road to progress. These groups could make much stronger progress if they were more seriously supported.

In this light, the national confederation the Growth Management Leadership Alliance (GMLA) presents a model for strengthening and consolidating the movement toward changes in state and federal land-use law. Founded by 26 member organizations operating in 22 states, GMLA members have been at the center of most if not all significant statewide land-use reform efforts.

GMLA has taken the next step in this process, reaching out beyond its usual coalitions of environmentalists to the fully built communities, particularly those suffering the detrimental consequences of being left behind by sprawl. In Portland and the Twin Cities, this process is the farthest advanced. The Coalition for a Livable Future and the Alliance for Metropolitan Stability are multimember groups working toward a regional agenda connecting land use and urban interest. In Cleveland, Eco-City Cleveland has joined efforts with the First Suburbs Consortium and United WE-CAN! a church-based advocacy group. In Baltimore, the Chesapeake Bay Foundation is working with the Regional Partnership, the Citizens Planning and Housing Association, and other organizations toward a comprehensive regional agenda.[5]

STEP 4: RENEW THE CIVIL RIGHTS MOVEMENT AROUND A CAMPAIGN TO END HOUSING DISCRIMINATION

There must be a renewed civil rights movement that is centered on ending racial discrimination in U.S. housing markets and in educating U.S. citizens about the consequences of continuing racial segregation in an increasingly diverse society. Race is the most intransigent dilemma confronting the United States. The nation took a century to abolish slavery and another century to grudgingly begin the process of allowing full citizenship to blacks.

5. For more information on the GMLA, see their web site at www.gmla.org.

Most discriminated groups have eventually blended into the larger U.S. society by moving out of segregated neighborhoods and into the mainstream of geographic opportunity.

Twice before in U.S. history—against seemingly insuperable odds, significant civil rights movements made significant gains. The abolition movement occurred between 1829 and 1876. The other significant movement was the push toward equality during the twentieth century by the NAACP, the Southern Christian Leadership Conference, and many other affiliated groups in a large multiracial civil rights movement. Both movements were built on facts and well-constructed arguments, but only after organizations mobilized in a highly public campaign of creative nonviolent action did real political progress occur. In both movements, broad segments of the U.S. church community were centrally involved in the public campaign to change opinion and law. Churches have unique power, because they are broadly based, respected institutions that speak with authority about a higher truth and moral purpose. Recent studies of the life and work of the abolitionist William Lloyd Garrison and David Garrow's chronicles of the American civil rights movement reveal the depth and power of the secular and church-based movement to achieve racial equality.[6]

Most of the groups discriminated against in the United States have eventually blended into the larger society by moving out of segregated neighborhoods into the mainstream of geographic opportunity. This is true of the Irish, Italians, East Europeans, Jews, and, more recently, many Asian groups. Through this blending comes membership and opportunity. Casting aside laments about cultural preservation—which are real and important—no other model has yet been created for achieving true equity and opportunity in the United States. Historically, every group kept separate has been held behind. Separate in the United States has never been equal. First American blacks and now Latinos have a unique history of separation based upon layers and layers of discrimination in the housing and employment markets.

How does a group position itself for progress in the face of such constant rejection and separation? It hedges its bets. It has two approaches that wax and wane. One approach asks for inclusion in the society on the same terms as all other groups of citizens in the United States. The other, in the face of constant rejection, asks for special help in self-improvement as a separate society. The first objective is clearer and, if understood by the public, more likely to achieve broad support. It responds to the classic American promise of opportunity. In the initial stage however, the first message can be exceptionally controversial and

6. See Branch (1988; 1998); Mayer (1998).

hard fought by powerful irrational forces. Many large institutions, like existing governmental officials and philanthropy, shun controversy—therefore making support for progress on this front hard to find. The second approach is less immediately controversial and thus more likely to achieve support from philanthropic groups and the government. However, it is unlikely to make much difference for blacks or Latinos left behind in segregated conditions. Moreover, because the second approach asks for special help to a community separate from the majority—in the words of polarizing commentators "for privileges rather than common rights"—it will never win much broad public support. Such strategies are likely to become a target for political leaders seeking to appeal to struggling white voters who want scapegoats for their own condition. In the end, such strategies often benefit demagogues more than the groups they were designed to help.

To judge by the current web pages of the NAACP and the Urban League, the modern civil rights movement has become largely an effort to preserve the gains from the initial movement toward racial equality, to maintain embattled affirmative action programs, and to gather support for community-development activities. New antidiscrimination initiatives are more likely to center on police profiling and disparate health risks for people of color than on segregation in the housing market—a form of discrimination that lies at the center of the black and Latino condition in the United States.

Ironically, at the millennium, the U.S. civil rights agenda labors under the twin detriments of being relatively unimportant in terms of making progress for blacks and Latinos and being increasingly radioactive to swing voters and hence to most powerful politicians. The political battle against affirmative action is being waged in many states, where demagogues are gaining political advantage by whipping up white resentment against imagined special privileges. Although this strategy may have backfired in California and was pointedly rejected by President George W. Bush when he was governor of Texas, it remains a powerful political wedge in many parts of this country.

Governmental support for the community-development movement has been waning for decades. There is little support and no present political strategy to get a majority of any state or the national government to provide anything more than token financial help. More and more activists and organizations representing people of color and poor urban neighborhoods fight among themselves, standing on the melting ice cube of the urban tax base as the governmental resources of the metropolitan economy sprawl away from them.

179

The mainline civil rights organizations should be brought into this discussion. The former abolitionist movement and the Southern Christian Leadership Conference should be a model. A renewed civil rights effort against housing discrimination should begin. Like the models in the abolitionist movement, it should be a partnership with religious and secular antidiscrimination organizations. The churches stood at the core of the modern civil rights movement, providing the moral foundation and fortitude for the struggles necessary to win civil rights. The churches also provide one of the only organizing bases to think about these issues, and they are one of the few organizations busy suburbanites still join.[7] The new civil rights movement needs to pursue housing opportunity with the same resolve and tactics used earlier in the struggles against slavery and discrimination in public accommodations and barriers to the vote. The classic strategy of creative nonviolent protest, legislation, and, if necessary, litigation should be resumed.

At present, the possibility for this renewal lies in the work of groups like the Gamaliel Foundation, a multiracial city-suburban church-based alliance headquartered in Chicago. Gamaliel is a network of multiracial religious leaders, professional community organizers, and other community leaders working to "rebuild urban and older suburban communities" throughout the country. Gamaliel has successfully organized strategies around tax equity, land-use planning, transit, and regional governance throughout its regional network of some forty grass-roots organizations in 11 states. It works in virtually every major metropolitan area in the Midwest, the western regions of New York and Pennsylvania, and Oakland, California, and is aggressively seeking to expand its base of operations. Gamaliel is one of the only organizations in the nation with broad multiracial leadership focused on a regional reform agenda.[8]

LESSONS ON REGIONAL COALITION BUILDING

In an earlier volume, I laid out 11 lessons on regional coalition building.[9] Here they are again—revised to reflect what I have learned since 1997.

7. See Putnam (2000).
8. A full list of Gamaliel organizations can be found at www.gamaliel.org.
9. Orfield (1997).

Lesson 1: Understand the Region's Demographics and Make Maps

Look for the at-risk suburbs, bedroom-developing communities, and affluent job centers. Understand the local fiscal equity questions, whether they center around improving school aid or the potential to improve or create an aid system to cities and suburbs. Understand also the local issues surrounding growth management and transportation/transit planning. Measure road spending and land use. Seek out other regions' studies; finance and conduct others. Bring in the best scholars at area universities. In short, develop the most accurate and comprehensive picture of the region possible.

Use color maps to show trends. They are inexpensive to create, easy to reproduce for meetings or presentations, and truly worth a thousand words. Politicians, newspaper reporters, citizens' groups, and other potential allies will not necessarily read reports or speeches, but they will look at color maps, over and over again. These maps will persuade them. MARC has created these maps with accompanying reports for more than 30 U.S. regions. The maps of the 25 largest U.S. regions created for this volume can be found at www.metroresearch.org.

Lesson 2: Reach Out and Organize the Issue on a Personal Level

Political reform is about ideas, but it is also about personal relationships and trust. Political persuasion is about selling an idea to another person or group that has power. This cannot be done over the Internet, by mail, or through publication of big new ideas. It has to be done in person. When regional trends are satisfactorily described, some individual or group of people has to reach out, person to person, to make contact with the individuals and groups affected by them. Do not announce problems and disparities until the people and groups affected have been met.

Invite input from all these individuals. Then lay out broad themes and the areas where regional progress is necessary—namely, tax policy and reinvestment, land-use planning and affordable housing, regional governance, and transportation/transit planning. Talk about the experience of other states. Engage all affected constituencies in the crafting of legislation. This gives them all ownership and allows for adjustment to the economic, physical, cultural, and political peculiarities of their localities—which they know best.

Lesson 3: Build a Broad, Inclusive Coalition

The coalition should stress two themes: it is in the entire region's long-term interest to solve the problems of polarization; it is also in the immediate short-term interest of most of the region. The first argument is important for the long haul; the second gets the ball rolling.

A regional agenda, at the beginning, finds few elected altruistic supporters. The early political support for regional reform in the Twin Cities and most other places came entirely from legislators who believed their districts would benefit immediately or soon from part or all of our policy package. The politics of self-interest was particularly apparent in the housing bill, where the decisive suburban political support was largely defensive in character. The supporters believed that as long as the affluent, developing part of the region did not accept its fair share of affordable housing, the burden would fall on the older parts of the Twin Cities region. The suburbs with a low tax base supported tax-base sharing, because it gave them lower taxes and better services. Places supported land-use planning to protect natural places they valued.

Lesson 4: "It's the Suburbs, Stupid!"

Regional reformers should tape this message to their mirrors: The at-risk and bedroom-developing suburbs are the pivotal point in American politics and the reformers' key political allies. They were instrumental in electing Presidents Nixon, Carter, Reagan, Clinton, and Bush and an endless procession of officials in state office. The support of these suburbs alters the political dynamics. When regionalism becomes a suburban issue, it becomes possible. As long as regionalism is portrayed as a conflict between city and suburbs, the debate is over before it starts.

In this light, do not accept early rejection by working-class, at-risk suburbs. These communities have been polarized for more than a generation. Residential turnover and the growing impoverishment of their communities, the downturn in the U.S. economy for low-skilled workers, and relentless class- and raced-based political appeals have made many residents calloused. Keep talking, keep trying. Eventually you will connect.

Bedroom-developing suburbs need money for schools and infrastructure. High-growth places are often choking on growing congestion and loss of open space. Beneath it all, these various communities will soon realize that they need regionalism to have healthy, stable communities. They will come around as they come to see that a better future is possible, their alternatives are limited, cooperation will produce measurable benefits, and they have long-term, trustworthy friends in the promoters of regionalism.

Lesson 5: Reach into the Central Cities to Make Sure the Message Is Understood

Central cities have a volatile political landscape. Without person-to-person contact in the inner city, the message will be misunderstood. Regionalism, if misperceived, threatens the power base of officials elected by poor, segregated constituencies. In this light, as in the older suburbs, the patterns of regional polarization must be reemphasized and the hopelessness of the present course revealed. Metropolitan reforms must not be presented as alternatives to existing programs competing for resources and power. Instead, they need to be seen as complements that would gradually reduce overwhelming central-city problems to manageable size and provide resources for community redevelopment through metropolitan equity. Fair housing is not an attempt to force poor minority communities to disperse but to allow individuals to choose—whether to remain or seek out opportunity, wherever it may be. Increasingly, U.S. mayors are getting the message of regionalism. Significantly, African American mayors like Dennis Archer of Detroit, Sharon Sayles Belton of Minneapolis, Bill Johnson of Rochester, New York, Wellington Webb of Denver, and former Seattle mayor Norm Rice have become strong advocates of regionalism. The writings of john powell of the University of Minnesota's Center for Race and Poverty and Robert Bullard at Clark Atlanta University have made powerful and new compelling arguments regarding the importance of regionalism to communities of color.

Lesson 6: Seek Out the Region's Religious Community

Politicians and self-interest arguments can move the agenda forward in the city and older suburbs. But they will not build a base of understanding in the affluent areas, and their determined opposition will slow progress. Churches and other houses of worship and religious organizations can bring a powerful new dimension to the debate—the moral dimension. How moral is it, they will ask, to divide a region into two communities, one prospering and enjoying all the benefits of metropolitan citizenship while the other bears most of its burdens? How moral is it to strand the region's poor people on a melting ice cube of resources at the region's core or to destroy forests and farmland, while older cities decline? Churches will broaden the reach of a regional movement. They can provide a legitimacy for its message in distrustful blue-collar suburbs, and understanding and a sense of responsibility and fair play in more affluent ones. Without the churches, the Twin Cities housing bill would not have been signed. Churches could also become part of a renewed American civil rights movement.

Lesson 7: Seek out the Philanthropic Community, Established Reform Groups, and Business Leaders

Every day philanthropic organizations face the consequences of regional polarization, and their mission statements are often in line with regional reform. They can be important sources of financing for research and nonprofit activities in support of regional solutions. Large American philanthropies are beginning to center new giving in the area of regionalism and smart growth.

The League of Women Voters can be helpful, as can entities such as the National Civic League and established reform groups. All of these groups can confer establishment respectability on the regional cause. Many of these groups, by themselves, have been working on regional reform for a generation. In this light, seek their counsel as well as their support.

Business leadership has led many important initiatives in support of regional reform. The support of business leaders can also be critical to advancing metropolitan reform. Prominent leaders include the Silicon Valley Manufacturing Group in California, the Greater Baltimore Committee, and the Greater Milwaukee Committee.[10] None has been as influential and important as the work of Chicago Metropolis 20/20. Here the business leaders of the nation's third largest region, under the leadership of Elmer Johnson, former general counsel of General Motors, and later George Ranney, chairman of the board of Inland Steel, retraced the steps of Daniel Burnham's turn-of-the-century Plan of Chicago. In the early twenty-first century, Chicago Metropolis 20/20 found that the region needed tax reform, land-use planning reform, and a more firm and representative regional structure. The report has had broad influence in Chicago and throughout the nation.[11] Leadership like this is indispensable in moving a regional agenda along.

10. All these organizations have web sites: see, for example, the Silicon Valley Manufacturing Group in California (www.svmg.org) and the Greater Baltimore Committee (www.gbc.org/reports/regionalism.htm).

11. See Metropolis Principles (www.chicagometropolis2020.org/plan.pdf).

Lesson 8: Draw in Distinct but Compatible Issues and Organizations

In addition to the churches, the communities of color have a deep stake in this agenda, as do land-use groups and a broad variety of environmental organizations that can reach into affluent suburbia. Women's and senior citizens' organizations, for example, want a variety of housing types in all communities for single mothers and retired people who cannot remain in their homes. These groups also want better transit. The preservationist movement, as led by the National Trust for Historic Preservation and all its local affiliates, is interested in preserving strong cities and maintaining important rural and open spaces at the region's edge. They would also like to see suburban planning that can respect the density and pedestrian orientation of old cities now becoming part of the metropolitan orbit. Regionalism is a multifaceted gemstone. In the power of its comprehensive solutions, it can show a bright face to many different constituencies to build broad support.

Lesson 9: With the Coalition, Seek out the Media

Using factual information, suburban officials, churches, philanthropists, reform groups, and business leaders, seek out editorial boards, which by necessity must have a broad, far-reaching vision for the region. Reporters are always looking for something new and potentially controversial. They will like the maps, and straightforward news releases without too much theoretical discussion will get the message across The best news sources to contact include major daily newspapers and public radio and television. Concentrate on the reporters with a suburban beat and any reporter who writes on demographics. Likewise, public radio and television can offer a fair and interested forum.

Both newspapers and public radio lead other news. Spend lots of time with these sources. Give them lots of information. They are the only media that will try to take the time to understand what you are talking about.

Be careful and well prepared with local commercial TV. It is best if the newspapers, public radio, and television are allowed to set the tone for commercial television. Local commercial TV reporters can spiral off in unpredictable ways, and television is enormously powerful. For commercial television, focus your message into short clear ideas and make sure they cannot be perceived as threatening the suburbs.

Finally, do not seek out talk radio, but be prepared to show the flag and participate if invited. Your goal is to prevent distortions, to clarify the suburban interest in this (particularly the blue-collar suburban interest)—that is, lower taxes, more stable residential markets, and better public services—not to win the hearts and minds of the far right.

Lesson 10: Prepare for Controversy

Professional regionalists have, over the years, explained away Minnesota's and Oregon's success with reforms as being the result of people having reached some happy Olympian consensus. This is not true. Each reform was a tough battle, and each group of leaders had to build coalitions to weather intense opposition and controversy. This is how any important reform in politics comes about—from labor reform, to civil rights, to the women's movement. Reform never happens effortlessly or overnight. It entails building coalitions, creating power, and engaging in strenuous political struggle. In the midst of a campaign and controversy, it is important to constantly emphasize the message of the common good and the benefits of these reforms to the region as a whole.

Lesson 11: Move Simultaneously on Several Fronts and Accept Good Compromises

Get as many issues moving as can effectively be managed, but not so many that nothing happens. Keep opponents busy and on the defensive. When many bills were moving in the Minnesota legislature, rarely were we completely defeated in any session. The governor of Minnesota vetoed the housing bill in 1993 but signed a land-use reform bill. He vetoed housing in 1994 but signed the Metro Reorganization Act. He vetoed tax-base sharing in 1995 but signed the housing bill. Had these bills not all been moving at once, no bill would have been signed. The same is true in all other states with participation in regional reform efforts. A platform for progress can be built step by step, bill by bill, session by session. Frequently, an advocacy group gets a bill on the legislative agenda that moves or threatens to move. Another group, opposed to progress, initiates its own bill, which claims progress on the same issue—but does very little. Out of these two positions is fashioned a compromise. In this light, it is important to keep the initial purer idea alive and potentially threatening as long as possible. Maintaining even a small chance that the original idea may pass will keep the compromise as strong as possible.

CONCLUSIONS

Our society is overwhelmingly metropolitan and will continue to grow more metropolitan, but government is fragmented and increasingly unequal among jurisdictions in the nation's large regions. This sort of organization may fit some Americans' idealized notion of small government and local control. For many other Americans, however, the reality of regional fragmentation means living in declining communities, paying more taxes for less service, and putting up with a deteriorating quality of life—powerless to reverse the course. For others living on the fringes of metropolitan America, fragmented, warring governments mean inadequate school spending, polluted wells and lakes, and commutes stretching into hours of dense gridlock. Even in the small areas of fiscal strength, "local government" often means submitting to a metro growth machine, grinding down local amenities and living conditions, with no prospect of resisting or deflecting its titanic force.

The goals of regionalism offer the best hope of taking back and keeping local control. Regionalism is not a sea change in the nature of local government but a strengthening and refocusing of existing, if weak, systems for cooperation. In this light, the movement toward regionalism is comparable to the nation's early transition from the Articles of Confederation to the Constitution. The new nation, a loose consortium of independent countries, could not protect itself from outside threats or function without a coordinated economic marketplace within its boundaries. The Constitution, with its important but explicitly limited shift of power to the center, may have weakened the power of the states, but it ultimately and immeasurably strengthened the nation and its constituent states. As the Constitution of 1787 had to be invented to protect the early nation from threats from without, a new form of regional confederation in each American region is needed to protect all citizens from the threats within.

TAX-CAPACITY CALCULATIONS

In this work a municipality's *tax capacity* is defined as the revenue that would be forthcoming if that municipality applied metropolitan-wide average tax rates to each tax base available to it under state law. Included in the analysis are property, sales, and income taxes. *Total revenue capacity* is defined as tax capacity plus state aid. These four revenue sources constituted roughly two thirds of local general revenue in the United States in 1996. The remaining third came largely from assorted fees and charges.

Charges and fees were excluded from this analysis for two reasons, the first conceptual, the second practical. The conceptual difficulties involve defining capacity in this context. Because fees and charges are assessed in many different ways, it is difficult to define the base on which the fee or charge is calculated (to compute a "tax rate"). Income might serve as a reasonable measure of the base for fees associated with consumption of specific services (for example, water fees based on usage rates). However, income would not serve as a good measure of the base for impact fees, that is, fees assessed on new housing or business development to offset infrastructure or other public costs associated with the development. Some measure of the potential value of new development would serve best for those types of fees. It would be difficult theoretically to measure this potential and nearly impossible in practice.

The practical difficulties are associated primarily with data availability. Adequate revenue and base data for fees and charges are not generally available at the local level. Most local revenue data sources do not report revenues separately from the different types of fees. When such distinctions can be made, it is often because the revenues are reported separately for various enterprise funds. However, such data are often difficult to interpret, because net revenues from such funds are commonly transferred from one fund to another. Nor are reliable recent data for the potential base for such revenues generally available. Local income data are available for all localities only in national census years. Measures of the potential base for impact or development fees are even more difficult to come by. For instance, the extent and value of land available for development are obtainable only in select cases from land-use surveys. Comparable data for all the municipalities in the 25 largest metropolitan areas are simply not available.

Both conceptual and practical concerns were also involved in the decision to use metropolitan average tax rates (rather than national average rates) in the capacity calculation. Conceptually, one could argue that applying national average rates to local bases for all three of the taxes is preferable, because that procedure would generate tax capacities that were comparable across metropolitan areas. However, this measure would provide tax capacities that were comparable only assuming that all tax bases were available to all municipalities. State laws limit local taxing powers in different ways in different states, and these distinctions are important when considering local tax capacities. For instance, if Boston ranked high among large cities in income-tax capacity but low in property-tax capacity, its overall tax capacity might rank fairly high. However, this would be of limited relevance to policymakers in Boston, because under Massachusetts law only the property tax is available to them. In addition, it can be argued that the best universe of comparison for local tax capacities is the metropolitan area, because the labor and housing markets most significantly affected by differences in capacities and costs (and the resulting differences in tax rates) are metropolitan in scope.

However one decides the conceptual issues, practical issues militate against applying national average rates to all three bases in all of the municipalities in the sample. In practice, tax-base data are available in a state only for the taxes in common usage in that state. For instance, base data on a local sales tax are not generally available in states where municipalities are not granted the power to tax sales.

Property-tax capacity was calculated using *effective tax rates* (revenues as a percentage of market value) in all cases to control for the fact that assessment ratios vary across (and, in some cases, within) states. Effective sales and income-tax bases were also used to control for differences in the coverage of the taxes across states. These decisions reflect the fact that the overall objective of the capacity calculations is to estimate each municipality's capacity to raise revenues within the context of the state laws governing its taxing behavior. Average tax rates for each base were calculated as the mean rate for 1993 and 1998. This measure was used so that the measured growth rate in tax capacity would reflect only changes in tax bases (and not in tax rates).

In the 19 metropolitan areas where more than one tax was available to some or all municipalities, the tax-capacity calculation was adjusted to reflect the fact that revenues from one tax do not displace or augment revenues from other taxes dollar for dollar. For example, if a locality that has access to only the property tax gains access to a new tax, its total tax revenues are unlikely to increase by exactly the amount of the revenues from the new tax. Instead, one would expect the property-tax rate to decline with the addition of the new revenues from the new tax base. Put another way, the property-tax rate (and therefore revenues) will be lower in a locality that also taxes sales than it would be in the absence of the sales-tax revenues. The difference in property-tax revenues between the two situations is likely to be some fraction (between 0 and 1) of the sales-tax revenues.

This fraction was estimated for both sales and income taxes from a regression analysis of all of the municipalities in the 25 metropolitan areas. This analysis implied that, all else equal, local property-tax revenues decline by $0.373 for each $1.00 of local sales-tax revenue and by $0.310 for each dollar of local income-tax revenues.[1]

These revenue displacement rates were converted into a commensurate adjustment to the property-tax base, jurisdiction by jurisdiction, by the following formula:

(A-1) $PBASE^*_i = PBASE_i - \{(t^S_i/t^P_i)\ (SBASE_i)(.373)\} - \{(t^I_i/t^P_i)\ (IBASE_i)(.310)\}$

Where $PBASE_i$ = property-tax base in jurisdiction i;
$PBASE^*_i$ = revised property-tax base in i;
t^S_i = sales-tax rate in i;
t^I_i = income-tax rate in i;
t^P_i = property-tax rate in i;
$SBASE_i$ = sales-tax base in i; and
$IBASE_i$ = income-tax base in i

1. The regression modeled property-tax revenues per household (dependent variable) as a function of median household income, *tax price* (the property-tax share of a median value home), intergovernmental aid per household, sales-tax revenues per household, income-tax revenues per household, average household size, the percentage of housing units that are owner-occupied, population density, poverty rate, age of the housing stock, and the statewide average local share of state and local direct expenditures.

PBASE$_i^*$ was then used to calculate property-tax capacity. In some cases, the adjustment resulted in a *PBASE*$_i^*$ less than zero. In those cases, the property-tax base in the community was set to zero (which implies a property-tax capacity of zero). This adjustment was used in metropolitan areas where all jurisdictions used sales or income taxes and in cases where only a subset of jurisdictions used sales or income taxes but tax-base data for the "extra" tax were not available for all places.

Four other situations also required special procedures: (1) areas where only one locality had access to a specific tax; (2) combined city-counties; (3) Washington, D.C. (which has no state); (4) areas with classified property-tax systems (different tax rates for different classes of property).

1. Localities with special access to a specific tax. In several metropolitan areas, a single municipality has the authority to levy a tax not generally available to local governments in the state or metropolitan area. This was the case in the Washington, D.C., Kansas City, and St. Louis metropolitan areas. In each of these three cases, only one city (the District of Columbia and, in Missouri, Kansas City and St. Louis), has the authority to use a local income tax. In these cases property-tax capacity in the locality with special access to the income tax was calculated using equation A-1, with income-tax capacity set equal to income-tax revenues.

2. Combined city-counties. In this sample, the cities of Baltimore, Denver, New York, Philadelphia, San Francisco, and St. Louis are combined city-counties. This means that revenues (both taxes and aid) in these cities reflect the fact that they have greater expenditure responsibilities than other municipalities in their states and metropolitan areas. To correct for this, tax and aid revenues for these cities were multiplied by the statewide average local share of total local plus county revenues for the relevant source. This correction affects the tax-capacity estimates only indirectly, through its impact on the calculation of the regionwide average tax rate. It affects the calculation of total revenue capacity (tax capacity plus aid) directly by decreasing the amount of aid to the relevant city included in the calculation. The procedure is meant to isolate revenue for municipal functions from aid for county functions.

3. Washington, D.C. The nation's capital, a federal territory, is not part of a state. It therefore has expenditure responsibilities that other cities do not have, and it does not share its income- and sales-tax bases with a state as other cities do. Sales and income-tax revenues for the city were therefore scaled by the average local share of each tax for the nation as a whole. This affects the capacity calculation for Washington, D.C., directly because the income tax is not in general use in the metropolitan area. This means that the tax-capacity calculation for the city uses revenues from this tax directly (as described above under category 2).

Washington, D.C., also receives federal aid meant to replace the state aid that it does not receive. However, it is difficult to disentangle this aid from the "normal" federal aid that many cities receive (and that is not counted in total revenue capacity). In addition, it has often been argued that, for a variety of reasons, the District receives much less of this aid than it should. Federal aid is meant to compensate the city both for federal buildings, representing large amounts of potential property-tax base, which are exempt from local taxation, and for the aid that states normally receive. Analysts generally agree this aid is adequate to cover either of these cost categories alone, but not both.[2] For these reasons, federal aid was not included in the total revenue-capacity calculation for Washington, D.C.

4. *Classified property-tax systems.* In states where localities may assess different tax rates on different types of property, the calculation of property–tax capacity was modified to allow the capacities to reflect differences in the mix of property types across places. Average tax rates were calculated separately for different types of property. Tax capacity was then calculated separately for each type of property for each jurisdiction. Total property-tax capacity was the sum of capacities for each property type.

---

2. It has also been argued that Washington, D.C., has been undercompensated for its welfare expenses. Welfare programs represent a major portion of federal aid to states. Historically, these funds were provided on a matching basis with the federal share determined state by state, with low-income states receiving a larger match than high-income states. Washington's matching rate has usually been determined independently and the rate has usually been commensurate with high-income states when actual income levels in the District would have justified a more generous match.

TAX-BASE-SHARING
SIMULATIONS

The tax-base-sharing simulations show the effects on the intrametropolitan distribution of local tax capacity of pooling 10 percent of each jurisdiction's tax capacity (from all bases combined) into a regionwide pool. This capacity is then redistributed back to municipalities, on the basis of a formula like the one employed by the Twin Cities Fiscal Disparities Program (below). With this distribution formula, the share a municipality receives is determined by the ratio of the metropolitan area average tax capacity per household and the municipality's tax base per household.

Contribution to the
pool by municipality i $\qquad = C_i = (.1) * (TXCAP_i)$

Total size of the pool $\qquad = \Sigma \, C_i$

Distributions from the pool:

Distribution index
  for municipality i $\quad = I_i = (HH_i) * \dfrac{\Sigma \, TXCAP_i \, / \, \Sigma \, HH_i}{TXCAP_i \, / \, HH_i}$

Distribution to municipality i $\qquad = D_i = \dfrac{I_i}{\Sigma \, I_i} * (\Sigma \, C_i)$

The formulation guarantees that $\Sigma \, C_i = \Sigma \, D_i$ (total contributions = total distributions).

APPENDIX C

MARC PROJECTS COMPLETED OR IN PROGRESS

MARC Projects Completed or in Progress[a]

Project	Date	Local Partner(s)	Funder(s)
American Metropolitics, social and fiscal analysis of 25 largest U.S. regions; 500+ maps	Jan-01	Brookings Institution	Charles Stewart Mott Foundation, Deutsche Bank, Ford Foundation, John D. and Catherine T. MacArthur Foundation, Local Initiatives Support Corporation (LISC), McKnight Foundation, Mid-America Regional Council, Rockefeller Foundation, U.S. Department of Housing and Urban Development
Atlanta	Dec-98	Atlanta Regional Commission	Turner Foundation
Baltimore	Mar-98	Citizens Planning and Housing Association	The Abell Foundation, Inc.
Boston	Oct-01	Citizens' Housing and Planning Association	Harvard University
California Central Valley	Jan-01	Great Valley Center	David and Lucile Packard Foundation
California, short report	Sep-00	Great Valley Center	David and Lucile Packard Foundation
California, statewide study	Mar-02	Great Valley Center, San Diego Dialogue, Urban Habitat Program	William and Flora Hewlett Foundation
Canada-U.S., health indicators study	Oct-01	University of British Columbia	Canadian Population Health Initiative
Chicago	Oct-96	John D. and Catherine T. MacArthur Foundation	Gaylord and Dorothy Donnelley Foundation, John D. and Catherine T. MacArthur Foundation
Chicago, maps only	Nov-00	Chicago Metropolis 2020	Chicago Metropolis 2020
Chicago, congressional districts	Feb-98	Brookings Institution	Brookings Institution
Cincinnati	Aug-01	Citizens for Civic Renewal	Regional Initiatives Fund of Greater Cincinnati Foundation
Cleveland	Jul-01	United WE-CAN!	Cleveland State University, George Gund Foundation
Cleveland, maps only	Mar-98	Cleveland State University	Cleveland State University
Community Typology, 50 largest regions	**	Brookings Institution	Brookings Institution
Connecticut, maps/ reforms	**	Archdiocese of Hartford	Archdiocese of Hartford
Denver	Apr-00	Center for Regional and Neighborhood Action, Metro Mayors Caucus	City and County of Denver, Denver Regional Council of Governments

MARC Projects Completed or in Progress[a] (*continued*)

Project	Date	Local Partner(s)	Funder(s)
Detroit	Jan-99	Archdiocese of Detroit	Archdiocese of Detroit
Erie, Pa.	Oct-01	County of Erie	County of Erie
Gainesville, Ga., redistricting maps	Jun-01	Lawyers' Committee for Civil Rights Under Law	Lawyers' Committee for Civil Rights Under Law
Gary, maps only	Jul-97	Northwest Indiana Interfaith Federation	Northwest Indiana Interfaith Federation
Grand Rapids	May-99	Grand Valley Metropolitan Council	Frey Foundation
Kentucky, rural-urban analysis	May-00	Mountain Association for Community Economic Development, Southern Rural Development Initiative	Ford Foundation
Kentucky, fiscal analysis of northern cities	Dec-01	Forward Quest	Forward Quest
Los Angeles	May-00	None	ARCO Foundation, Rockefeller Foundation
Miami	Jun-98	Collins Center for Public Policy, Inc.	John D. and Catherine T. MacArthur Foundation
Michigan, statewide study	**	Archdiocese of Detroit, Center for Applied Environmental Research, Ezekiel Project, Grand Valley Metropolitan Council, ISAAC, Michigan Environmental Council, Michigan Land Use Institute, Michigan Local Government Management Association, Michigan Municipal League, MOSES	Archdiocese of Detroit, Diocese of Saginaw, Kalamazoo Community Foundation (other funders pending at time of publication)
Milwaukee	May-98	Center on Wisconsin Strategy	University of Wisconsin
Mississippi, redistricting maps	**	Lawyers' Committee for Civil Rights Under Law	Lawyers' Committee for Civil Rights Under Law
17 regions mapped	Dec-01	Fannie Mae Foundation	Fannie Mae Foundation, U.S. Department of Housing and Urban Development
Ohio, statewide study	**	ACTION, Citizens for Civic Renewal, Sierra Club-Ohio Chapter, United WE-CAN!	Cleveland Foundation (other funders pending at time of publication)
Pennsylvania, statewide study	**	Pennsylvania Environmental Council, 10,000 Friends of Pennsylvania	William Penn Foundation
Philadelphia	Mar-97	Pennsylvania Environmental Council	Claniel Foundation, The Energy Foundation, William Penn Foundation
Pittsburgh	Jun-9	Heinz Endowments	Heinz Endowments

MARC Projects Completed or in Progress[a] (*continued*)

Project	Date	Local Partner(s)	Funder(s)
Portland	Jul-98	Coalition for a Livable Future	Northwest Area Foundation, U.S. Department of Housing and Urban Development
Saginaw	Oct-00	Ezekiel Project, Diocese of Saginaw	Charles Stewart Mott Foundation
San Diego	Dec-99	San Diego Dialogue	ARCO Foundation, The James Irvine Foundation
San Francisco	May-98	Urban Habitat Program	Nathan Cummings Foundation, Richard and Rhoda Goldman Fund
Seattle	May-99	Institute for Washington's Future	Northwest Area Foundation, The Energy Foundation
Seattle, update and report	**	Northwest Area Foundation	Northwest Area Foundation
St. Louis	Aug-99	Metropolitan Congregations United for St. Louis	St. Louis City Community Development Agency, St. Louis County Economic Council, and other local contributors
Washington, D.C.	Jul-99	Brookings Institution	Annie E. Casey Foundation, Robert P. Kogod, Meyer Foundation, The Morris and Gwendolyn Cafritz Foundation, Prince Charitable Trust, Philip L. Graham Foundation, W. Russell and Norma Ramsey Foundation
Wisconsin, statewide study	Feb-02	Citizens for a Better Environment, Greater Milwaukee Committee, Wisconsin Sustainable Cities, Inc.	Joyce Foundation
Working families, 26 regions mapped	Mar-01	Brookings Institution	Annie E. Casey Foundation, John S. and James L. Knight Foundation
Youngstown	Sep-01	ACTION	ACTION, the City of Youngstown, the City of East Liverpool, LISC, Mahoning County Board of Commissioners, Mahoning Valley Economic Development Corporation

a. All are studies of social separation and sprawl in metropolitan areas unless noted.
** Indicates project in progress.

REFERENCES

Albert, Alan Dale. 1979. "Sharing Suburbia's Wealth: The Political Economy of Tax-Base Sharing in the Twin Cities." Harvard University, Government Department.

Altshuler, Alan, William Morril, Harold Wolman, and Faith Mitchell, eds. 1999. *Governance and Opportunity in Metropolitan America.* Washington: National Academy Press.

American Planning Association. 1998. "Growing Smart Legislative Guidebook." Chicago.

Anderson, Elijah. 1989. "Sex Codes and Family Life among Poor Inner-City Youths." *Annals of the American Academy of Political and Social Science* 501 (January): 59–78.

———. 1991. "Neighborhood Effects on Teenage Pregnancy." In *The Urban Underclass*, edited by Christopher Jencks and Paul E. Peterson. Brookings.

Anderson, Martin. 1964. *The Federal Bulldozer: A Critical Analysis of Urban Renewal 1949–1962.* MIT Press.

Baker, Karen, and Steve Hinze. 1995. "Minnesota Fiscal Disparities Program." Saint Paul: Minnesota House of Representatives Research Department.

Bartik, Timothy J. 1991. *Who Benefits from State and Local Economic Development Policies?* Kalamazoo, Mich.: W. E. Upjohn Institute for Employment Research.

Baugh, John. 1983. *Black Street Sopeech: Its History, Structure, and Survival.* University of Texas Press.

Beckman, Norman. 1964. "Alternative Approaches for Metropolitan Reorganization." *Public Management* 46: 130.

Berke, Richard L. 2000. "The 2000 Candidates—For the Last Dance Candidates Eye the Wallflower." *New York Times*, September 3.

Branch, Taylor. 1988. *Parting the Waters: America in the King Years 1954–63*. New York: Touchstone.

———. 1998. *Pillar of Fire: America in the King Years 1963–65*. Simon and Schuster.

Brookings Center on Urban and Metropolitan Policy. 1999. "A Region Divided: The State of Growth in Greater Washington, D.C." (www.brook.edu/es/urban/dc/regiondivided.htm).

———. 2000. "Moving beyond Sprawl: The Challenge for Metropolitan Atlanta" (www.brook.edu/es/urban/atlanta/toc.htm).

Burchell, Robert W. 1990. "Fiscal Impact Analysis: State of the Art and State of the Practice." In *Financing Growth: Who Benefits? Who Pays? And How Much?* edited by Susan G. Robinson. Chicago: Government Finance Officers Association.

———. 1992. "Impact Assessment of the New Jersey Interim State Development and Redevelopment Plan."

———. 1997a. "Fiscal Impacts of Alternative Land Development Patterns in Michigan: The Costs of Current Development versus Compact Growth."

———. 1997b. "South Carolina Infrastructure Study: Projection of Statewide Infrastructure Costs 1995–2015."

Burchell, Robert W., and David Listokin. 1995. "Land, Infrastructure, Housing Costs, and Fiscal Impacts Associated with Growth: The Literature on the Impacts of Traditional versus Managed Growth." In *Costs of Sprawl Revisited*, edited by Robert W. Burchell and others. Brookings.

Calthorpe, Peter, and William Fulton. 2000. *The Regional City*. Washington: Island Press.

Caraley, Demetrios. 1992. "Washington Abandons the Cities." *Political Science Quarterly* 107 (1): 1–30.

Cervero, Robert. 1989. "Jobs, Housing Balance and Regional Mobility." *Journal of the American Planning Association* 55 (2): 136–50.

Citizens' Housing and Planning Association. 1999. "Using Chapter 40b to Create Affordable Housing in Suburban and Rural Communities of Massachusetts: Lessons Learned and Recommendations for the Future." Boston.

Citizens Research Council of Michigan. 2000. "Michigan's Unrestricted Revenue Sharing Program: Retrospect and Prospect." Livonia, Mich.

Clinton, William. 1994. "Leadership and Coordination of Fair Housing in Federal Programs: Affirmatively Furthering Fair Housing, Executive Order 12892 of January 17, 1994." *Weekly Compilation of Presidential Documents*, pp. 110–14.

Conley, Dalton. 1999. *Being Black, Living in the Red: Race, Wealth, and Social Policy in America.* University of California Press.

Crane, Jonathan. 1991. "Effects of Neighborhoods on Dropping Out of School and Teenage Childbearing." In *The Urban Underclass,* edited by Christopher Jencks and Paul E. Peterson. Brookings.

Davis, Mike. 1993. "Who Killed L.A.? The War against the Cities." *Crossroads* 32: 2–19.

de Oliver, Miguel, and Teresa Dawson-Munoz. 1996. "Place-Not-Race? The Inadequacy of Geography to Address Racial Disparities." *Journal of Black Political Economy* 25 (2): 37–60.

Downs, Anthony. 1994. *New Visions for Metropolitan America.* Brookings.

———. 1999. "Comment on Kenneth T. Rosen and Ted Dienstfrey's 'Housing Services in Low-Income Neighborhoods.'" In *Urban Problems and Community Development,* edited by Ronald F. Ferguson and William T. Dickens. Brookings.

Dreier, Peter. 1999. "Comment on Margaret Weir's 'Power, Money, and Politics in Community Development.'" In *Urban Problems and Community Development,* edited by Ronald F. Ferguson and William T. Dickens. Brookings.

Duncan, James E., and others. 1989. *The Search for Efficient Urban Growth Patterns.* Prepared for The Governor's Task Force on Urban Growth Patterns. Tallahassee, Fla.: Department of Consumer Affairs (June 30).

Farris, Charles L. 1989. "Urban Renewal: An Administrator Remembers." *Journal of Housing* 46 (4).

Fischel, William A. 1998. "Metropolitan Sharing of Local Property Tax Bases: Maybe Not Such a Good Idea After All." *The Value of Land: 1998 Annual Review.* Cambridge, Mass.: Lincoln Land Institute.

———. 1999. "Does the American Way of Zoning Cause the Suburbs of Metropolitan Areas to Be Too Spread Out?" In *Governance and Opportunity in Metropolitan America,* edited by Alan Altshuler, William Morril, Harold Wolman, and Faith Mitchell. Washington: National Academy Press.

Fisher, Ronald C. 1996. *State and Local Public Finance.* 2d ed. Irwin.

Flanigan, William H., and Nancy H. Zingle. 1974. "Measures of Electoral Competition." *Political Methodology* 1 (Fall): 31–60.

Frank, James E. 1989. *The Costs of Alternative Development Patterns: A Review of the Literature.* Washington: Urban Land Institute.

Fulton, William. 1997. *The Reluctant Metropolis.* Point Arena, Calif.: Solano Press Books.

Fulton, William, Rolf Pendel, Mai Nguyen, and Alicia Harrison. 2000. "Who Sprawls Most? How Growth Patterns Differ across the U.S." Brookings Center on Urban and Metropolitan Policy (www.brook.edu/es/urban/publications/fulton.pdf).

Fulton, William, Paul Shigley, Alicia Harrison, and Peter Sezzi. 2000. "Trends in Local Land Use: Ballot Measures, 1986–2000: An Analysis of City, County and Statewide Trends" (www.cp-dr.com/pdfs/ballotmeasures/ballotmeasurerprt.pdf).

Furstenburg, Frank F., and others. 1987. "Race Differences in the Timing of Adolescent Intercourse." *American Sociological Review* 52 (August): 511–18.

Galster, George C. 1992. "A Cumulative Causation Model of the Underclass: Implications for Urban Economic Development Policy." In *The Metropolis in Black and White: Place, Power and Polarization*, edited by George C. Galster and Edward W. Hill. New Brunswick, N.J.: Center for Urban Policy Research.

Garreau, Joel. 1992. *Edge City: Life on the New Frontier*. Doubleday.

Gittell, Marilyn, Kathe Newman, Janice Bockmeyer, and Robert Lindsay. 1998. "Expanding Civic Opportunity: Urban Empowerment Zones." *Urban Affairs Review* 33 (4): 530–57.

Greenberg, Stanley B. 1995. *Middle-Class Dreams: The Politics and Power of the New American Mayoralty*. Random House.

Hinze, Steve, and Karen Baker. 2000. *The Minnesota Fiscal Disparities Program*. Report prepared for the Minnesota House of Representatives Research Department.

Hogan, Dennis P., and Evelyn M. Kitagawa. 1985. "The Impact of Social Status, Family Structure, and Neighborhood on the Fertility of Black Adolescents." *American Journal of Sociology* 90 (4): 825–55.

Jackson, Kenneth T. 1985. *Crabgrass Frontier: The Suburbanization of the United States*. Oxford University Press.

Jargowsky, Paul A. 1996. "Take the Money and Run: Economic Segregation in U.S. Metropolitan Areas." *American Sociological Review* 61: 984–98.

———. 1997. *Poverty and Place: Ghettos, Barrios, and the American City*. New York: Russell Sage Foundation.

Kain, John F., and Joseph J. Persky. 1969. "Alternatives to the Gilded Ghetto." *Public Interest* (Winter): 74–88.

Kasarda, John D. 1985. "Urban Change and Minority Opportunities." In *The New Urban Reality*, edited by Paul E. Peterson. Brookings.

———. 1989. "Urban Industrial Transition and the Underclass." *Annals of the American Academy of Political and Social Science* 501: 26–47.

Katz, Bruce, and Amy Liu. 2000. "Moving beyond Sprawl: Toward a Broader Metropolitan Agenda." *Brookings Review* (Spring): 31.

Keating, W. Dennis. 1994. *The Suburban Racial Dilemma: Housing and Neighborhoods.* Temple University Press.

Kelly, Eric Damian. 1993. *Managing Community Growth: Policies, Techniques, and Impacts.* Westport, Conn.: Praeger.

Kennedy, Maureen, and Paul Leondard. 2001. "Dealing with Neighborhood Change: A Primer on Gentrification and Policy Choices." Paper prepared for the Brookings Center on Urban and Metropolitan Policy and Policy Link (April) (www.policylink.org/pdfs/brookingsgentrification.pdf).

Kirschenman, Joleen, and Kathryn M. Neckerman. 1991. "'We'd Love to Hire Them, But. . .': The Meaning of Race for Employers." In *The Urban Underclass,* edited by Christopher Jencks an Paul E. Peterson. Brookings.

Labov, William. 1972. *Language in the Inner City: Studies in the Black English Vernacular.* University of Pennsylvania Press.

———. 1980. *Locating Language in Time and Space.* Academic Press.

———. 1986. "The Logic of Nonstandard English." In *Black American English: Its Background and Its Usage in the Schools and in the Literature,* edited by Paul Stoller. Dell.

Labov, William, and Wendell Harris. 1986. "Defacto Segregation of Black and White Vernaculars." In *Diversity and Diachrony,* edited by David Sankoff. Current Issues in Linguistic Theory Series, vol. 53. Philadelphia: Benjamins.

Ladd, Helen F. 1994a. "Fiscal Impacts of Local Population Growth: A Conceptual and Empirical Analysis." *Regional Science and Urban Economics* 24: 661–86.

Ladd, Helen F. 1994b. "Spatially Targeted Economic Development Strategies: Do They Work?" *Cityscape* 1 (1).

Ladd, Helen F., and John Yinger. 1989. *America's Ailing Cities: Fiscal Health and the Design of Urban Policy.* Johns Hopkins University Press.

Landis, John D. 1995. "Imagining Land Use Futures: Applying the California Urban Futures Model." *Journal of the American Planning Association* 61 (Autumn): 438–57.

Land Trust Alliance. 2000. (www.lta.org/censum.html [December 1, 2000]).

———. 2001. *Summary of Data from the 1998 National Land Trust Census.* Washington (www.lta.org [September 21]).

Lemann, Nicholas. 1986. "The Origins of the Underclass." *Atlantic Monthly* 257: 31–55.

———. 1991. *The Promised Land: The Great Black Migration and How It Changed America*. Vintage Books.

———. 1994. "The Myth of Community Development." *New York Times Sunday Magazine,* January 9, pp. 27–31, 50, 54, 60.

Luce, Thomas. 1998. "Regional Tax-Base Sharing: The Twin Cities Experience." In *Local Government Tax and Land Use Policies in the United States,* edited by Wallace E. Oates. Northampton, Mass.: Edward Elgar.

Madden, Janice. 2000. *Changes in Income Inequity within U.S. Metropolitan Areas.* Kalamazoo, Mich.: W. E. Upjohn Institute for Employment Research.

Marcuse, Peter. 1998. "Mainstreaming Public Housing: A Proposal for a Comprehensive Approach to Housing Policy." In *New Directions in Public Housing,* edited by David P. Varady, Wolfgang F. E. Prieser, and Francis P. Russell. New Brunswick, N.J.: Center for Urban Policy Research.

Massey, Douglas S., and Nancy A. Denton. 1993. *American Apartheid: Segregation and the Making of the Underclass.* Harvard University Press.

Mayer, Henry. 1998. *William Lloyd Garrison and the Abolition of Slavery.* St. Martin's Press.

Mayer, Susan. 1991. "How Much Does a High School's Racial and Socioeconomic Mix Affect Graduation and Teenage Fertility Rates?" In *The Urban Underclass,* edited by Christopher Jencks and Paul E. Peterson. Brookings.

McDowell, Bruce. 1984. "The Metropolitan Planning Organization Role in the 1980s." *Journal of Advanced Transportation* 18 (2): 125–33.

McLanahan, Sara, and Irwin Garfinkel. 1989. "Single Mothers, the Underclass, and Social Policy." *Annals of the American Academy of Political and Social Science* 501 (January): 92–104.

Meehan, Eugene J. 1980. "Urban Development: An Alternative Strategy." In *Urban Revitalization,* edited by Donald B Rosenthal. Beverly Hills, Calif.: Sage Publications.

Melton, Hope. 1993. "Ghettos of the Nineties: The Consequences of Concentrated Poverty." St. Paul, Minn.: Department of Planning and Economic Development (November 10).

Minnesota Legislative Commission on Planning and Fiscal Policy. 1991. *Measuring the Fiscal Condition of Cities in Minnesota.* St. Paul.

Minnesota Planning. 2000. "Minnesota by Design: Options for a State Development Strategy." St. Paul.

Myers, Phyllis. 2000. *Green Ballot Measures, Election Day 1999: A Catalyst for Local Action to Shape Growth.* Washington: Brookings Center on Urban and Metropolitan Policy.

Myers, Phyllis, and Robert Puentes. 2000. "Growth at the Ballot Box: Electing the Shape of Communities" (November) (www.brook.edu/es/urban/ballotbox/finalreport.pdf).

National Association of Regional Councils. 1989. *Regional Council Programs and Activities: 1988 Survey.* Washington.

National Low Income Housing Coalition. 1998. "Worst Case Needs Study Underscores Housing Budget Shortfalls, Hard Work of Community Based Development Organizations" (www.nlihc.org/news/worst.htm).

National Resources Defense Council (NRDC). 2001. "A Guide to Water Quality at Vacation Beaches" (www.nrdc.org/water/oceans/ttw/titinx.asp).

O'Connor, Alice. 1999. "Swimming against the Tide: A Brief History of Federal Policy in Poor Communities." In *Urban Problems and Community Development,* edited by Ronald F. Ferguson and William T. Dickens, 77–137. Brookings.

O'Neill, David. 1999. *Smart Growth: Myth and Fact.* Washington: Urban Land Institute.

Orfield, Gary. 1985. "Ghettoization and Its Alternatives." In *The New Urban Reality,* edited by Paul Peterson. Brookings.

Orfield, Gary, and Carole Ashkinase. 1991. *The Closing Door: Conservative Policy and Black Opportunity.* University of Chicago Press.

Orfield, Gary, and John T. Yun. 1999. *Resegregation in American Schools.* The Civil Rights Project (www.law.harvard.edu/civilrights/publications/resegregation99.html [June]).

Orfield, Myron. 1996. Chicago Metropolitics (MAP/NGMLP) (www.metroresearch.org).

———. 1997. "Washington Metropolitics: A Regional Agenda for Community and Stability." Brookings (www.brook.edu/es/urban/myron.pdf).

———. 1998. "Chicago Metropolitics: A Regional Agenda for Members of the U.S. Congress" (www.brook.edu/es/urban/congrep6.pdf).

Orfield, Myron, and Thomas Luce. 2001. *Boston Metropatterns: A Regional Agenda for Community and Stability in Greater Boston.* Minneapolis: Metropolitan Area Research Corporation.

Pack, Janet Rothenberg. 1995. "Poverty and Urban Expenditures." University of Pennsylvania, Wharton Real Estate Center.

207

Penn, Mark J. 2001. "Penn's Poll—Turning a Win into a Draw." Special Issue. *Blueprint Magazine*, January 24.

Porter, Douglas. 1997. *Managing Growth in America's Communities*. Washington: Island Press.

powell, john a. Forthcoming. "Sprawl, Fragmentation and the Persistence of Racial Inequality: Limiting Civil Rights by Fragmenting Space." In *Urban Sprawl: Causes, Consequences, and Policy*, edited by Gregory Squires.

Puentes, Robert. 2000. "Flexible Funding for Transit: Who Uses It?" Brookings Survey Series (www.brook.edu/es/urban/flexfunding.pdf).

Putnam, Robert. 2000. *Bowling Alone: The Collapse and Revival of American Community*. Simon and Schuster.

Rich, Michael J. 1995. "Community Building and Empowerment: An Assessment of Neighborhood Transformation Initiatives in American Cities." Paper presented at the Annual Meeting of the Association for Public Policy Analysis and Management.

Richmond, Henry R. 1997. "Program Design: The American Land Institute." Report to the Steering Committee, American Land Institute. Unpublished manuscript.

Riposa, Gerry. 1996, "From Enterprise Zones to Empowerment Zones." *American Behavioral Scientist* 39 (5): 536–55.

Rolleston, Barbara Sherman. "Determinants of Restrictive Suburban Zoning: An Empirical Analysis." *Journal of Urban Economics* 21 (1987): 1–21.

Rosenbaum, James E., and Julie Kaufman. 1991. "Educational and Occupational Achievement of Low-Income Black Youth in White Suburbs." Paper presented at the annual meeting of the American Sociological Association, Cincinnati, Ohio (October).

Rosenbaum, James E., Marilyn J. Kulieke, and Leonard S. Rubinowitz. 1988. "White Suburban Schools' Responses to Low-Income Black Children: Sources of Successes and Problems." *Urban Review* 20 (1): 28–41.

Rosenbaum, James E., and Susan Popkin. 1991. "Black Pioneers: Do Their Moves to the Suburbs Increase Economic Opportunity for Mothers and Children?" *Housing Policy Debate* 2 (4): 1179–1213.

———. 1991. "Employment and Earnings of Low-Income Blacks Who Move to Middle-Class Suburbs." In *The Urban Underclass*, edited by Christopher Jencks and Paul E. Peterson. Brookings.

Rosenbaum, James E., Susan Popkin, Julie Kaufman, and Jennifer Rusin. 1991. "Social Integration of Low-Income Black Adults in Middle-Class White Suburbs." *Social Problems* 38 (4): 448–61.

Rubin, Marylin Marks. 1994. "Can Reorchestration of Historical Themes Reinvent Government? A Case Study of the Empowerment Zones and Enterprise Communities Act of 1993." *Public Administration Review* 54 (2): 161–69.

Rusk, David. 1993. *Cities without Suburbs.* Washington: Woodrow Wilson Center Press.

———. 1999. *Inside Game/Outside Game: Winning Strategies for Saving Urban America.* Brookings.

Sanders, Heywood T. 1980. "Urban Renewal and the Revitalized City: A Reconsideration of Recent History." In *Urban Revitalization,* edited by Donald B. Rosenthal. Beverly Hills, Calif.: Sage Publications.

Savitch, H. V., D. Collins, D. Sanders, and J. P. Markham. 1993. "Ties That Bind: Central Cities, Suburbs, and the New Metropolitan Region." *Economic Development Quarterly* 7 (4): 341–57.

Schroeder, Dana. 2000. "Fiscal Disparities Pool Grows 10% after 2-Year Decline." *Minnesota Journal* (February).

Shuy, Robert. 1975. "Teacher Training and Urban Language Problems." In *Black American English: Its Background and Its Usage in the Schools and in Literature,* edited by Paul Stoller. Dell.

Skogan, Wesley G. 1992. *Disorder and Decline: Crime and the Spiral of Decay in American Neighborhoods.* University of California Press.

Solof, Mark. 2001. "History of MPOs." *NJTPA Quarterly* (February).

Stoutland, Sara E. 1999. "Community Development Corporations: Mission, Strategy, and Accomplishments." In *Urban Problems and Community Development,* edited by Ronald F. Ferguson and William T. Dickens. Brookings.

Taylor, Ralon B., Stephen D. Gottfredson, and Sidney Brower. 1985. "Attachment to Place: Discriminant Validity, and Impacts of Disorder and Diversity." *American Journal of Community Psychology* 13 (5): 525–42.

Traynor, W. 1992. "Community Development: Does It Need to Change?" *Neighborhood Works* (April-May): 9–10, 22–23.

U.S. Bureau of the Census. 2000. *1997 Census of Governments.* Washington: U.S. Department of Commerce.

U.S. Department of Housing and Urban Development (HUD), Advisory Commission on Regulatory Barriers to Affordable Housing. 1991. " 'Not in My Back Yard': Removing Barriers to Affordable Housing." Government Printing Office.

Varady, David P., Wolfgang F. E. Prieser, and Francis P. Russell. 1998. *New Directions in Public Housing.* New Brunswick, N.J.: W. E. Upjohn Center for Urban Policy Research.

Vidal, A. C. 1992. "Rebuilding Communities: A National Study of Urban Community Development Corporations." New York: New School for Social Research, Community Development Research Center, Graduate School of Management and Urban Policy.

Voith, Richard. 1995. "Do Suburbs Need Cities?" *Journal of Regional Science* 38 (3).

von Hoffman, Alexander. 1998. "High Ambitions: The Past and Future of American Low-Income Housing Policy." In *New Directions in Public Housing,* edited by Wolfgang F. E. Prieser, David P. Varady, and Francis P. Russell. New Brunswick, N.J.: Center for Urban Policy Research.

Wasylenko, M. 1980. "Evidence of Fiscal Differentials and Intra-metropolitan Firm Relocation." *Land Economics* 56 (1980): 339–56.

Weiner, Edward. 1992. *Urban Transportation Planning in the United States: A Historical Overview.* Washington: U.S. Department of Transportation.

Weir, Margaret. 1999. "Power, Money, and Politics in Community Development." In *Urban Problems and Community Development,* edited by Ronald F. Ferguson and William T. Dickens. Brookings.

Wikstrom, Nelson. 1977. *Councils of Governments: A Study in Political Incrementalism.* Chicago: Nelson-Hall.

Wilson, William Julius. 1987. *The Truly Disadvantaged: The Inner City, the Underclass, and Public Policy.* University of Chicago Press.

Winsor, Diane. 1979. *Fiscal Zoning in Suburban Communities.* Lexington, Mass.: Lexington Books.

Wisconsin Department of Revenue. 2001. "State Shared Revenues Division of Research and Analysis, 2001" (www.dor.state.wi.us/ra/shrev00.html [February 5, 2001]).

Yinger, John. 1982. "Capitalization and the Theory of Local Public Finance." *Journal of Political Economy* 90: 917–43.

———. 1995. *Closed Doors, Opportunities Lost: The Continuing Costs of Housing Discrimination.* New York: Russell Sage Foundation.

Ziegler, Donald J., and Stanley D. Brunn. 1980. "Geopolitical Fragmentation and the Pattern of Growth and Need: Defining the Cleavage between Sunbelt and Frostbelt Metropolises." In *The American Metropolitan System : Present and Future,* edited by James O. Wheeler and Stanley D. Brunn. London: V. H. Winston & Sons.

Zuckman, Jill. 1992. "Enterprise Zone Alchemy: '90s-Style Urban Renewal." *Congressional Quarterly Weekly* 50: 2354–57.

INDEX

Affluent job centers, 44–46; ballot initiatives, 172; designation, 32; distribution, 46–48; gains from regional reform, 153, 171–72; growth moratoriums, 112; office space, 33; political affiliations, 157; problems, 3; swing districts, 158

Affordable housing, 76, 121–25; in at-risk communities, 164–165; community development corporations, 79–83. *See also* Housing discrimination; *specific housing legislation*

African Americans: civil rights movement, 178–80; in regional coalition building, 183, 185; school segregation, 49. *See also* Housing discrimination; Race and ethnicity; Segregation

Agenda for regional reform, 173–87

Agricultural land and open space preservation, 117–18, 120, 127

Air quality, state implementation plans for, 146

Alliance for Metropolitan Stability, 177

American Farmland Trust, 117

Annexation, 73, 133–35

At-risk suburbs, 35–42; affordable housing in, 164–65; association for governments of, 175–76; designation, 32; distribution, 34–35, 46–48; fiscal equity for, 163, 164, 168–69; and fragmentation of metropolitan governance, 130; gains from regional reform, 162–71; infrastructure needs, 97, 166–67, 169–70; land-use planning and transportation needs, 163, 164, 170–71; low-density communities, 11–42, 168–71; managed integration, 166; office space, 33; older communities, 38–41, 162–67; political affiliations, 157–62; problems, 2, 70; in regional coalition building, 182; schools and infrastructure, 42–44, 168–70; segregated communities, 37–38, 162–67; as swing districts, 158–60; types of communities, 36–42

Atlanta metropolitan area: at-risk low-density suburbs, 42; at-risk segregated communities in, 37; distribution of types of communities, 47–48; "edge cities," 44; political party affiliations, 160;

211